THE BEST BIKE RIDES IN NEW ENGLAND

Best Bike Rides Series

THE BEST BIKE RIDES IN NEW ENGLAND

Third Edition

Connecticut • Maine
Massachusetts • New Hampshire
Rhode Island • Vermont

by
Paul Thomas

edited by
Paul Angiolillo

A Voyager Book

Old Saybrook, Connecticut

Photo credits: pp. xii, 13, 47, 77, 203: courtesy Dennis Coello; p. 145: courtesy William C. Roy; p. 191: courtesy Dennis Curran; p. 254: courtesy Jamie King, Charles River Wheelmen.

Library of Congress Cataloging-in-Publication Data is available.
ISBN 1-56440-877-9

♻ This book is printed on recycled paper.
Manufactured in the United States of America
Third Edition/Second Printing

for Sarah

and for Dea and David

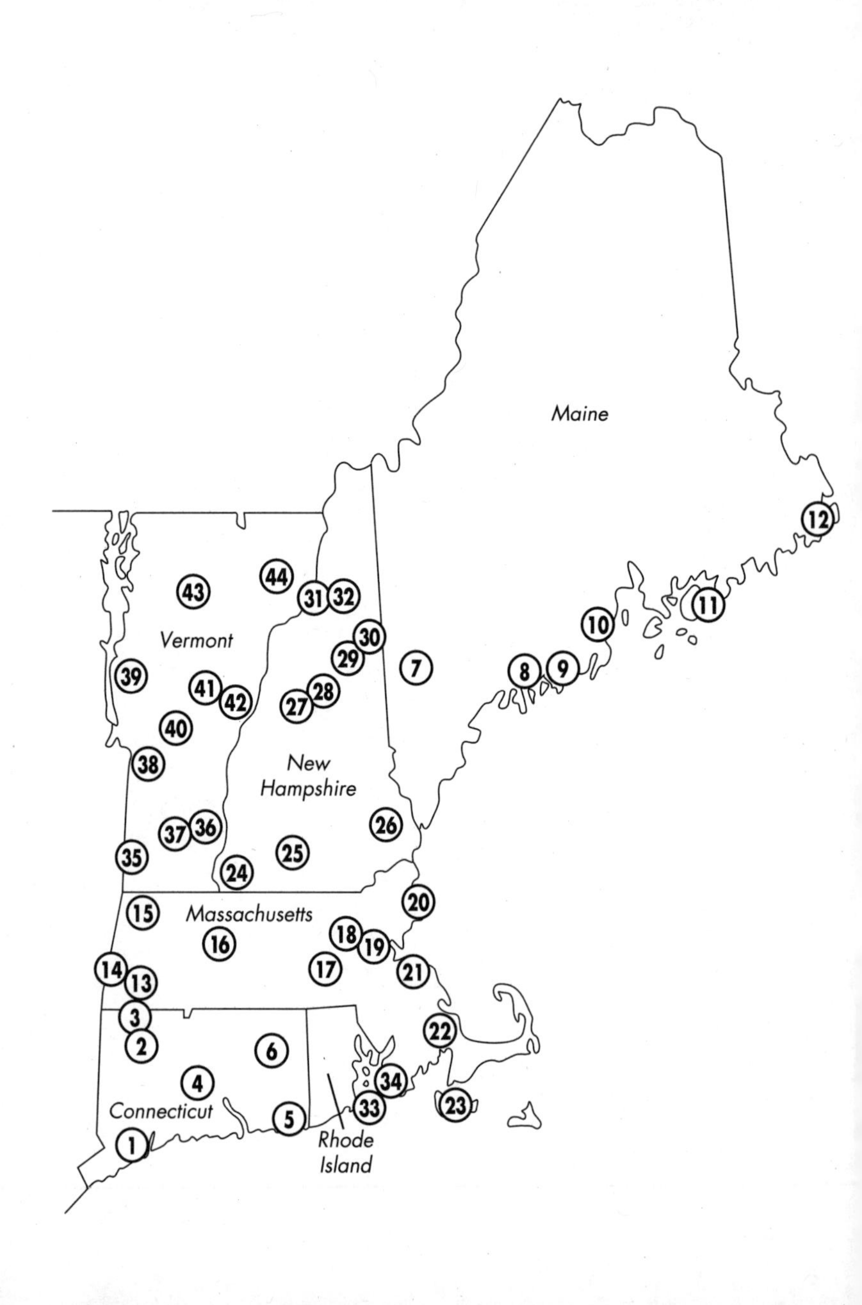
Maine
Vermont
New Hampshire
Massachusetts
Connecticut
Rhode Island
1
2
3
4
5
6
7
8
9
10
11
12
13
14
15
16
17
18
19
20
21
22
23
24
25
26
27
28
29
30
31
32
33
34
35
36
37
38
39
40
41
42
43
44

Contents

Preface to the Third Edition x

Introduction 1

A Brief History of Bicycle Touring in New England 1
Tips for a Safer and More Exhilarating Ride 2
How to Use this Book 9

Bike Rides 13

Connecticut 13

1. Westport Ramble 16
2. Music Mountain Cruise 21
3. Salisbury Ramble 27
4. A Midstate Cruise 31
5. Mystic Seaport Ramble 37
6. Mansfield Hollow Cruise 41

Maine 47

7. Moose Country Challenge 50
8. Kennebec Crossing Challenge 54
9. Pemaquid Point Cruise 58
10. Camden Hills and Coastal Cruise 63
11. Acadia National Park Cruise 69
12. Sunrise County Challenge 73

Massachusetts 77
13. Monument Valley Ramble 80
14. Great Barrington Cruise 85
15. Mount Greylock Classic 90
16. Five-College to Quabbin Reservoir Challenge 94
17. Sudbury Reservoir Ramble 100
18. Lincoln to Great Brook Farm Ramble 105
19. Walden Pond Cruise 110
20. Cape Ann Cruise 116
21. South Shore–Wompatuck State Park Ramble 122
22. Cape in a Day (or Two) Classic 129
23. Martha's Vineyard: Two Tours 134
The Vineyard: Gay Head Cruise 136
The Vineyard: Edgartown Ramble 140

New Hampshire 145
24. Covered Bridge Cruise 148
25. A Yankee Cruise 153
26. Town and Country Cruise 158
27. Kinsman Region Classic 163
28. Waterville Valley Challenge 168
29. Bear Notch Challenge 173
30. White Mountains Triple-Notch Classic 178
31. Cherry Mountain Ramble 184
32. North Country Challenge 187

Rhode Island 191
33. Newport (and Beyond) Ramble 194
34. Sakonnet Point Ramble 199

Vermont 203
35. Bennington to Battenkill River Challenge 206
36. Chester Country Weekend: Saxtons River Cruise 212

37. Chester Country Weekend: West River Challenge 217
38. Middletown Springs Cruise 222
39. Champlain Valley Cruise 227
40. Tour of Scenic Rural Vermont Classic 231
41. Randolph Challenge 235
42. Orange County Challenge 239
43. Smuggler's Notch Challenge 243
44. Northeast Kingdom Challenge 248

Appendix: Bicycling and Touring Resources
in New England and Beyond *253*

Preface to the Third Edition

While simply getting on your bike and exploring new ground can be a lot of fun, it can also be a less than pleasant experience—if you're unfamiliar with the territory. That's where a book like this one is useful.

Of course, it's difficult to build a 45-mile ride that avoids all the busier or otherwise less than perfect roads in a well-settled region like New England. But the forty-four rides in this book have been fine-tuned to offer you some of the best routes.

How does this book differ from cycling guidebooks for, say, Vermont or Massachusetts (besides covering all six New England states)? For one thing, it has substantial rides—anywhere from 25 to 100 miles—and provides at least one shorter option for most of them, so that both the beginner and the more experienced cyclist can use it—and even do a ride together. At the same time, pedaling the longer rides in this book will familiarize you with opportunities for other excursions in a "miniregion."

In this edition I have added six entirely new rides (replacing six old ones), as well a new category in each ride, labeled "Traffic/Safety," that should make for safer touring.

Although this is a book of paved road rides (except for the Acadia National Park Cruise on packed dirt and gravel roads and a handful of other rides with short stretches on smooth dirt roads), a mountain or hybrid bike is excellent for doing all of these tours. Many rides in New England tackle roads with narrower shoulders or a steep climb or two, or they pass a forest or park with mountain-biking trails. Today mountain bikers are rapidly discovering the joys of road riding. So pump up those fat tires and hit the road.

Instead of trying to be an expert on all sections of New England, I took advantage of experienced local cyclists (mostly via the Internet) to review the current rides in this book. Several dozen people helped, updating and revising exhaustively. My deep appreciation to the following people:

Pamela Blalock
Ed Cote
Seth Davis
Karen Dodge
Roger Duchesneau
Susan Genser
Ron Goodman
Karen Haas
Mary Haggerty
Edward Hoffer
Ed Jette
Michael Kiernan
Barbara Knauff
Jeff Korenstein
Timothy Lucia
Walter McNeil
Bill Meduski
Stephen Moriarty
Barry, Linda, and Gene Nelson
Penny Newbury
Fred Oliver
Bruce and Lisa Packard
John Peipon
Jerry Sabath
Robin Schulman
Sandra Seymour
Phillip and Roy Stern
Dave Tier
Lynne Tolman
Beth and Arthur Tracy
Harry and Dan Wolfson
Dara Zuckernick

—Paul Angiolillo

Introduction

A Brief History of Bicycle Touring in New England

New England isn't only the cradle of liberty—it's also the birthplace of bicycling in America. The Boston Bicycle Club, founded in 1878 by 14 high-wheeled cyclists, was the country's first bike club. (Its first ride went from Boston to neighboring Brookline.)

New England can boast of other cycling firsts as well. According to the *Wheel,* a popular cycling journal of the day, "The first bicycle rider in this country was Alfred Chandler, now an eminent Boston lawyer." The first "remarkable ride" was W. R. Pitman's tour from Boston to Haverhill, a distance exceeding 42 miles, which he covered in five hours and forty minutes. That must have been a great training ride, for Pitman went on to win the first amateur race, run in Lynn, Massachusetts, on July 4, 1878.

If only these two gentlemen were with us today. They could trade in their hundred-pound high-wheelers for high-performance machines, exchange their wool knickers for Lycra cycling shorts, and enjoy weekly races and "remarkable rides" the whole year round. For company on the road, they could join any of several dozen New England–area touring and racing clubs. To revisit some of their familiar haunts, they might sign up for a weekend-long, inn-to-inn cycling expedition, during which they could rest every night in lodgings that were historical even a hundred years ago.

Reflecting the new vitality and sophistication of cycling in its second century, *The Best Bike Rides in New England* is the first all-new guide to cycling the entire six-state region to be published in many years. Today's cyclists include weekend tourists and competitive racers alike, women and men who want to know where the best rides are—where the roads offer beautiful and varied scenery, challenges they can rise to, a perfect day of solitude or camaraderie.

Regional cycling clubs, inn-to-inn tour leaders, and a host of cycling fans have contributed their favorites to this collection of 44 tours. Ranging in length from 20 to more than 100 miles, these bike rides have proven appeal to active weekend riders and competitive racers alike:

Here's a short sample:

- The Walden Pond Cruise is the all-time favorite training ride of John Allis, three-time Olympic cyclist and Boston-area racing coach.
- The Acadia National Park Cruise has special appeal for New England's growing number of fat-tire bike enthusiasts.
- The Northeast Kingdom Challenge includes the favorite ride of many tour leaders in Vermont.

Before pedaling down the road, review the following tips. They will help make every ride a great ride.

Tips for a Safer and More Exhilarating Ride

Riding a bicycle—a combination of sport, transportation, and exploration—can be a rewarding and exhilarating experience. Mental, physical, and material preparation, though, are critical to safety and enjoyment. Experts have written volumes about touring and racing technique, training strategy, bicycle maintenance, and sports nutrition. Cycling magazines publish regular features on these topics and countless others. The most important lessons, however, can be summarized in the following tips. Cyclists just beginning to ride distances longer than 20 miles should read these carefully. Even the most experienced rider can benefit from a quick review.

Pace yourself to last the distance. On long tours, start out slowly. You will have plenty of time to test your speed once you have stretched out, warmed up, and settled into the ride.

- If you are tackling a longer ride for the first time, don't hesitate to stop and enjoy some of the scenery along the way. Dismount, stretch, and walk around every 10 or 20 miles. You'll find that you can ride comfortably for hours if you take these short breaks.
- Drink plenty of water as you ride. Take frequent small sips, drinking much more often than you feel you need to. It's easy

to become dehydrated on a long ride, because the breeze you create helps evaporate perspiration. Never wait for signs of thirst before taking a pull from your water bottle.

Tune up your cycling technique. Here are some pointers to help you go farther faster with less energy.

- Use the full range of your pedal stroke. Toe clips and cycling shoes will help you apply even pressure throughout the pedal's revolution.
- Maintain higher revolutions per minute (rpms). You should pedal at a cadence of about 90 rpms. This means selecting a relatively easy gear and spinning your cranks. This may seem awkward at first, but you will soon get used to it and appreciate why racers often train in this manner. The inexperienced rider tends to push too hard a gear too early in a ride, placing stress on the knees and the lower back. Maintaining a high pedal revolution provides a better aerobic workout for your heart and lungs.
- Practice the above rule especially in colder weather. Riding at a fast cadence in a low gear will keep you warm and your muscles loose.
- On long climbs, alternate between sitting and spinning in a low gear and standing on the pedals to push a higher gear. If you feel like walking up a particularly tough climb, try stopping for a minute-long stretch and then remounting your bike to try again. The secret to making it up any climb is to always use a lower gear than you need. Start out easy and increase your pace only as you near the top.
- Relax your elbows and shoulders, and vary your hand position. Grip your handlebars on top, around the brake hoods, in the drops, and at every point in between. Keeping your arms loose and alternating your hand position often help to ward off muscle fatigue on longer rides.
- Brake in short bursts to avoid locking up your wheels. Use both front and rear brakes. Because your front brake catches your forward momentum, it provides more braking power than your rear brake.

Share the road with others, as you would have them share it with you.

- Obey traffic laws, not only for your own safety but also to earn the respect of drivers. Use brief stops at traffic lights to drink water, stretch, or wait for your riding partners to catch up.
- Ride to be predictable. Ride single file on the right side of the road. Never swerve suddenly into the road. Use hand signals. This is just common sense. Cars signal turns and stops, and cyclists should too.
- Turning left is the most dangerous maneuver in bicycling. Always look behind you before turning left, taking care that you don't drift into the road as you do so. Never turn left suddenly from the far right side of the road. When approaching a left turn, move to the left turn lane or the center of the road after checking for traffic behind you. On busy roads pull off to the right, onto the road's shoulder, and wait until traffic is clear in both directions before crossing. A rearview mirror attached to your left handlebar plug or your helmet will help you keep an eye on traffic.

Wear a helmet. It could save your life.

- Contemporary cycling helmets are feather-light, well ventilated, extremely comfortable, and appealing. There is no excuse for not wearing one. A good helmet can cost more than $50, but it is also your single most important investment in the sport. Don't skimp on safety.

Equip yourself properly. Ride prepared for every contingency.

- It is not necessary to own an expensive bicycle to enjoy riding. It is important, though, that whatever bike you ride be well maintained and safe. Make certain that your brakes and derailleurs are adjusted properly. Spray and wipe your chain regularly with a light-grade lubricant. Check your tires for embedded bits of glass and stone before every ride.
- Carry a pump and a spare tire or tube on every ride. Know how to fix a flat tire. Riding through glass can either cause a minor annoyance or ruin your ride, depending on how prepared you are.
- Carry some personal identification, a few extra dollars, and change for a telephone call. Many experienced riders keep these items in a waterproof sandwich bag to carry on every ride. If you are cycling alone from a vacation home, a friend's house, or a

hotel or inn, always jot down the address, the phone number, and your name on a piece of paper to slip in your jersey pocket before you set out.

- Considering the unpredictability of New England weather, it's a wise idea to carry a lightweight, packable rain jacket on spring and fall rides. This item will fit easily into a small pack that attaches beneath your bicycle seat.

Adjust your bike so it fits. Don't let it misadjust you.

- Saddle height and tilt are the most critical factors for a comfortable riding position. When the balls of your feet are on the pedals, your knees should be just slightly bent at the bottom of each stroke. Your seat is too high if your hips rock as you pedal. To determine your saddle's proper tilt, balance a yardstick lengthwise along its nose and back. The stick should be level, parallel to your bike's top tube. Many riders make the mistake of tilting their seats slightly forward, thrusting too much weight and stress onto their shoulders, arms, and hands.
- Your reach to the handlebars and your handlebar height are also important. When you are in the normal riding position with your hands on your brake hoods, your front wheel's hub should be hidden behind or just visible in front of your handlebars' cross section. Overextending your back and arms to reach your bars will cause discomfort and stiffness. The top of your bars should be level with or about 1 inch below the top of your seat.
- An increasing number of bike shops now offer precision fitting services to adjust your bicycle to your body proportions. If you are having difficulty finding a comfortable riding position, consult a quality bike shop in your area.

Dress for the sport. Bicycle clothing is more than a current fashion craze. Proper shorts, jerseys, shoes, and gloves, besides looking good, provide a more comfortable ride. None of these items are absolutely necessary, but on a longer ride especially, you'll be glad you are wearing them.

- Skintight shorts, most commonly black but now sold in a rainbow of colors, prevent chafing and provide a more aerodynamic profile. They also provide padding at those vital contact points.
- Bright jerseys make you visible on the road, and the pockets in

back are convenient for carrying your wallet, some food, and a map (or this book).

- Cycling shoes are available in racing or touring models. Both feature stiff soles that provide more comfort and transfer more of your leg power to the pedals. Proper cycling shoes also feature special grooves or cleats that securely engage the pedals for steady leg power all around the stroke.
- Padded gloves absorb road shock and protect against abrasions should you stop a fall with the palm of your hand.
- Eyewear for cycling shields against sun, wind, bugs, and dirt. Wear sunglasses, or choose specially designed cycling glasses that have interchangeable light and dark lenses.
- Always wear more rather than less. In raw weather the wind you create while riding will accentuate the cold. Riding in cold conditions can be fun but only if you dress appropriately. Wear a cap beneath your helmet. Cotton gardening gloves that fit over regular cycling gloves are an inexpensive substitute for winter cycling gloves. Wear a second jersey or a sweatshirt, sweater, or jacket. In a pinch you can even stuff a sheet of newspaper inside your jersey, covering your chest and stomach. (It's an old trick, and it really works!) Wool or polypropylene cycling tights will keep your legs warm. A quality bike shop is the best source for winter clothing designed specifically for the sport.

Practice group riding etiquette. The company of other riders can make any tour more enjoyable. Riding in a group, though, requires extra attention and a certain amount of courtesy.

- Whether you are an experienced cyclist comfortable with drafting in the slipstream of others or a recreational cyclist out with a large group for the first time, obey these five rules: Always ride in a straight line, avoiding any sudden swerves to either side. Never stop suddenly; if you must stop, pull all the way off the road to the right. Riding in a tight group, point out obstacles, shouting "glass," "rocks," and so forth. Warn other cyclists of an approaching car by shouting "car back" or "car up." Never ride through a traffic light, and never make a left turn in traffic unless the whole group can make it at once.
- Arrive prepared for the ride. Don't make others wait while you

take care of adjustments that should have been made earlier. Carry a pump, spare tire, cash, food, and water. Don't count on borrowing any of these from another rider.

Eat well on and off the bike.

- Eat small snacks on rides longer than two hours. You need to replace the blood sugar depleted through constant exertion. Bananas, oranges, raisins, and energy bars are favorite on-the-bike snacks of experienced cyclists. Many riders also swear by glucose- or fructose-based drinks.
- Don't combine cycling and dieting. Dieting will sap you of needed strength. And anyway, if you ride regularly, dieting will be unnecessary.
- Minimize your alcohol intake for at least two days before a big ride. Alcohol disturbs your body's chemistry and makes you more susceptible to becoming dehydrated while you ride.

Know your limits.

- A long ride requires preparation and training. Never ride a tour more than 20 miles longer than one you have ridden comfortably before. All of the rides in this book are divided into Rambles (easy), Cruises (intermediate), Challenges (difficult), and Classics (expert). If you are just beginning to ride longer distances, work your way up through these categories. Always begin your season with many short rides ridden in an easy gear.

Get (and stay) fit. The pleasure you get out of cycling will increase in direct proportion to your level of fitness.

- Racers ride more than 300 miles per week in daily training sessions. Don't worry about trying to match that pace, but do think about getting some form of exercise every day. Jog, swim, play tennis, attend aerobics classes—do anything to get your heart and lungs working hard for at least a half hour every day. And keep up your regimen throughout the winter to get a head start on the next cycling season.
- The best way to train for cycling, of course, is to ride regularly. Don't limit cycling to weekends. Commute by bike, or throw the bike in your car for a short lunchtime ride. Even a half-hour spin a few times during the week will improve your stamina and strengthen your legs.

- If you are a competitive cyclist, be careful not to overtrain. Riding hard every day can easily result in physical and mental fatigue. Take one day off every week, perhaps using the opportunity to play softball, volleyball, or any other sport with your noncycling friends.

Get your mind right. Mental fitness is as important as physical ability.

- One cycling magazine conducted a poll of its readers that showed attitude to be as important as fitness to the enjoyment of bike riding. Before you set off, prepare yourself mentally for the challenge ahead. Visualize the ride. If you have never ridden the course before, study the map and directions so that you will know where the difficult stretches are and can pace yourself accordingly. *Don't be goaded by others into riding a tour that you feel unprepared for.*
- Search out new rides. Every rider has his or her favorite local loop, but exploring new routes can make cycling fresher and more adventurous. Start with some of the rides in this book. Plan a cycling weekend in the Berkshires or the White Mountains, by the Atlantic or along Lake Champlain. The exhilaration you feel in cycling through newly discovered countryside will carry over into your regular neighborhood rides.

Join a club.

- Touring clubs organize regular weekend and occasional weekday evening rides throughout the year. These are often listed in local newspapers. Touring clubs also publish newsletters, organize rallies, offer equipment discounts, and host dinners throughout the year.
- If you are interested in cycling competitively, join a racing club. There is no substitute for the formal and informal coaching, training rides, races, and cycling clinics that are a part of most club programs. Larger clubs offer programs for all levels of cyclists.
- This book's appendix presents a state-by-state listing of New England's cycling and touring resources.

How to Use This Book

The Best Bike Rides in New England places each ride in one of our categories according to the ride's degree of difficulty—easy, intermediate, difficult, or expert. Each ride's name indicates its rating. Most rides also offer shorter (and sometimes longer) options.

Rambles are this collection's easiest rides, perfect for the beginning cyclist or for the experienced rider looking for a relaxed, scenic outing. All Rambles are less than 35 miles long and cover flat or rolling terrain.

Cruises are intermediate rides for those ready to test their legs over moderate distances and eager to tackle a hill or two. Cruises generally measure between 25 and 50 miles and cross rolling or hilly terrain.

Challenges require adequate training and preparation beforehand. These 40- to 70-mile routes commonly feature long climbs that, however scenic, may prove too difficult for the inexperienced cyclist. But the active rider should view these tours, which explore some of New England's most picturesque regions, as welcome challenges.

Classics are the black diamond slopes of bicycling. Most Classics earn this rating, though, less for the steepness of their descents than for the difficulty of their climbs or for their sheer length. Classic rides generally exceed 60 miles and cross hilly or mountainous terrain. Some shorter rides, such as the Mount Greylock Classic, qualify for this experts-only rating as well.

Most rides offer shorter and longer options; these options are noted in their directions. Some Challenges, for example, feature shorter loops that would qualify as Cruises or even Rambles. In selecting a ride, look not only at its rating but also at the different lengths of its various options.

Keep in mind that these ratings represent guidelines rather than rules. What may be a fun, moderately challenging ride for one rider can prove an unpleasant endurance test for another. Remember: Know your limits and be careful not to set out for a tour that is twice as long or hilly as any you have ever completed. Read each ride's description and directions before rolling down the road. All major climbs are noted so that you may pace yourself appropriately.

For each ride in this book, directions include the cumulative mileage at each turn. One small and relatively inexpensive piece of equipment will help you keep track of your mileage and will make these directions easier to follow. This is a cyclometer, essentially a digital wristwatch for your bike's handlebars. Besides telling time, a cyclometer displays your speed and the elapsed distance for a ride. (More sophisticated and expensive models can also display your cadence, or the rate of revolution for your pedals, and your heart rate.)

Your bike shop is likely to carry a half dozen different cyclometer brands. The simplest models, which display trip distance, speed, and time, are generally the least expensive and most reliable. The Avocet, favored by most racers, is one of these. It is particularly compact, about the size of an Oreo cookie, and costs approximately $35.

Acknowledgments

This book could never have been written without the generous contributions, comments, and moral support of individuals, clubs, and cycling organizations throughout New England. I would like to thank in particular Dennis and Ellen Curran of Maine Coast Cyclers; Bob Maynard of Vermont Country Cyclers; Bill Perry and Steve Bushey of Vermont Bicycle Touring; Linda Harvey and Adolphe Bernotas of the Granite State Wheelmen; all the folks with my local club, the Charles River Wheelmen; Wally Bugbee and Ken Bell, ride leaders for the Penobscot Wheelmen; John Fletcher of the Pequot Cyclists; Al Lester of the American Youth Hostels, Greater Boston Council; Mike Farney of the Lincoln Guide Service shop; coach and teacher Leif Thorne-Thomsen; and John Allis, who actually pushed me the final 5 miles back to his Belmont Wheelworks shop after my back and legs had given out for the day.

Thanks also to my pack of fact-checking cyclists—Lindy and

Jamie King, Bob Kearney, Jon Day, Alice Sawyer, Sharman Lappin, Richard Buck, Joe Repole, and Andrew deGarmo. Thank you all for your enthusiasm, your comments, and your corrections.

My thanks also to the countless shopkeepers, innkeepers, motorists, and passersby whom I met while scouting out these routes. Whether offering directions, advising me of road conditions ahead, or providing a hot cup of coffee on a cold day, you all contributed immeasurably to this effort.

Disclaimer

Connecticut

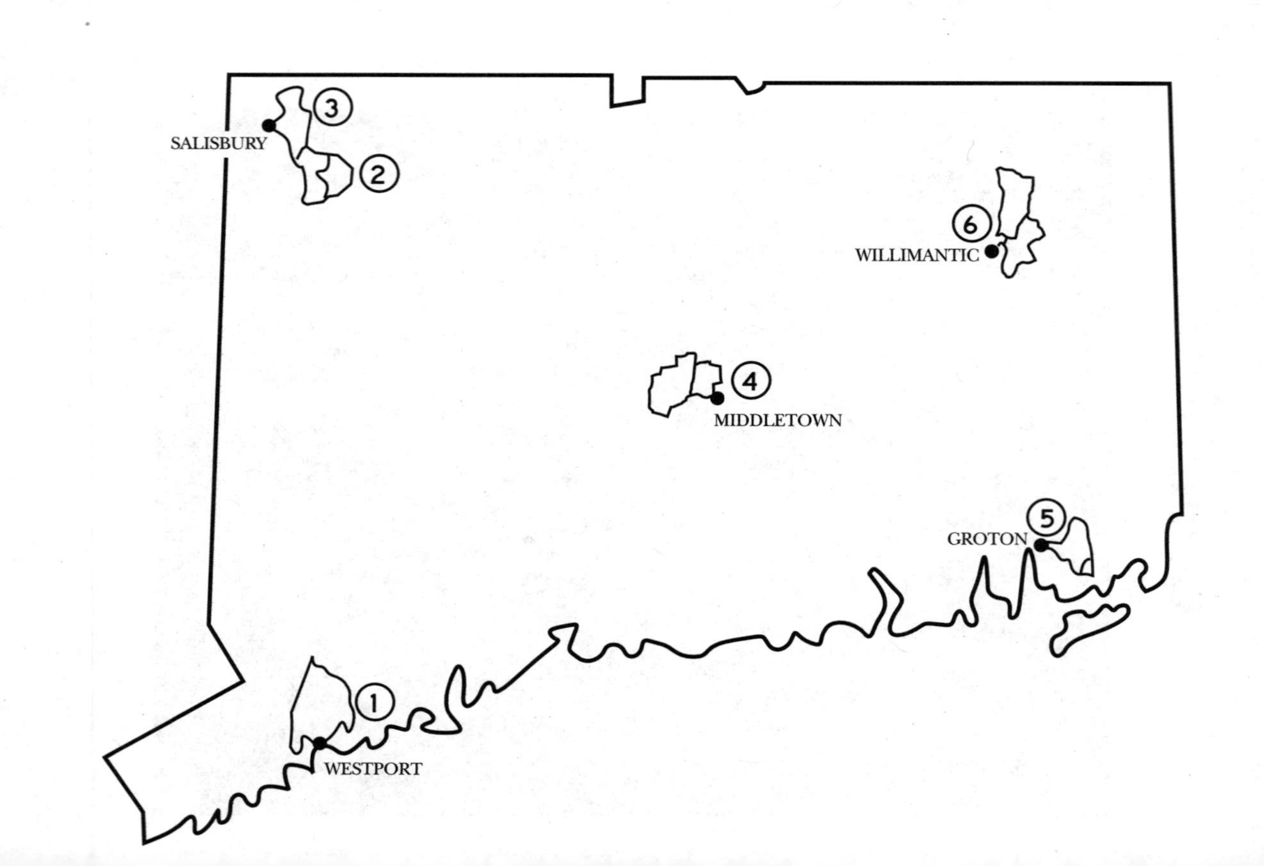

3
SALISBURY
2
6
WILLIMANTIC
4
MIDDLETOWN
5
GROTON
1
WESTPORT

Connecticut

1. Westport Ramble 16
2. Music Mountain Cruise 21
3. Salisbury Ramble 27
4. A Midstate Cruise 31
5. Mystic Seaport Ramble 37
6. Mansfield Hollow Cruise 41

1

Westport Ramble

Westport—Aspetuck—Fairfield—Southport—Westport

Whether you're seeking an invigorating ride into the countryside or a leisurely ramble along the coast, this ride will satisfy. It begins near a large park on Long Island Sound, Sherwood Island State Park. From there the ride rolls for about 5 miles along residential streets that sometimes hug the shoreline in the handsome town of Westport. Next you'll explore well-paved, shady stretches of two scenic inland highways that meet near a large reservoir. After that 14-mile inland loop, the ride follows the shoreline again, this time in well-to-do Fairfield.

You will undoubtedly pass other cyclists along this ride—it's a popular route for two-wheeled sightseeing. What's more, famous people live in Westport and Fairfield—you might keep an eye out for the likes of Robert Redford or Paul Newman. You'll also pass dozens of spectacular homes along lanes lined with huge maple trees—a blend of restrained New England taste and sheer prosperity. During the summer the town of Westport comes alive with free concerts and other cultural events, so be sure to make a short side trip into the "strip" in Westport, to admire its fancy shops and to partake of its pleasures.

Finally, of course, there's the ocean. Take a break at one or two of the beaches or harbors along this ride. Watch the sea's timeless comings and goings. Or cruise into large Sherwood Island State Park, which for bicyclists waives the $8.00 nonresident admission fee. You may never live in a place like Fairfield or Westport, but you can always experience their beauty and charm from a bike.

The Basics

Start: At a park-and-ride lot just off exit 18 on I–95. From the exit turn north (toward U.S. 1). After 0.4 mile you will reach the parking lot on the right.
Length: 25.3 miles or, if you take only the roads south of U.S. 1, about 11 miles.
Terrain: Rolling lanes through well-kept communities, and two well-paved rural highways with good shoulders and an occasional modest climb.
Food: There are food stores at 4.7 miles at the junction of Rte. 136 and U.S. 1 and at 16.4 miles at the intersection of Routes 58 and 135.
Traffic/Safety: This is a well-settled area, with plenty of traffic, especially in the summer. There are bike route signs along some of the ride—but always ride single file and stay alert.

Miles and Directions

- 0.0 Turn left out of the parking lot, southward toward I–95.
- 0.1 At the first stoplight, turn right onto Greens Farms Rd.
- 0.5 Fork left, staying on Greens Farms Rd.
- 1.0 At a four-way intersection, turn left onto Hills Point Rd., and cross I–95. You will begin to see the ocean and reach Compo Beach (where there is a bike path on the other side of the road).
- 2.0 Fork right, heading away from the shoreline, on S. Compo Rd., with a bike route sign on it. (After another 0.5 mile you will pass a statue of a Minuteman at a road on the left. You can turn left here to do a short loop along Compo Beach Rd.)
- 3.3 Go straight at a stop sign at a four-way intersection, with Rte. 136S to the left and Greens Farms Rd. to the right. Straight ahead is Rte. 136N.
- 4.7 Head straight across U.S. 1, onto N. Compo Rd., which is also Rte. 136N.

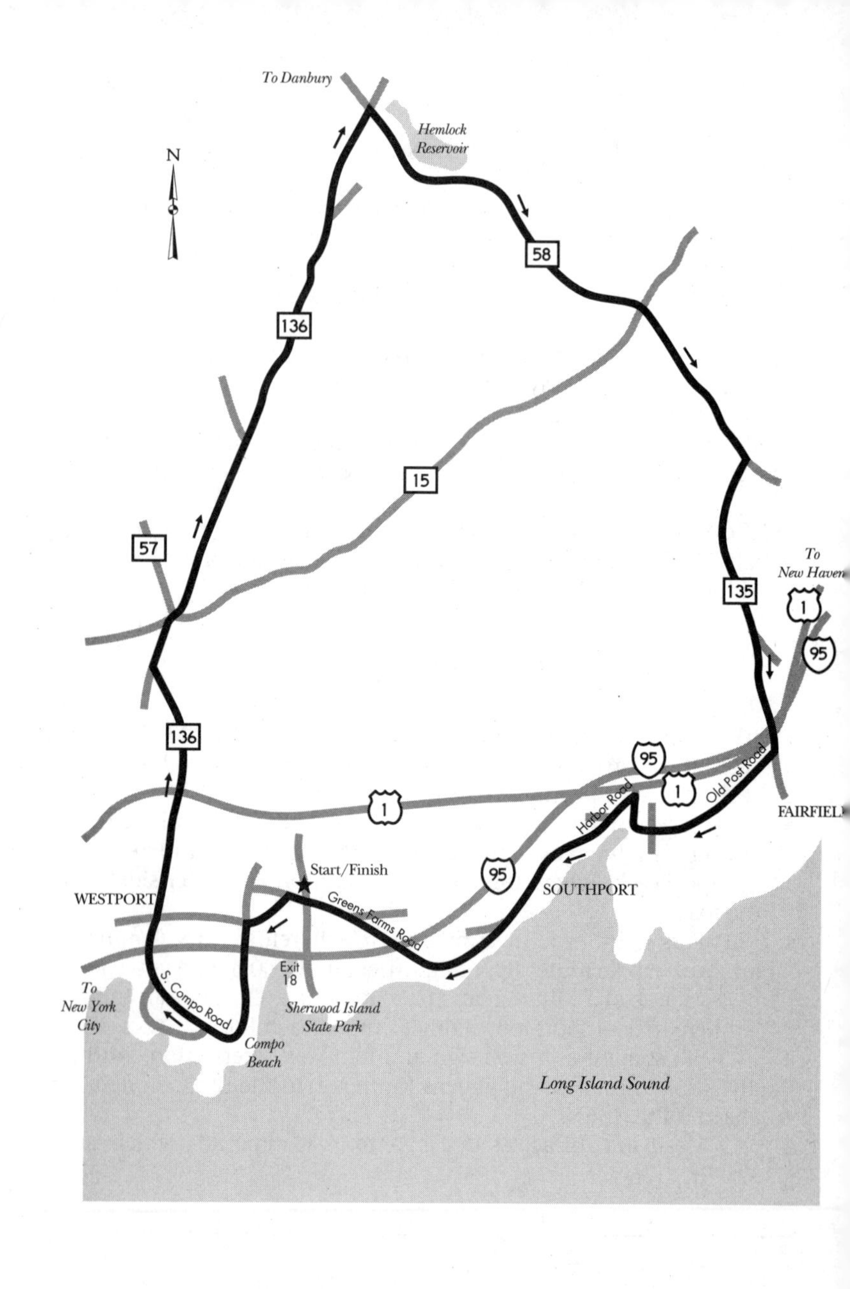
To Danbury
Hemlock Reservoir
N
58
136
15
57
135
To New Haven
1
95
136
95
1
Old Post Road
Harbor Road
1
FAIRFIELD
Start/Finish
95
SOUTHPORT
WESTPORT
Greens Farms Road
Exit 18
To New York City
S. Compo Road
Sherwood Island State Park
Compo Beach
Long Island Sound

If you turn left on U.S. 1, you will reach the center of attractive Westport, with its many shops and eateries. Or, for a shorter out-and-back ride, simply turn around and retrace your route along the coast.

- 6.0 Turn right onto Routes 57 and 136N.
- 6.3 At a light go straight, staying on Rte. 136N.
- 7.4 Go straight at a junction with North Ave. on the left. (Rte. 136 is now Easton Rd.)
- 8.0 Fork left, staying on Rte. 136 (now Westport Turnpike). Watch for spectacular homes.
- 11.3 At a stoplight turn right onto Rte. 58S. Watch for good views of Hemlock Reservoir on the left, just beyond stands of large pine trees.
- 14.7 Pass underneath Rte. 15. *Caution:* Watch for traffic merging from Rte. 15.
- 16.4 Turn right onto Rte. 135S at an intersection with many stores, including eateries.
- 17.0 Fork left, following Rte. 135. Pass Fairfield University on the right, cross underneath I–95, and then cross U.S. 1 at a stoplight.
- 19.1 Turn right onto Old Post Rd. in Fairfield. (For a short side trip to a beach, keep going straight, until you reach a dead-end road. Then return to Old Post Rd.) You will pass several handsome churches, Fairfield Town Hall, and more spectacular homes. Then keep going straight, on Old Field Rd., as Old Post Rd. turns to the right.
- 20.8 At a T turn right onto Sasco Hill Rd.
- 21.1 Turn left onto (unmarked) Harbor Rd.
- 21.2 Fork left at a stop sign.
- 21.8 Veer to the left, still following the shoreline.
- 21.9 Fork to the right on Old South Rd., and soon left onto Pequot Ave.
- 22.8 At the end of a beach, fork left onto Sasco Creek Rd.
- 24.0 Fork left onto Beach side Ave., which climbs and crosses I–95.
- 24.3 Continue straight, as Greens Farms Rd. comes in from the right.

- 25.1 Turn right onto the access road for I–95.

  Turning left and riding across I–95, you arrive at Sherwood Island State Park, which for bicyclists waives the entrance fee. (Be sure to slow down and thank the attendant as you enter.)

- 25.3 Arrive back at the park-and-ride parking lot on the right.

2

Music Mountain Cruise

Salisbury—Lime Rock—Falls Village—Cornwall—
West Cornwall—Lime Rock—Salisbury

The Music Mountain Cruise rolls south from Salisbury to West Cornwall. Here when autumn sets the foliage ablaze, a covered bridge across the Housatonic River attracts just about as many visitors as this small village can handle. Cars line up along Route 7, and weekending New Yorkers crows the few stores. Hikers and campers on their way into the surrounding woods pass through the bridge, fishermen cast for trout lurking in the shadows of its span, and kayakers float by. The Music Mountain Cruise descends into this throng, providing an exhilarating interlude midway through an otherwise quiet ride.

This is the second ride starting and ending in the southern Berkshires town of Salisbury, which in the summer and fall is a hub of cultural and artistic activity. This ride follows the same path as the shorter Salisbury Ramble as far as Falls Village. From there, however, it diverges to explore the hills and river valley farther south, including Music Mountain, so named because it is the site of one of the oldest chamber music performance sheds in the nation. World-renowned musicians perform there on summer weekends.

Just outside Falls Village the cruise divides, offering two options for arriving in West Cornwall. The shorter ride turns right on a backroad for a challenging climb up Music Mountain, a green knob rising abruptly from the river. The route passes through a magnificent century-old row of sugar maples leading to a hilltop dairy farm and then plunges down the other side. This first option makes up for the miles saved with its quite steep 3-mile climb. The longer option skirts Music Mountain, with a short climb after 10 gradually rolling miles.

The two routes rejoin on the descent into West Cornwall, then follow the Housatonic River back through Lime Rock to Salisbury.

The Basics

Start: Salisbury, the most northwesterly town in Connecticut. From New York follow Rte. 22 to Millerton, then turn east on Rte. 44 into Connecticut and through Lakeville to Salisbury. From Connecticut or Massachusetts follow Rte. 7 to Canaan, then turn west onto Rte. 44 into Salisbury. Combined Routes 44 and 41 become Main St. Park on either side or behind the new Town Hall at the town's southern end.
Length: 31 or 35 miles.
Terrain: Rolling roads. The shorter option crosses Music Mountain, a challenging 3-mile climb in two big steps. The longer option features one short climb.
Food: The covered bridge at West Cornwall is an ideal spot to stop for a rest and a bite to eat. Either pack your snack or patronize one of the village's stores. There are picnic tables on the grassy riverbank to the right just before the bridge.
Traffic/Safety: Watch for faster-moving traffic on Routes 63 and 43.

Miles and Directions

- 0.0 Start at Salisbury Town Hall, in town center on west side of combined Routes 41 and 44, here named Main St. Ride south on Main St. toward Lakeville.
- 0.2 Turn left off Main St., just beyond town center, onto Salmon Kill Rd. *Caution:* This is a narrow, winding road with little shoulder.
- 2.4 Continue straight on Salmon Kill Rd. as Farnum Rd. goes right to Lakeville through scenic farmland.

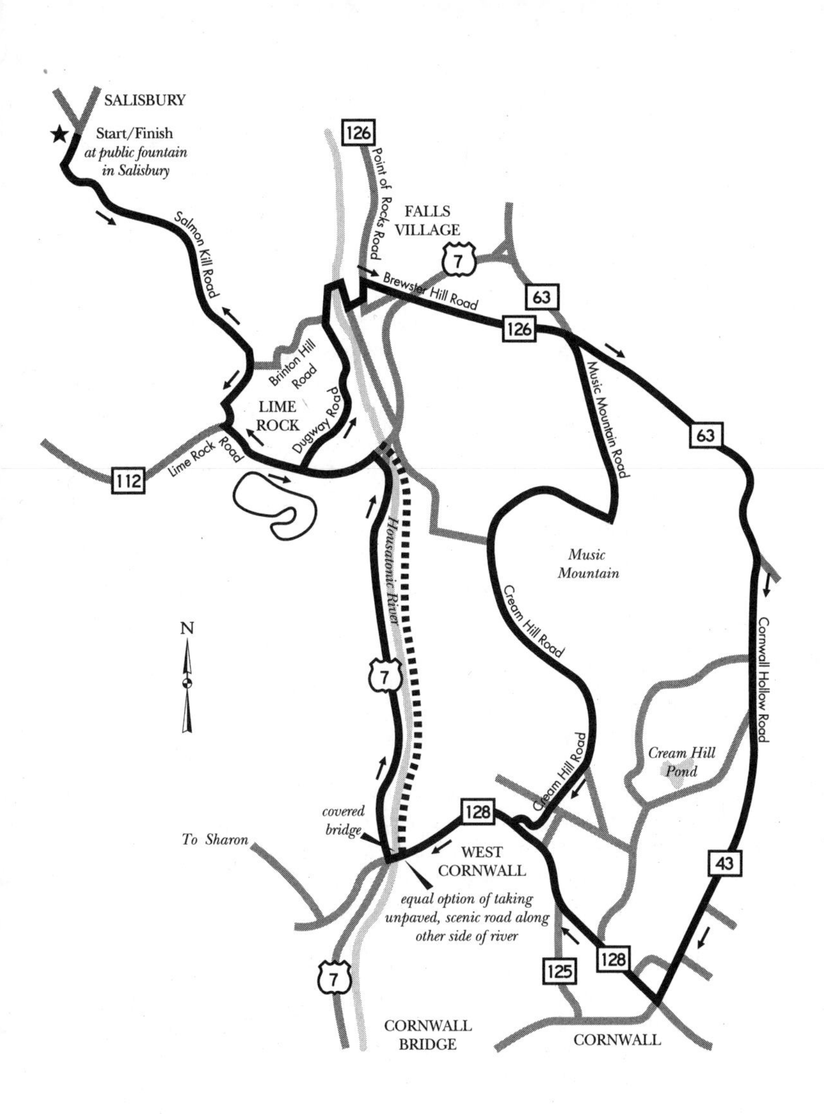

SALISBURY
Start/Finish
at public fountain
in Salisbury
Salmon Kill Road
126
Point of Rocks Road
FALLS
VILLAGE
7
Brewster Hill Road
63
126
Brinton Hill
Road
LIME
ROCK
Dugway Road
Music Mountain Road
63
Lime Rock Road
112
Housatonic River
Music
Mountain
Cream Hill Road
Cornwall Hollow Road
N
7
Cream Hill
Pond
Cream Hill Road
covered
bridge
128
To Sharon
WEST
CORNWALL
43
equal option of taking
unpaved, scenic road along
other side of river
128
125
7
CORNWALL
BRIDGE
CORNWALL

- 3.6 Stay right with Salmon Kill Rd., riding alongside Salmon Creek on the right.
- 4.4 Left on Rte. 112, Lime Rock Rd., at T after a quick downhill.
- 4.7 Enter Lime Rock, continuing straight on Rte. 112 as White Hollow Rd. bears off to right.
- 5.3 Left onto Dugway Rd., toward Amesville, directly opposite entrance to Lime Rock Park motor speedway.
- 7.6 Turn right, toward Rte. 7, onto the blue iron trestle bridge crossing the Housatonic. Stay right on Water St. coming off the bridge.
- 7.9 Prepare for two successive left turns: Stay left with Water St. as it passes beneath stone railway bridge; then turn left at the yield sign onto an unnamed road.
- 8.1 Right onto Brewster Hill Rd. (Rte. 126) as Point of Rocks Rd. (also Rte. 126) goes left. (This is where the Salisbury Ramble turns left.)
- 8.3 Merge left at stop sign onto Main St.
- 8.6 Cross Rte. 7, continuing straight. *Caution:* Watch out for traffic on Rte. 7.
- 10.6 Merge right onto Rte. 63.

From here the two options to this ride diverge. The shorter ride makes up for the miles saved with a steep climb for the next 3 miles. Caution: *If the temperature and humidity are high, be sure to carry plenty of water—or take the longer option. The longer option skirts the hills and requires only a short climb 10 miles from here.*

Option One

- 10.8 Turn right onto Music Mountain Rd. almost immediately after merging into Rte. 63.
- 14.8 Turn sharply left, uphill, onto unmarked Cream Hill Rd. Be careful not to follow Music Mountain Rd. downhill to the right. (Look for a stop sign on Cream Hill Rd. facing the opposite way.)
- 17.2 Sharp right at bottom of long, steep descent, staying on Cream Hill Rd. Approach turn with caution. Continue straight

through intersection in 1 mile. Pass Rattlesnake Rd. on the right.

- 18.0 Merge right onto Rte. 128, a well-paved road that swoops downhill to the Housatonic. (Option Two joins here from the left.)
- 20.0 Slow down for the blind curve into West Cornwall at bottom of descent. Mingle with sightseers among the many quaint shops and eateries.

There are two options for riding north out of West Cornwall: Rte. 7N or a scenic, partly unpaved road along the east bank of the river. To take this unpaved road, turn right after the railroad tracks and before the covered bridge. After 5 miles you will be on paved Lime Rock Station Rd., which comes out on Rte. 7.

- 20.2 Cross covered bridge over the Housatonic and turn right onto Rte. 7N toward Lime Rock and Canaan. Rte. 7 rolls along the western side of the Housatonic for the next 5 miles.
- 24.9 Turn left at the short cutoff to Rte. 112 toward Lime Rock. Watch out for traffic from both directions here.
- 25.7 Pass the Lime Rock Park raceway on the left and begin to retrace route to Salisbury.
- 26.7 Right onto Salmon Kill Rd. Follow winding route for next 4 miles.
- 30.8 Right onto combined Routes 41 and 44 into Salisbury.
- 31.0 Return to Salisbury public fountain.

Option Two

- 10.6 Continue straight on Rte. 63 toward Cornwall Hollow and Goshen after merge. *Caution:* This road has fast traffic and a narrow shoulder.
- 14.2 Bear right onto Rte. 43, Cornwall Hollow Rd., toward Cornwall Hollow and Cornwall.
- 19.3 Turn right at blinking light onto Rte. 128 toward West Cornwall.
- 20.1 Stay right with Rte. 128 as Rte. 125 joins from the left.
- 22.0 Continue straight as the Option One route, Cream Hill Rd., merges into Rte. 128 from the right.

- 23.0 Slow down for the blind curve into West Cornwall at bottom of descent. From here turn right onto either Rte. 7 or an unpaved rural road, following the directions under Option One, starting at 20.2 miles, back to Salisbury. Just add 4 miles to the mileage at each direction. That's the extra distance you've picked up by circling rather than climbing Music Mountain.

3

Salisbury Ramble

Salisbury—Lime Rock—Falls Village—Salisbury

The rolling roads of the Housatonic Valley in Connecticut's far northwest corner provide the ideal setting for cycling. The Salisbury Ramble and the Music Mountain Cruise both start and end in the town of Salisbury, only two hours north of—but a world away from—New York City. So pack your bags and bikes for a weekend in the southern Berkshires. Stay in one of the many local inns or B&B accommodations. Then follow these rides through the flatlands and hills surrounding Connecticut's "Hoosie River."

Starting from Salisbury, where the town fountain provides springwater, the ramble leads first to the town of Lime Rock, home of actor Paul Newman's favorite auto racing track. The region is full of attractions: chamber music at Music Mountain, summer camps, antiques, first-class inns, crafts, and summer theater. And Mr. Newman has neighbors like Meryl Streep, Kevin Bacon, Tom Brokaw, Whoopi Goldberg, and George Segal.

From Lime Rock this course crosses over the Housatonic River itself. It passes alongside the river for just over a mile, at the end of which are a grassy bank and picnic area overlooking kayak gates strung across the water. This is the best spot along the route to pause: while watching the kayakers paddle their nimble craft through the river's rapids, you can eat any snacks you packed. Also look for blue herons on rocks in the river, wild turkey along the shore, and leashed golden retrievers.

The next destination is the Twin Lakes. Lakes Washining and Washinee lie only a quarter mile apart, the bulge of one fitting into the curve of the other. Twin Lakes Road and then Taconic Road trace a rolling route around this pair, ending in Route 44, just a mile north of the public fountain in Salisbury center.

The Basics

Start: Salisbury, the most northwesterly town in Connecticut. From New York follow Rte. 22 to Millerton, then turn east on Rte. 44 into Connecticut and through Lakeville to Salisbury. From Connecticut or Massachusetts follow Rte. 7 to Canaan, then turn west onto Rte. 44 into Salisbury.Combined Routes 44 and 41 become Main St. Park on either side or behind the new Town Hall at the town's southern end.
Length: 21 miles.
Terrain: Mildly rolling roads; no major climbs. You might want to check beforehand on local road conditions, since these rural roads are sometimes being repaired.
Food: There is a restaurant at 15.0 miles. Salisbury is the biggest town on this ride. You may want to pack a snack to eat on the grassy banks of the Housatonic, at 7.2 miles, or at the Twin Lakes dock, at 14.1 miles.
Traffic/Safety: Care must be taken on the narrower rural roads (mentioned below). It's always a good idea to dress in bright colors and otherwise make yourself visible.

Miles and Directions

- 0.0 Start at Salisbury Town Hall, in town center on west side of combined Routes 44 and 41, here named Main St. Fill water bottles at spring-fed fountain. Ride south on Main St. toward Lakeville.
- 0.2 Turn left off Main Street, just beyond town center, onto Salmon Kill Rd. *Caution:* This road is narrow and winding, with a narrow shoulder.
- 2.4 Continue straight on Salmon Kill Rd., as Farnum Rd. goes right to Lakeville through rolling farmland.

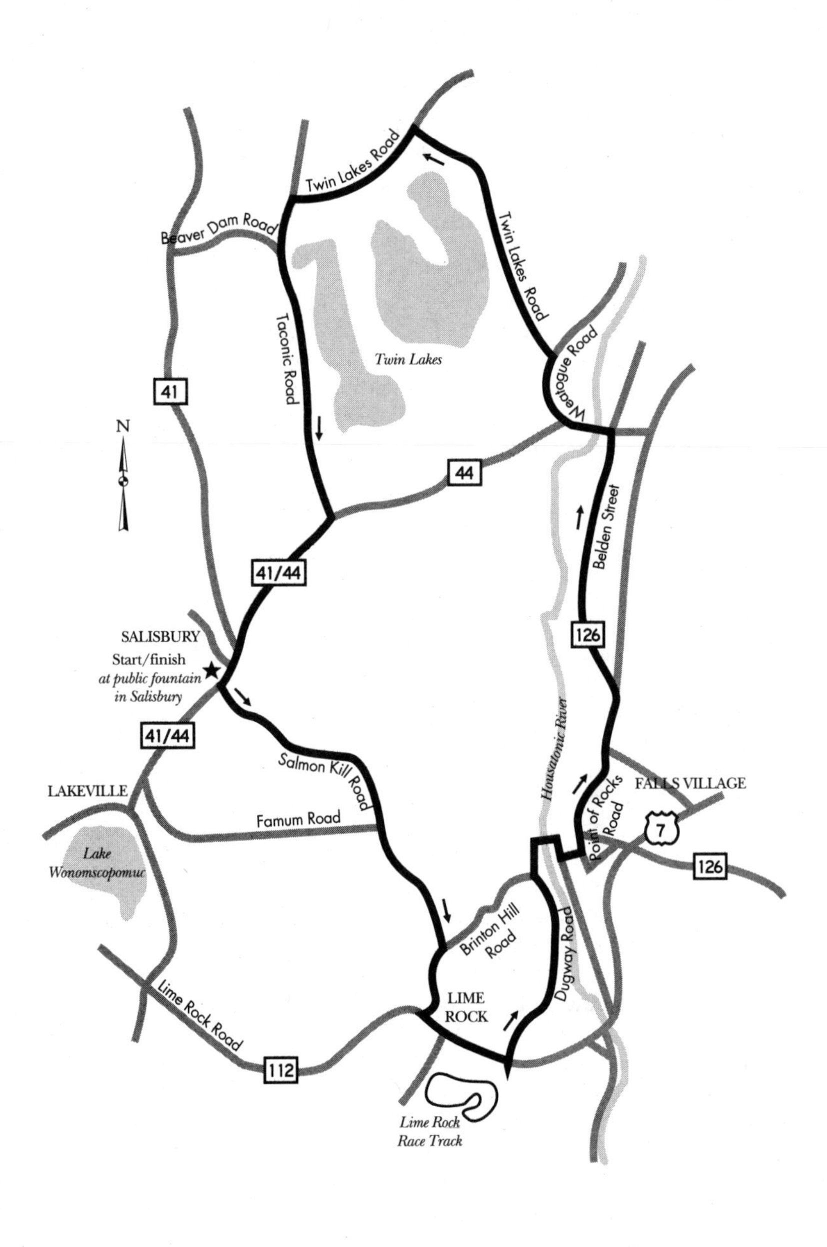
Twin Lakes Road
Beaver Dam Road
Twin Lakes Road
Taconic Road
Twin Lakes
Weatogue Road
41
N
44
Belden Street
41/44
126
SALISBURY
Start/finish
at public fountain
in Salisbury
41/44
Salmon Kill Road
Housatonic River
Point of Rocks Road
FALLS VILLAGE
LAKEVILLE
Famum Road
7
126
Lake
Wonomscopomuc
Brinton Hill Road
Dugway Road
LIME
ROCK
Lime Rock Road
112
Lime Rock
Race Track

- 3.6 Stay right with Salmon Kill Rd., riding alongside Salmon Creek on the right. Brinton Hill Rd. will come in on the left.
- 4.4 Left onto Rte. 112, Lime Rock Rd., at T after quick downhill.
- 4.7 Enter Lime Rock, continuing straight on Rte. 112 as White Hollow Rd. bears off to right.
- 5.3 Left onto Dugway Rd., toward Amesville, directly opposite entrance to Lime Rock Park motor speedway and Trinity Church. This road section is narrow and curving. At 7.0 miles there is a turnout on the right with a view of the river below.
- 7.6 Right, toward Rte. 7, onto the blue iron trestle bridge crossing the Housatonic. Stay right on Water St. coming off the bridge.
- 7.9 Prepare for three successive left turns: Stay left with Water St. as it passes beneath stone railway bridge; turn left at the yield sign onto an unnamed road; then turn left onto Point of Rocks Rd. (Rte. 126) as Brewster Hill Rd. (also Rte. 126) goes right.
- 9.5 Bear left with Rte. 126 (here named Belden St.) as it crosses railroad tracks. Sand Rd. bears off to right.
- 11.7 Left onto Rte. 44 at stop sign, passing over short stone bridge over Housatonic.
- 12.0 Right onto Weatogue Rd., the first turn after crossing the river.
- 12.8 Left onto Twin Lakes Rd. as Weatogue Rd. goes right.
- 14.9 Stay left on Twin Lakes Rd. after passing public boat launch area on left. There is a restaurant on the right.
- 15.3 Stay left again where Cooper Hill Rd. joins from the right.
- 16.7 Bear left at fork, staying on Twin Lakes Rd., at large grassy island. Then turn left, toward Salisbury and Lakeville, at the stop sign that immediately follows.
- 17.1 Continue straight onto Taconic Rd. at intersection. Beaver Dam Rd. turns right.
- 19.3 Right onto Rte. 44 at the end of Taconic Rd. Ride on the shoulder here, as the traffic is fast.
- 20.8 Enter Salisbury, passing the White Hart Inn on the right as Rte. 44 merges into Rte. 41S.
- 21.0 Arrive back at Salisbury Town Hall.

4

A Midstate Cruise

Middletown—Meriden—Berlin—
Cromwell—Middletown

Many of the rides in this book are favorites of local cycling clubs and touring groups. (It's one reason they're "the best.") But individual cyclists also have their favorite rides, of course—loops they know well, tackle regularly, and love. Here's such a personal favorite, from a young cyclist in Connecticut, Jeff Korenstein, who rides any way he can: on large fund-raising tours, with friends, and solo.

This first-rate excursion—it's scenic, varied, and exhilarating—is located just outside Middletown, home of Wesleyan University, halfway between Hartford and New Haven and just off three major highways, Routes 91, 15, and 9. Jeff created this ride by using the Connecticut Bicycle Map and a detailed street atlas, he says, and by "hooking together the best roads . . . and I did some exploring."

The 28-mile cruise begins on the outskirts of Middletown, at a shopping mall (a convenient place to rendezvous with other riders). From there the tour almost immediately heads to a pastoral landscape of fields, farms, and light woods. Along the way it also passes next to, through, and under a working quarry (you'll have to see it), where rock hounds can call ahead to go on a group tour and take home a souvenir.

The shorter, 13-mile loop climbs to a scenic ridge before returning through rolling countryside. ("I wanted one ride I could do after work and another one for the weekends," Jeff explains.)

After 9 miles the longer loop enters the city of Meriden. Once known as the Silver City because of its key role in the silver manufacturing industry in New England back in the mid-1800s, Meriden, like many other small U.S. cities, is today surviving with high-tech and biotechnology manufacturing and other smaller industries. Take time to admire some of the city's fine old brick buildings.

Just outside Meriden the tour passes through large, green Hubbard Park, the site of an annual spring festival in late April. The Daffodil Festival draws thousands of celebrants, dozens of floats and crafts vendors, and live music. If it's before 5:00 P.M. , the ride then takes a quiet, secluded access road along a reservoir, with an optional steep climb to a stone tower that affords a panoramic view of the countryside.

From that halfway point on the longer ride, it's 14 miles of scenic cruising, past a Christmas tree farm, another large park, a pick-your-own orchard, golf courses, farm stands, suburbs, and the town of Berlin—before you return to "civilization."

The Basics

Start: At a large shopping center parking lot at the junction of Routes 372 and 3, just off both Rte. 9 and I–91. From I–91 take exit 21 and head toward Cromwell on Rte. 372E. You will reach the shopping plaza on the right.
Length: 28.0 or 13.5 miles.
Terrain: The ride alternates between paved rural, suburban, and urban roads, all in relatively good shape. There are a few hills, mainly at the beginning of the ride. The shorter option has a modest climb to a ridge.
Food: There are plenty of places to pick up a snack or meal along Rte. 5 in Meriden at 9 miles and on Rte. 372 in Berlin at 21 miles. On the shorter ride there's a small convenience store/deli at 10 miles at the junction of Savage Hill and Berlin roads.
Traffic/Safety: Be prepared for changes in road conditions, from less busy, secluded rural roads to some urban traffic in Meriden.

Miles and Directions

- 0.0 Turn south on Rte. 3.
- 0.2 Turn left at the stoplight, staying on Rte. 3.
- 1.2 Right at the stoplight onto Mile Ln.
- 2.2 At a T and stop sign, turn left onto Ridgewood Rd. Watch for the good view on the left.
- 3.4 At another T and stop sign, turn right onto unmarked Westfield St.
- 4.0 Continue straight at the stop sign, onto Country Club Rd.
- 5.4 At the stop sign at I–91, keep going straight.

For a shorter, 13.5-mile loop, at 6.4 miles turn right onto Atkins St. When you reach the top of the ridge, you can take a side road on the left for good views of the surrounding country side. After 3.5 miles on Atkins St., which becomes Savage Hill Rd., turn right onto Berlin Rd., which comes just after Mill St. (There might be a deli and bike shop at this junction.) Then pick up the directions at 25.8 miles below.

- 7.5 Pass a large quarry on either side of the road and soon a park and a golf course on the right.
- 8.3 At the stop sign turn right onto Westfield Rd. Then pass under Rte. 15 and keep going straight.
- 9.2 At the stoplight turn left onto U.S. 5.
- 10.4 Turn right onto W. Main St. Note the large stone Town Hall and several handsome churches.
- 11.2 Veer right at a fork.
- 11.7 Pass Rte. 71 (Chamberlain Hwy.) on the right.

If it's after about 4:45 P.M. or between November and March, turn right onto Rte. 71. The access road into the Merimere Reservoir area closes promptly at 5:00 P.M. each day and is closed during the winter. After 2 miles on Rte. 71, watch for a left fork onto Butler St. After another 0.2 mile turn left onto Park Dr. and then right onto Edgewood Rd. Pick up the ride directions below at 16.4 miles.

- 11.9 Turn right onto Fowler Ave., a small residential street.

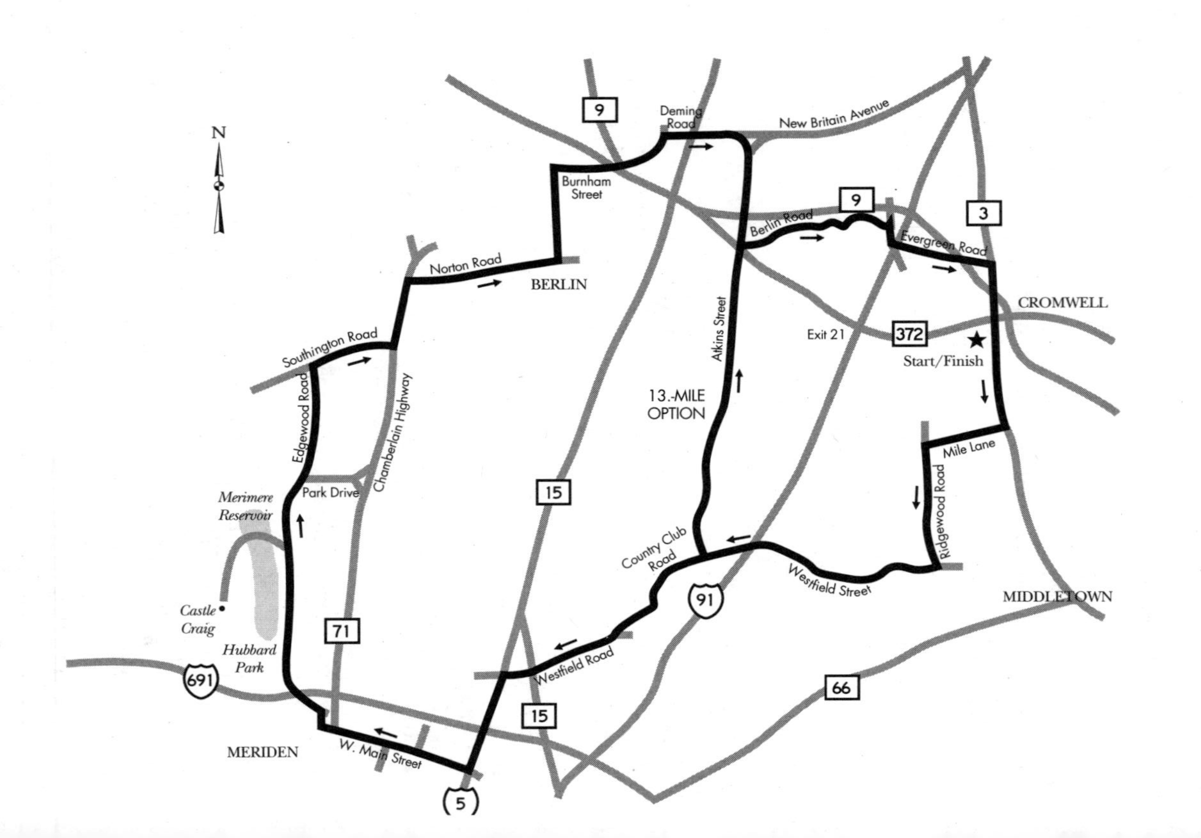
N
9
Deming Road
New Britain Avenue
Burnham Street
9
Berlin Road
3
Evergreen Road
Norton Road
BERLIN
CROMWELL
Atkins Street
Exit 21
372
Start/Finish
Southington Road
13.-MILE OPTION
Edgewood Road
Chamberlain Highway
Mile Lane
Ridgewood Road
Park Drive
15
Merimere Reservoir
Country Club Road
Westfield Street
91
MIDDLETOWN
Castle Craig
71
Hubbard Park
Westfield Road
691
66
15
MERIDEN
W. Main Street
5

- 12.1 Take the first left onto unmarked Reservoir Ave.
- 12.7 You will reach a dead end, with a pathway for bicycles and pedestrians around it. Just ahead on the right, underneath Rte. 691, is the gated access road into the reservoir area. On the left is Hubbard Park, with a large pond and picnic tables. Ride around the dead end and turn right underneath the highway, onto the access road, Percival Park Rd., and climb next to the reservoir on the left. Watch for the stone castle, Castle Craig, on top of the cliff on the other side of the reservoir.
- 14.0 Reach a fork, marked by three large cement cinder blocks across a road on the right and a bridge over the reservoir on the left. This ride continues through the cinder blocks on the right.

  For a short, steep side trip, turn left and climb for about 2 miles to Castle Craig, a stone tower that you can ascend for a panoramic view.

- 14.3 Turn left onto Edgewood Rd. You will pass a Christmas tree farm.
- 16.4 At the T turn right onto Southington Rd.
- 16.9 Pass Timberlin Park on the left. Although it looks like merely a golf course, this park also has a pond, trails, several drinking fountains, soda machines, and a lounge and restaurant. It's open seven days a week, beginning in April.
- 17.5 At another T turn left onto Chamberlain Hwy. (Rte. 71). Watch for a pear orchard on the right, where you can pick pears on the weekends (beginning in mid-August).
- 18.0 Turn right onto Norton Rd.
- 19.6 Turn left onto Four Rod Rd. You might see black-and-white Holstein cows grazing nearby.
- 20.7 At the T turn right onto Burnham St. Cross Rte. 372.
- 21.4 Fork left at the stop sign. Cross Rte. 9.
- 22.0 Turn right at a T onto Deming Rd. Cross Rte. 15.
- 23.5 Watch for a right turn, across from an industrial park, onto small Bacon Ln.

  For a slightly longer, "no-brainer" ride, keep going straight on New

Britain Ave. until it intersects busier Rte. 3. Turn onto Rte. 3 and crank back to the shopping plaza.

- 23.6 Turn right onto Wethersfield Rd.
- 23.8 Fork left onto Beckley Rd.
- 25.3 Turn left onto Berlin Rd.
- 25.8 Turn right onto North Rd.
- 26.0 While going uphill, turn left onto Evergreen Rd. Go through two stop signs, and cross Rte. 9.
- 27.3 At a stoplight turn right onto Rte. 3.
- 28.0 Arrive back at the shopping center.

5

Mystic Seaport Ramble

Center Groton—Mystic—Stonington—Center Groton

The Mystic Seaport Ramble is modeled after a shorter ride offered by the Pequot Cyclists on the day of the club's annual Seaport Metric Century ride (which we've mapped out along with the ramble in case you want to attempt it yourself). The ramble follows the same route as the Century ride through the historic towns of Mystic and Stonington. It then circles inland and back to Center Groton.

With no major hills, this leisurely tour leaves plenty of time to explore the two historic seaport towns on its route. In Mystic you can detour onto Route 27S to visit Mystic Seaport, a museum-village that re-creates everyday life in a nineteenth-century maritime community, or just take in the free view from Gravel Street across the river. Stonington is an authentic modern maritime community of restored colonial homes, tasteful shops, and docks for the sailing crowd. Take time to explore this pretty coastal village too.

The Basics

Start: Groton Schwinn Cyclery on Rte. 184 in Center Groton. Take exit 88 off I–95 onto Rte. 117N. Turn right onto Rte. 184 for 0.5 mile. The shop will be on your left. Park on side streets or in the office building lot across the street.
Length: 27.8 miles.

Terrain: Flat seacoast and rolling coastal inlands.
Food: Food in Mystic, including an ice cream parlor near the bridge.
Traffic/Safety: Be prepared for regular narrow, windy roads with narrow shoulders. Also, Mystic is busy on summer weekends, and Rte. 1 between Mystic and N. Water St. (Rte. 1A) has traffic and a narrow shoulder.

Miles and Directions

- 0.0 Ride east (away from the Rte. 117 intersection) on Rte. 184.
- 0.9 Right on Flanders at top of short rise.
- 1.5 Left on Noank Ledyard Rd.; orchards on the left.
- 2.2 Left on Sandy Hollow Rd.
- 2.9 Cross Allyn St.
- 3.3 Left on High St.
- 3.4 Right on Bindloss St.
- 3.6 Right on River Rd.
- 4.2 Left on Starr St., then bear right into Pearl St.
- 4.5 Left on Eldredge St.
- 4.6 Right on Gravel St., which passes along the riverfront opposite Old Mystic Village.
- 4.8 Left on Main St., Rte. 1, through Mystic, crossing the iron grate drawbridge over the Mystic River. Be careful crossing the grating.
- 8.8 right on North Water St. (Rte. 1A) toward Stonington Village.
- 9.4 Left on Trumbull St.
- 9.5 Right on Alpha St., crossing railroad overpass.
- 9.8 Left onto Water St., continuing straight through Stonington to its waterfront. When you reach the parking area jutting into the harbor, turn around and return along Water St.
- 10.1 Right onto Cannon Square.
- 10.2 Left on Main St.
- 10.7 turn left onto Broad St. at St. Mary's Church, to circle Stonington Green.

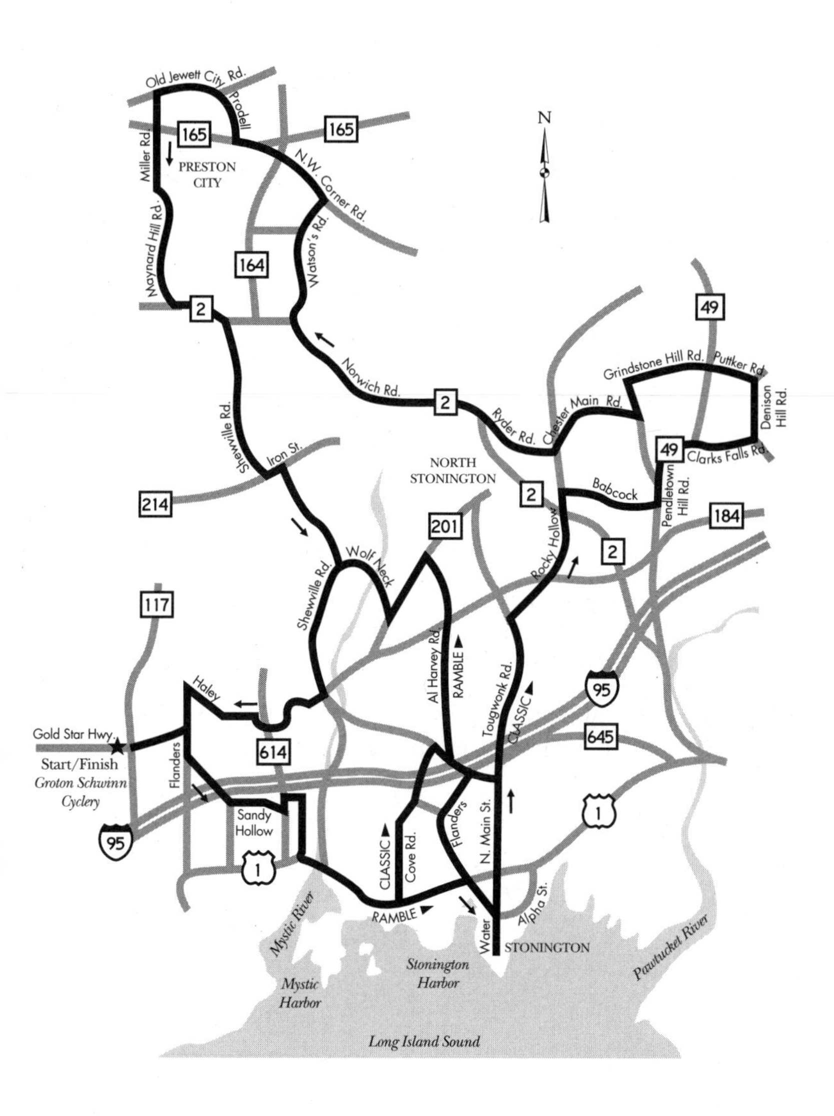

Old Jewett City Rd.
Prodell
165
165
Miller Rd.
PRESTON
CITY
N.W. Corner Rd.
Watson's Rd.
Maynard Hill Rd.
164
N
2
49
Norwich Rd.
Grindstone Hill Rd.
Puttker Rd.
Denison Hill Rd.
2
Chester Main Rd.
Ryder Rd.
Shewville Rd.
49
Clarks Falls Rd.
Iron St.
NORTH
STONINGTON
214
2
Babcock
Pendletown Hill Rd.
184
201
Rocky Hollow
2
Wolf Neck
117
Shewville Rd.
Al Harvey Rd
RAMBLE
Tougwonk Rd.
95
Haley
CLASSIC
645
Gold Star Hwy.
Start/Finish
Groton Schwinn
Cyclery
614
Flanders
Sandy
Hollow
Flanders
N. Main St.
1
95
CLASSIC
Cove Rd.
1
Alpha St.
RAMBLE
Mystic River
Water
STONINGTON
Stonington
Harbor
Pawtucket River
Mystic
Harbor
Long Island Sound

- 10.8 Right onto Water St., then right back onto Alpha Ave. and cross the railroad overpass.
- 11.1 Left onto Trumbull St.
- 11.2 Right on N. Main St.
- 11.9 Straight across Rte. 1.
- 13.6 Left on the Pequot Trail, a scenic road.
- 14.8 Right on Al Harvey Rd.
- 17.3 Straight across Rte. 184.
- 18.7 Left on Rte. 201.
- 20.0 Right on Wolf Neck Rd.
- 21.0 Straight across Lantern Hill Rd.
- 21.5 Straight onto Shewville Rd.
- 23.5 Right onto Rte. 184, Gold Star Hwy. From here you can continue west on Rte. 184 to Groton Schwinn Cyclery. The following, less direct route uses side roads where possible.
- 23.8 Right on Welles Rd.
- 24.2 Cross Rte. 184 and then Cow Hill Rd.; then turn right at Y intersection with Godfrey Rd.
- 25.0 Left on Rte. 184.
- 25.6 Right on Haley Rd. at the flashing yellow light.
- 26.2 Left on Quaker Farm Rd.
- 26.3 Left on Lambtown Rd.
- 26.9 Right onto Rte. 184.
- 27.8 Ride ends back at Groton Schwinn Cyclery.

5

Mansfield Hollow Cruise

Mansfield Hollow State Park—Windham—Hampton—Eastford—Mansfield Hollow State Park

What features make up an ideal bike tour in New England? Plenty of cruising on secluded roads with little traffic. Riding past stone walls and old cemeteries, next to a river, and through a state forest. Several forays into towns or villages with well-preserved eighteenth- and nineteenth-century architecture. Throw in a few hills and a starting point at a tranquil lake.

Welcome to such a first-rate ride. It's located just 5 miles from lively Storrs (home of the large University of Connecticut), 10 miles from I–84, and 25 miles from Hartford. The ride begins next to a lake in Mansfield Hollow State Park, where a canoe regatta is held each year. (After doing the cruise, you might take a short side trip to explore the park itself, by riding Bassetts Bridge Road to the west, reaching a large dike used for flood control.)

From the lake the ride explores the lightly settled countryside for about 12 miles, including the attractive village of Hampton. Along the way you'll pass by the access road for James L. Goodwin State Forest. Back in 1913 Goodwin, Connecticut's first conservationist, wrote glowingly about the "abundance of picturesque hills and valleys and streams in the state, once thickly covered with dense forests where Indians roamed, and now rapidly becoming despoiled." Today his namesake forest acts as a center for environmental activities—as well as containing miles of secluded paved and dirt roads and trails for mountain biking and hiking. The park headquarters also has rest rooms and water.

After skirting the adjoining Natchaug State Forest, with its own sites for relaxing and unpaved roads for exploring, this ride enters another well-preserved small town, Eastford. In the countryside the ride passes impressive stone walls, inspiring churches, and at least a half dozen old cemeteries. Finally, like most "classic" bike rides in New England, this one has a straight stretch on a rural highway before it veers off onto less traveled roads. For those who enjoy touring in a large group, there's an annual fund-raising ride, the Steeple Chase Bike Tour (it has rest stops at many local churches), that uses many of these same roads.

The Basics

Start: In Mansfield Hollow State Park, in Mansfield, just north of Willimantic. From Rte. 6 to the south, take Rte. 195N and watch for the brown state park signs. Turn right onto Bassetts Bridge Rd., cross a dike, and continue straight until you reach a large parking lot at a lake on the left. From the north take exit 68 off I–84 onto Rte. 195S and keep going through Storrs until you reach Bassetts Bridge Rd. on the left.
Length: 40.4 or 23.4 miles.
Terrain: Rolling, well-maintained country roads, varying from smoother, faster byways to rougher, less traveled lanes. There are several extended, not-too-steep climbs on the longer ride.
Food: There's a good grocery store/deli in Eastford at 21.4 miles.
Traffic/Safety: Stay alert on narrower shoulders on the rural highways. Also, be sure always to cross railroad tracks perpendicular to the tracks.

Miles and Directions

- 0.0 Turn left out of the parking lot at the lake and immediately cross a bridge.
- 1.0 Fork right onto S. Bedlam Rd.
- 1.9 After crossing another bridge, reach a three-way intersection. Take the "soft" right turn.

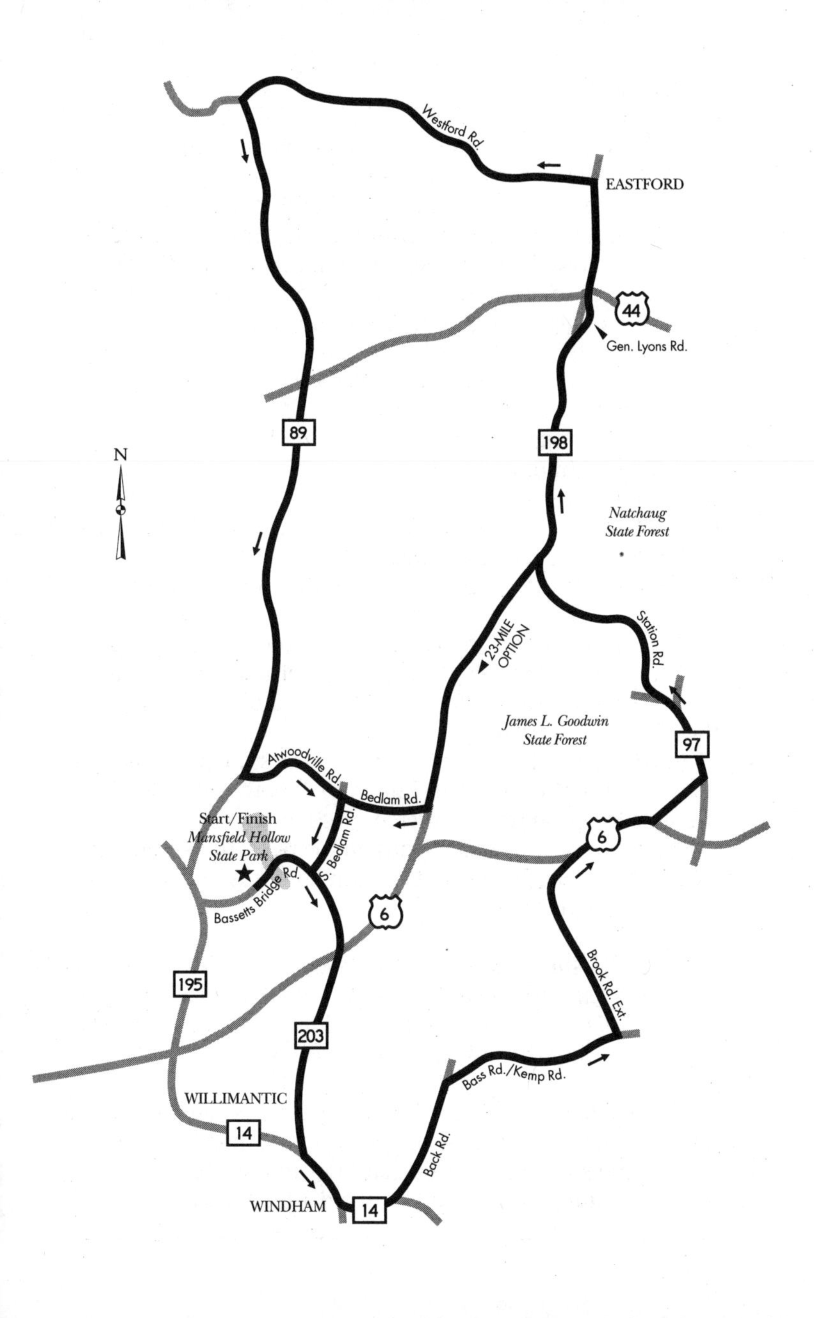
Westford Rd.
EASTFORD
44
Gen. Lyons Rd.
89
198
N
Natchaug State Forest
Station Rd.
23-MILE OPTION
James L. Goodwin State Forest
97
Atwoodville Rd.
Bedlam Rd.
Start/Finish
Mansfield Hollow State Park
S. Bedlam Rd.
6
Bassetts Bridge Rd.
6
Brook Rd. Ext.
195
203
Bass Rd./Kemp Rd.
WILLIMANTIC
14
Back Rd.
WINDHAM
14

- 2.2 Head straight across Rte. 6 at a stoplight, onto Rte. 203S.
- 4.6 Turn left onto Rte. 14E.
- 5.4 Turn left, staying on Rte. 14E. But first take a few minutes to admire the handsome nineteenth-century houses and Gothic-windowed church here in Windham. Also, as you leave the center of town, note the long, elaborate stone wall on the left—it's like something from medieval Europe.
- 6.1 Turn left onto Back Rd.
- 7.6 Turn right onto Bass Rd., which becomes Kemp Rd.
- 10.1 Turn left onto Brook Rd. Ext.
- 12.0 At a stop sign turn right onto S. Brook Rd.
- 12.8 Turn right onto Rte. 6.
- 13.5 On the other side of Rte. 6, see Potter Rd. This is the access road for James L. Goodwin State forest, which has a rest room and pleasant grounds for a break.
- 13.9 Turn left (it's a "soft" fork) off Rte. 6 onto an unmarked road.
- 15.0 Turn left at a T onto Rte. 97. Enter Hampton, "an unspoiled rural community," as a historical marker along Rte. 97 says. Hampton was settled in 1786, on land first inhabited by the Nipmuck Indians.
- 15.9 Fork left onto Station Rd. Notice the stone walls along the road. (A turnoff on the left, Estabrook Rd., would take you into the state forest on several interconnecting dirt and paved roads.) Next pass several gated dirt roads on the right; these lead into adjoining Natchaug State Forest. Station Rd. turns into Morey Rd.
- 16.3 Turn right onto Rte. 198.

For a shorter, 23.4-mile ride, turn left onto Rte. 198. After 3.8 miles, just before a bridge, turn right onto Bedlam Rd. After another 1.3 miles, turn left onto S. Bedlam Rd. and, after another 1 mile, right at a stop sign. In 1 mile you will reach the parking lot at the lake.

- 16.9 Pass the entrance for Natchaug State Forest. A short distance along the access road are picnic tables next to a stream. To explore the graded dirt roads that loop around this piney forest, you must climb for 0.5 mile on an old asphalt access road.

- 18.9 Turn right onto Gen. Lyon Rd., named after Gen. Nathaniel Lyons, "the saviour of Missouri to the Union cause and the first Northern general killed in the Civil War." (Note Pilfershire Rd. on the right—it comes down from Natchaug State Forest.)
- 19.4 At a stop sign turn right and immediately cross U.S. 44. Look for a cemetery on the right.
- 21.4 Reach Eastford, settled in 1710. This is a good place for a break—before tackling the last half of the ride. Check out the Eastford Village Store, which has a good food selection, as well as a small cafelike area where one can relax and watch the goings-on. (The store is closed on Sundays and open on Saturdays until 3:00 P.M.) Then turn right onto Westford Rd.
- 27.2 At a stop sign at a church, turn left onto Rte. 89. You pass more old cemeteries.
- 36.7 Watch for and turn left onto Atwoodville Rd.
- 37.4 Fork right, staying on Atwoodville Rd.
- 38.4 Turn right at a four-way intersection, onto S. Bedlam Rd.
- 39.5 At a three-way intersection, turn right.
- 40.4 Arrive back at the parking lot at the lake.

Maine

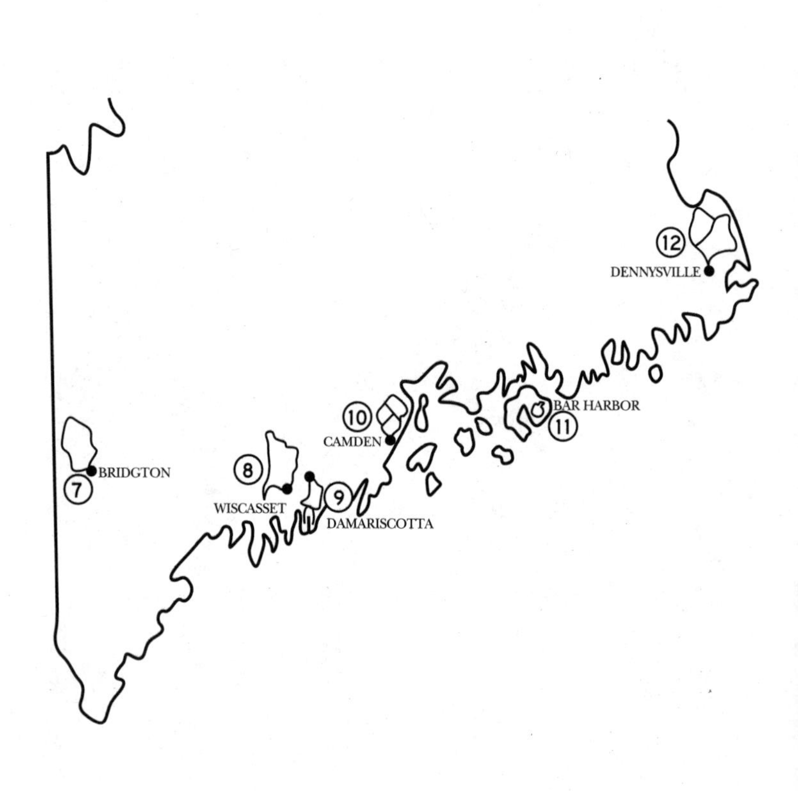
12
DENNYSVILLE
BAR HARBOR
11
10
CAMDEN
8
BRIDGTON
7
WISCASSET
9
DAMARISCOTTA

Maine

7. Moose Country Challenge 50
8. Kennebec Crossing Challenge 54
9. Pemaquid Point Cruise 58
10. Camden Hills and Coastal Cruise 63
11. Acadia National Park Cruise 69
12. Sunrise County Challenge 73

7

Moose Country Challenge

Bridgton—Lovell—Center Lovell—
East Stoneham—Waterford—Bridgton

The Moose Country Challenge, a 41-mile route, explores the pond-studded terrain between Sebago Lake and the White Mountains. On a sunny day in mid-March, this is the perfect ride from which to take in the scenes of a winter's end—skiers enjoying the last runs of the season on the slopes of Pleasant Mountain, snowmobilers zipping around widening patches of corn stubble, ice fishermen dragging their bobhouses off Moose Pond. In the summer the same lakes are playgrounds for boaters and swimmers.

This ride will appeal to cyclists wanting to enjoy alpine views without any more than a couple of short, steep climbs. It's a favorite inland tour of Maine's cycling clubs at any time in the cycling season.

Highlights of this trip are several pristine lakeside villages, including Waterford. First settled in 1775, this congregation of white clapboard buildings appears to have changed little in the last 200 years. It is now a National Historic Site. At the beginning and end of the loop, relax at lively Highland Lake Park, offering picnic tables, a beach, and a bike rack.

Local riders are not the only cyclists to have discovered Waterford. One clan rides across the continent from Portland, Oregon, to Portland, Maine, every year, stopping at the general store.

By the way, there are moose in these woods (as the numerous MOOSE CROSSING signs on Route 302 reveal). The best times to see them are early mornings and late afternoons.

The Basics

Start: Bridgton, just northwest of Sebago Lake. From Portland, Maine, take Rte. 302W directly into Bridgton, turn left with Rte. 302 as Rte. 117 continues straight, and park at the top of the hill, near the granite memorial. Bridgton can also be reached easily from Conway, New Hampshire, via Rte. 302E.
Length: 41.5 miles.
Terrain: Surprisingly flat, considering the terrific views of mountains all around. Two climbs, about 1 mile long each: from North Waterford to Waterford, at 26.0 miles, and from North Bridgton to Highland Ridge Rd., at 37.0 miles.
Food: Most of the towns along the route have a general store.
Traffic/Safety: Most of the roads have speed limits of 40 to 50 mph and narrow shoulders.

Miles and Directions

- 0.0 From the granite memorial in the center of Bridgton, ride west on Rte. 302, here called N. High St., toward Fryeburg. *Caution:* This first mile along Rte. 302 can have heavy traffic, so stay alert.
- 1.2 Bear left with Rte. 302W toward Fryeburg, as Rte. 93 forks right toward Sweden. (For an alternative, though hillier, initial 10 miles, turn right on Rte. 93. This backroad passes through Sweden on the way to rejoining the given route in Lovell.) Watch for Moose Pond on both sides of the road at 4.5 miles.
- 5.5 Right on Knights Hill Rd., opposite the Pleasant Mountain ski area. Knights Hill Rd. passes through mostly unpopulated woods, climbing gradually for half of its 5.8 miles, then descending for the other half.
- 11.4 At stop sign, left on Rte. 93, Lovell Rd., then bear right with the road into Lovell.
- 11.4 Right on Rte. 5N.
- 13.3 Stay with Rte. 5, following the sign toward Stoneham and Bethel, as Rte. 5A turns to the right. You will pass a turnoff for Kezar Lake.

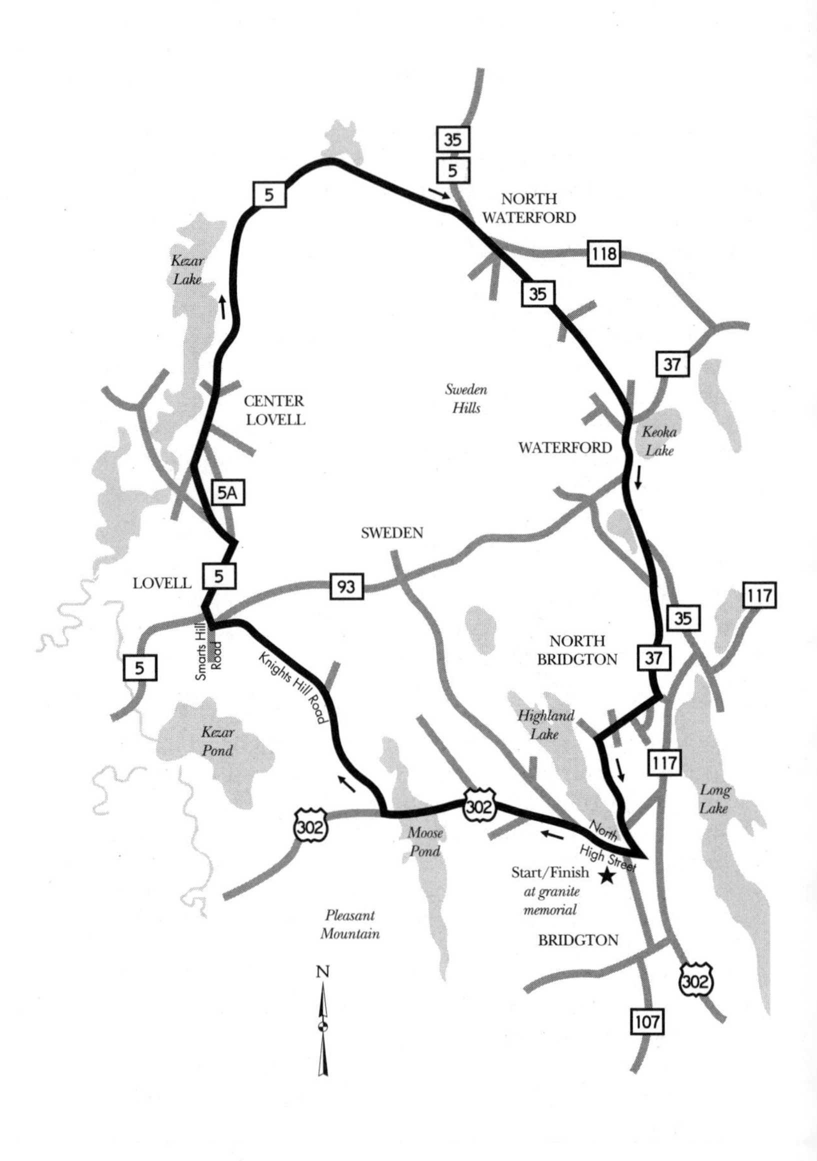
35
5
5
NORTH
WATERFORD
118
Kezar
Lake
35
37
CENTER
LOVELL
Sweden
Hills
Keoka
Lake
WATERFORD
5A
SWEDEN
LOVELL
5
93
117
35
5
Smarts Hill
Road
Knights Hill Road
NORTH
BRIDGTON
37
Highland
Lake
Kezar
Pond
117
Long
Lake
302
302
Moose
Pond
North
High Street
Start/Finish
at granite
memorial
Pleasant
Mountain
BRIDGTON
N
302
107

- 20.3 Pass through North Lovell on Rte. 5.
- 23.5 Pass Keewaydin Lake Dam on left, with picnic tables and swimming.
- 24.3 Pass through East Stoneham, with a country store on left. Rte. 5 straightens and flattens.
- 25.1 Arrive at the "international signpost" intersection. Continue straight onto Rte. 35S as Rte. 5N turns left.
- 26.7 Bear right and uphill at the fork, staying on Rte. 35S toward Waterford and Harrison. Rte. 118 bears left.
- 26.9 Pass through North Waterford. Tut's General Store offers drinks and snacks.
- 31.4 Right at bottom of hill into downtown Waterford. Rte. 35 merges into Rte. 37 here. Town beach on Keoka Lake in a few hundred yards.
- 32.5 Stay left with combined Routes 35 and 37 as Sweden Rd. turns right.
- 34.0 Fork right with Rte. 37S toward Bridgton as Rte. 35 turns left toward Harrison. Bear Pond on right.
- 37.3 Enter North Bridgton and turn right, proceeding steeply uphill on Chadbourne Hill Rd., which borders the grounds of Bridgton Academy.
- 38.7 Left at T. This is Highland Ridge Rd. (although it is unmarked here). You will soon pass a scenic mountain view in North Bridgton, then Highland Lake Park.
- 41.4 Right at T, immediately following Highland Lake Park on the right. This is Rte. 302W, in downtown Bridgton.
- 41.5 Arrive at granite memorial at intersection of N. and S. High streets in Bridgton.

8

Kennebec Crossing Challenge

Wiscasset—Whitefield—Gardiner—Richmond—Days Ferry—Wiscasset

This exhilarating and challenging tour circumvents the thumb of land formed by the Sheepscot and Kennebec rivers as they rush down to the tangle of islands between Bath and Boothbay Harbor. Its 55 miles of rolling roads lead from the historic seafaring town of Wiscasset to modest farming communities inland and the old mill town of Richmond before following the Kennebec River back to the sea.

The ride avoids Maine's crowded coastal roads, opting instead for a riverine landscape. It's a good excursion for September and October, when the weather turns crisp, brilliant leaves begin to rattle off the trees, and the season's crops of pumpkin and squash dot the acres of fields that slope toward the Kennebec River. (Keep an eye on the weather, though, as gales can come up.)

Be sure to stop and enjoy some of the sights along this rural route. Look for the Sheepscot Reversing Falls, reached by a short, dirtroad detour to the right 4 miles into the ride. A collection of monumental abstract sculptures unexpectedly grace the roadside leading into Whitefield. Pack a sandwich to eat along the banks of the Kennebec River. And leave plenty of time to explore historic Wiscasset itself. The elegant homes of nineteenth-century merchants and captains still grace this former seafaring town. And along its waterfront lie the weathered remains of the last two four-masted clipper ships known to exist. They're some reminders of a bygone era.

The Basics

Start: Wiscasset. From Rte. 95N take exit 22 toward Brunswick and Rte. 1. Follow Rte. 1 through Bath to Wiscasset. Park in Wiscasset town center—just be sure it's not a two-hour spot.
Length: 55.2 miles.
Terrain: Rolling hills between two rivers. No major climbs.
Food: There are several coffee shops on Water St., Gardiner's main street, midway at 23.3 miles. Wiscasset offers a variety of small cafes and restaurants for a meal before or after the ride.
Traffic/Safety: Watch for traffic on Rte. 27N through Gardiner, on Rte. 127N outside Days Ferry, and on Rte. 1 into Wiscasset. Also, be careful on the bridge on Rte. 197 outside Richmond.

Miles and Directions

- 0.0 Follow Rte. 218N out of Wiscasset, passing the town's nineteenth-century Old Jail, on a rise overlooking the Sheepscot River.
- 5.9 Continuing on Rte. 218N, pass the eighteenth-century Center School and Meeting House on left, just after Golden Ridge Road on the right. Look back over your shoulder. There's a view toward the ocean from here.
- 12.9 Pass Whitefield Ring *Cross* sculpture, cut from a 20-foot granite cemetery stone, on right. Look for other abstract sculptures in clearing on left just ahead.
- 13.2 Entering village of Whitefield, bear left on Rte. 194W toward Pittston. Routes 218 and 194E turn right on bridge across Sheepscot River. Rte. 194W traverses the rolling hills from the Sheepscot to the Kennebec River.
- 16.8 Bear left, staying with Rte. 194, a half mile after passing the Pittston General Store.

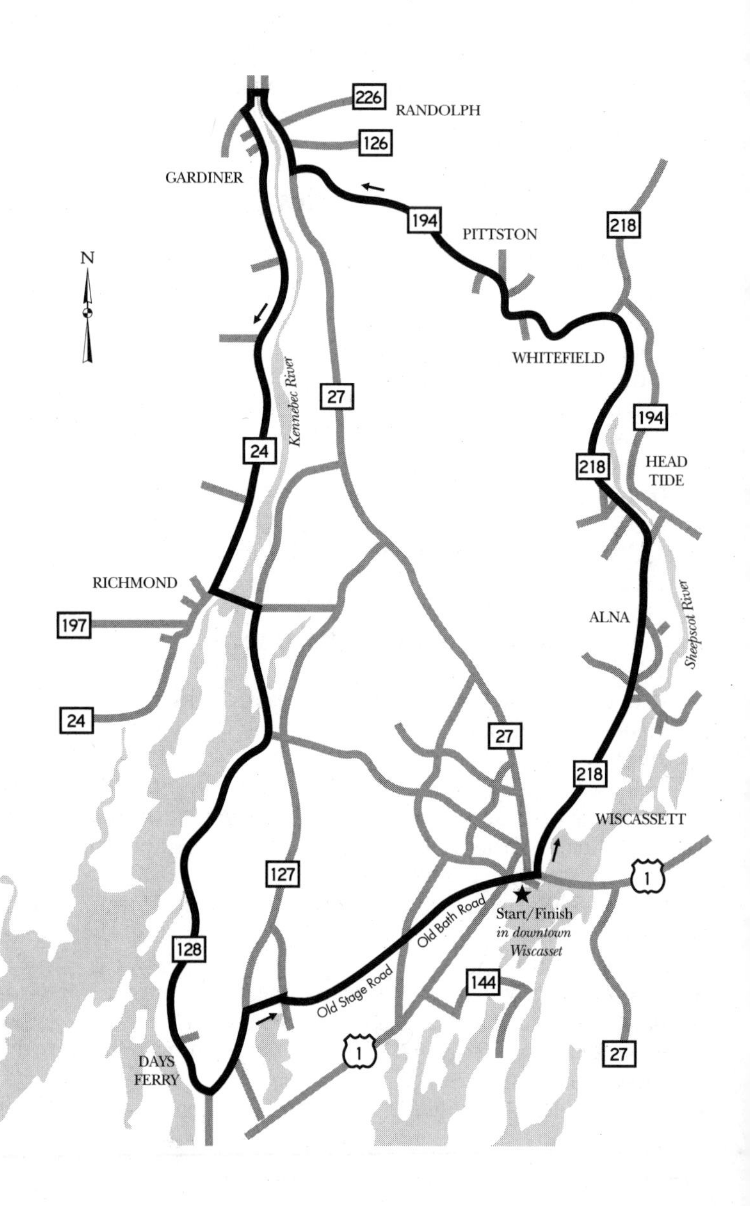
226
RANDOLPH
126
GARDINER
194
PITTSTON
218
N
WHITEFIELD
Kennebec River
27
194
24
218
HEAD
TIDE
RICHMOND
197
ALNA
Sheepscot River
24
27
218
WISCASSETT
127
1
Old Bath Road
Start/Finish
in downtown
Wiscasset
128
Old Stage Road
144
1
DAYS
FERRY
27

- 21.4 Right on Rte. 27N toward Randolph and Gardiner. Rte. 194 ends here.
- 22.7 Follow Rte. 27 as it turns left across bridge over Kennebec River and into Gardiner.
- 23.0 Immediate left onto Rte. 24, nearest the river, coming off bridge. *Note:* This can be a busy, tricky turn. You might also turn right and then double back—to avoid traffic waiting to turn left.
- 23.3 Follow Rte. 24 as it takes a quick right into the town's shopping district. Then immediately, at the stoplight, turn left with Rte. 24, here called Water St., to follow the Kennebec River south. Water St., both to the left and to the right of the light, is home to several casual lunch spots.
- 28.8 Continue straight up hill on Rte. 24 as Riverside Rd. curves left.
- 33.9 Following Rte. 24S from Gardiner, take a sharp left onto Rte. 197E, toward Dresden Mills, immediately after passing under railway tracks. (You have missed this turn if you enter Richmond.)
- 34.5 Rte. 197E crosses Kennebeck River. *Caution:* Walk your bike across iron grate if bridge is wet.
- 35.0 Right on Rte. 128S toward Woolwich.
- 45.9 Pass through Days Ferry, catching a glimpse of the Bath Iron Works downriver and smelling the ocean.
- 46.3 Left onto Rte. 127N at T. From here this ride follows a series of backroads home to Wiscasset rather than joining the more direct but heavily trafficked Rte. 1. Rte. 127 also has traffic, though.
- 48.3 Right onto Old Stage Rd., the second right off Rte. 127.
- 51.8 Bear left at stop sign.
- 51.9 Right at fork after passing cemetery on left.
- 53.4 At stop sign turn left on Old Bath Rd., which is also unmarked.
- 54.8 Left onto Rte. 1N for final stretch into Wiscasset. Watch out for traffic along this busy stretch of road.
- 55.2 Arrive in Wiscasset town center.

9

Pemaquid Point Cruise

*Damariscotta—Round Pond—New Harbor—
Pemaquid Point—South Bristol—Damariscotta*

Centuries ago glaciers carved out the rocky shoreline that distinguishes Maine's coast from that of the smoother Atlantic seaboard father south. Midcoast, between Brunswick and Belfast, the glaciers scooped out a series of distinct peninsulas reaching south into the ocean. One of these, the finger of land from Damariscotta to Pemaquid Point, offers excellent cycling.

A local newspaper, the *Maine Sunday Telegram,* calls this tour "the best one-day bike ride in Maine." The ride passes through traditional coastal villages, where fishing is still a way of life but is one that now coexists with a tourism industry. A lobster lunch, a lighthouse, spectacular ocean views, a sandy beach, a possible boat cruise, and historical sites will beckon you to stop regularly. With a longer option and several possible shortcuts, this easily becomes an all-day outing.

From Damariscotta to Muscongus Bay, the road crossing the peninsula's top passes by four ponds. Red-winged blackbirds, perched on reeds, survey the land while swaying in the wind. In Round Pond detour to the left for a quick visit to the town's crowded and picturesque harbor.

Riding south from Round Pond, you'll head inland through woods before reaching the water again at Long Cove. (The tide often leaves colorful dinghies grounded on this little inlet's gravelly bottom.) The road continues along the coast, passing the neat gardens of renovated clapboard homes outside New Harbor.

If you have a hankering for a lobster feast, try Shaw's restaurant in New Harbor. This casual lunch and dinner place is perched on a wharf overlooking the town's active harbor. You can select the lobster you want boiled and then eat it on the deck, pausing to watch the comings and goings of the boats. There's a popular boat cruise outfit that will take you out in the ocean for an hour ($8.00) or longer. You might see rare puffins or sea lions.

From New Harbor it is only a short stretch south to Pemaquid Point. The lighthouse here stands sentinel over a series of ledges, striped with black and white rock, that march into the sea. Also visit the small Fishermen's Museum inside the lighthouse itself ($1.00). Or stop here for lunch at the Seagull Restaurant.

Backtracking to New Harbor, the cruise turns left to Pemaquid Beach, a beautiful, crescent-shaped stretch of sand with a parking lot, snack bar, and rest rooms. Nearby Colonial Pemaquid, the excavated foundations of an old settlement, reveals that this peninsula was colonized as a station for European fishermen as early as the sixteenth century.

From Pemaquid Beach the route heads up the peninsula's western flank back to Damariscotta. If you have the time and energy, take the 15-mile round-trip detour to Christmas Cove. Named by Capt. John Smith, who spent a lonely Christmas Eve here while exploring the coast in 1614, Christmas Cove is located on a tiny island connected to the mainland by a short drawbridge. Also on this detour, and well worth a visit, is Thompson's Ice House. Built in 1826, Thompson's has been restored as a working ice-harvesting operation and museum.

The Pemaquid Point Cruise is a good ride for any cyclist—as long as he or she is in good shape. The many scenic spots will encourage one to stop, rest, and explore along the way. The Kennebec Crossing Challenge (Ride 8) explores the inland area near Wiscasset, the next town south on Route 1; it makes a good companion ride. Combine the two tours for a full weekend of cycling.

The Basics

Start: Damariscotta, located on Rte. 1B about 18 miles east of Bath. Park in a public lot in the center of town, on the south side of the road behind a row of stores and offices.
Length: 38.9 or 51.4 miles.
Terrain: Rolling coastal terrain with several steep and long hills (see "Miles and Directions").
Food: Every town on this route has at least one grocery store or snack bar. For lunch stop at either Shaw's in New Harbor, at 16.5 miles, or the Seagull Restaurant at Pemaquid Point, at 20.0 miles.
Traffic/Safety: Watch for faster-moving traffic on Routes 32 and 129.

Miles and Directions

- 0.0 Leaving the Damariscotta parking lot, turn right onto Rte. 1BN. Continue straight as Rte. 129 turns south.
- 1.2 Right onto Biscay Rd. toward Round Pond. Stay on this smooth, climbing, and rolling road as several back routes take off to either side. Halfway along you will skirt the northern tip of Biscay Pond.
- 6.4 Right on Rte. 32, continuing toward Round Pond. *Caution:* Watch for faster-moving traffic on Rte. 32.
- 10.3 Continue straight through Round Pond, a small lobster port, on Rte. 32. Detour to the left for a visit to the busy, compact harbor.
- 16.5 Pass New Harbor and Shaw's restaurant on left. Stop for sightseeing, ocean viewing, or lunch.
- 17.2 Just past New Harbor turn left onto Rte. 130 toward Pemaquid Point.
- 20.0 Bear left with the main road to the lighthouse. At the lighthouse you might explore its rocky surroundings down to the water. Then backtrack on Rte. 130 toward New Harbor.
- 22.6 Just before reaching the junction of Routes 130 and 32, turn left down an unmarked road to Pemaquid Beach.

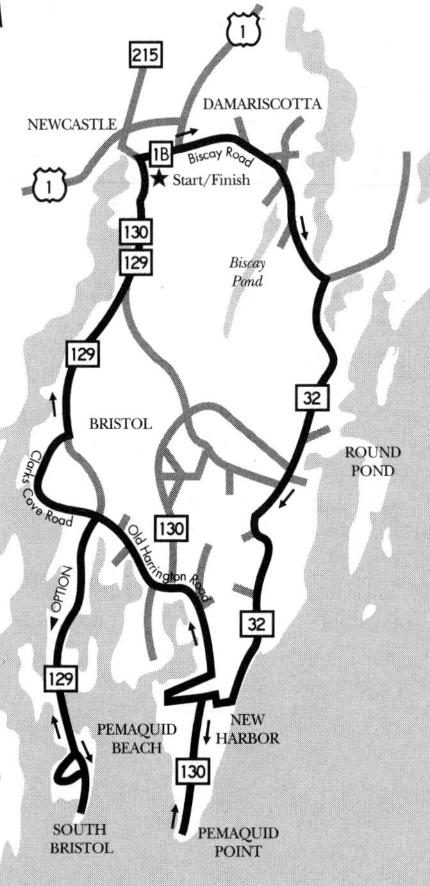
N
1
215
DAMARISCOTTA
NEWCASTLE
1B
Biscay Road
Start/Finish
1
130
129
Biscay
Pond
129
32
BRISTOL
ROUND
POND
Clarks Cove Road
130
Old Harrington Road
OPTION
32
129
NEW
HARBOR
PEMAQUID
BEACH
130
SOUTH
BRISTOL
PEMAQUID
POINT

- 23.6 Right at intersection after passing Pemaquid Beach on the left. Or detour straight to see the Colonial Pemaquid restoration, unearthed foundations of a seventeenth-century village with a small museum housing artifacts.
- 25.0 Left onto Rte. 130.
- 26.8 Left onto Old Harrington Rd., toward Bristol, immediately after Rte. 130 crosses Pemaquid River.
- 28.0 Bear right with Old Harrington Rd. as Harbor Rd. turns left. You will pass the eighteenth-century Harrington Meeting House, and then the road changes its name to Pemaquid Rd.
- 29.7 Straight across Rte. 129 onto Clarks Cove Rd. Be prepared for a steep hill. The road climbs, descends to a small cove, and then climbs again. This road leads back to Rte. 129 farther north.

Turn left on Rte. 129 for a scenic detour of 12.5 miles. Rte. 129 travels down a narrow finger of land, over a drawbridge at 5.0 miles, and into South Bristol. As you return, circle around W. Side Rd. to the left for 1.5 miles. This will put you back on Rte. 129, toward the junction with Clarks Cove Rd. Continue with the directions below, adding 12.5 miles.

- 32.5 Left onto Rte. 129, the final stretch back to Damariscotta.
- 35.7 Turn left at stop sign, staying on Rte. 129 to Damariscotta. Be ready for a long hill.
- 38.7 Left onto Rte. 1B.
- 38.9 Return to public parking lot on left in Damariscotta.

11

Acadia National Park Cruise

Local bike club members look forward eagerly to each year's first tour of the carriage paths lacing Acadia National Park, on Maine's famous Mount Desert Island. These dirt roads, winding through the island's interior forests and skirting its lakes and mountains, afford spectacular views of the Atlantic Ocean and are one of Acadia's unique features. John D. Rockefeller, Jr., financed and directed their construction between 1917 and 1933. The roads are superbly built, with gentle grades, stone culverts, and retaining walls. They cross sixteen stone bridges, each one individually and gracefully designed. Altogether the park boasts 170 miles of trails and bridle and carriage paths (some just for hiking).

This is as beautiful and unusual a tour on a sunny afternoon in August as it is on a dark and dripping early morning in April, when Acadia's forests and mountains take on an isolated magnificence most tourists miss. Highlights include spruce-framed views of Somes Sound and a dramatic passage along a ridge between Jordan Pond and the Penobscot Mountain.

The Acadia National Park Cruise covers nearly 30 miles of trails that are navigable by a bike with wide tires—either a mountain or a hybrid bike is highly preferable. Although these broad paths are even and packed, there are some loose spots. So take it easy, especially on downhill runs, and share the roads amicably with walkers and horseback riders. The maze of carriage roads can be confusing at some junctions; you may want to request a map a the visitor center to supplement the one in this book. If you want more exercise—and a great view—try climbing Cadillac Mountain.

The Basics

Start: There are several parking areas in the park. One is at the north end of the lot at the Acadia National Park Visitor Center, on Rte. 3 just north of Bar Harbor. (The center itself is open from mid-June through August.)
Length: 26 miles, in three interconnecting shorter loops.
Terrain: Hard-packed gravel and dirt roads, graded for bicycles. Several long but gradual climbs and descents.
Food: Be sure to pack a picnic lunch to enjoy at any of the numerous scenic spots. This is an energetic ride, and you should plan on devoting four to six hours to the tour. The ride passes Jordan Pond House, a sit-down restaurant operated by the National Park Service, at about 17 miles.
Traffic/Safety: You will share these carriage roads with many walkers and occasional horseback riders. A bell is useful. A few places in the roads have soft, sandy shoulders. Stay in control of your bike at all times.

Miles and Directions

- 0.0 *Note:* The numbers in parentheses in these directions correspond to the numbers on signposts at the actual intersections in the park. Follow the path away from the parking lot for half a mile to the end. This is uphill, with some steep pitches. But don't get discouraged; this is the worst hill on the ride.
- 0.5 Left for nine-tenths of a mile to the first left. There is a nice view from the top of the hill, with Frenchman Bay in the distance. (1)
- 1.4 Left, following the sign for Bar Harbor, Eagle Lake, and Duck Brook. Go 1 mile to the next road on the left, which crosses a stone bridge high above a brook. (3)
- 2.4 Bear right and continue for 1 mile to a fork. (5)
- 3.4 Bear left, following the sign for Eagle Lake and Seal Harbor, and continue to a stone bridge underpass. (4)
- 4.5 After passing beneath the stone bridge, continue *straight* to a small road on the right. (9)

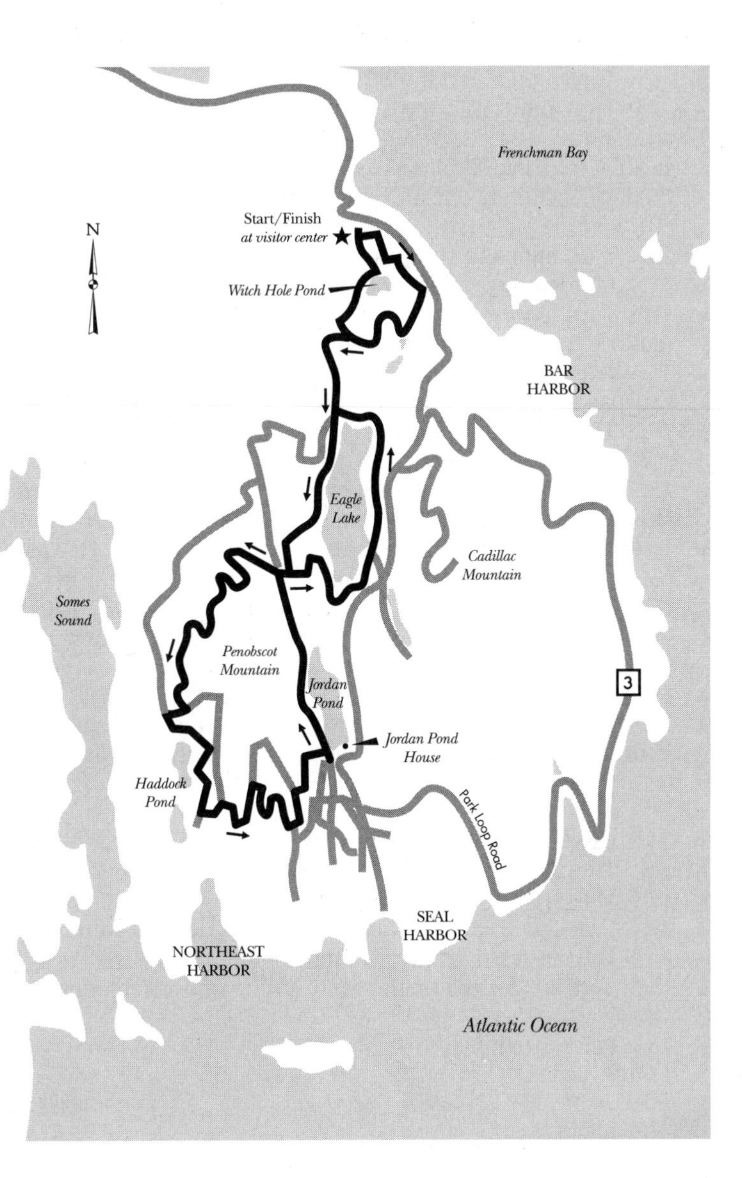

Frenchman Bay
N
Start/Finish
at visitor center
Witch Hole Pond
BAR
HARBOR
Eagle
Lake
Cadillac
Mountain
Somes
Sound
Penobscot
Mountain
Jordan
Pond
3
Jordan Pond
House
Haddock
Pond
Park Loop Road
SEAL
HARBOR
NORTHEAST
HARBOR
Atlantic Ocean

- 6.8 Turn right and ride to T intersection. (8)
- 7.0 Turn right at T and stay straight, following the sign for around mt., and ride 3 miles to the next turn. This path climbs steadily for about 2 miles. There are many beautiful views along the way, including one of Somes Sound. Enjoy the long descent. (10)
- 10.7 Turn right and continue to the next fork. (12)
- 11.0 Bear left toward Haddock Pond. (13)
- 12.5 Turn left for just a short distance, (18) then take the next right. (19)
- 13.6 Turn right and go to an intersection with signs indicating the road to right is off limits to bikes. (20)
- 19.9 Turn left and go sharply uphill for six-tenths of a mile. (22)
- 15.5 Take a sharp right, following the sign for Jordan Pond House, and continue to the next intersection. (21)
- 16.8 Turn left, riding to the crossroads at Eagle Lake. This road passes high above Jordan Pond to the right and beneath the cliffs of Penobscot Mt. on the left. You may want to visit the Jordan Pond House, a short distance to the right, before making this turn. (14)
- 19.3 Turn right. (10)
- 19.5 Turn right and follow the broad road around Eagle Lake, returning to the stone bridge underpass you passed through earlier. (8)
- 21.3 Bear left. (7)
- 23.3 Pass beneath the bridge and continue to a T. (6)
- 24.4 Turn left, following the sign for Witch Hole Pond on Paradise Hill. (4)
- 25.4 Keep left, following signs for Paradise Hill and Hulls Cove, until you reach a narrow path on the left. (2)
- 25.6 Turn left for the final descent to the visitor center parking lot. (1)
- 26.1 Return to the visitor center.

12

Sunrise County Challenge

Dennysville—Pembroke—Perry—Baring—
Moosehorn National Wildlife Refuge—
West Pembroke—Dennysville

Maine's "Sunrise County" is an unspoiled land of quiet natural beauty. Located at Maine's—and the country's—easternmost tip, this part of the state captures the spirit of the phrase "down east" (which actually refers to the sea breezes that come "down" from the East). Along its coastline, washed by the highest tides in the country, lie small fishing villages that rarely see visitors. Just inland are pristine forests, clear lakes, and thousands of acres of wild blueberry fields. Washington County, the region's official name, is an ideal place for carefree cycling: Traffic is never heavy, and the coast is not very hilly.

This circuit starts out relatively flat, winding through a landscape of blueberry fields, lakes, and sea. The longer ride begins to roll on the road toward the Moosehorn National Wildlife Refuge, after you've had a chance (in July or August) to refresh yourself with a swim at Round Lake's sandy beach. The refuge is a two-part wilderness, with 17,00 acres off U.S. 1 near Calais and 7,000 acres at Cobscook Bay south of Dennysville. It offers excellent birdwatching and hiking. For more information contact Refuge Manager, Moosehorn National Wildlife Refuge, P.O. Box 1077, Calais, ME 04619 (207–454–3521). The final 10-mile stretch along Route 214 features the most hills. These, though, provide splendid views east toward the islands of Cobscook Bay.

The Basics

Start: The Lincoln House Country Inn in Dennysville (207–726–3953). Dennysville is located approximately 115 miles east of Belfast along the easternmost section of Rte. 1. Turn west onto Rte. 86 for a short distance to reach the inn.
Length: 43.6 or 65.3 miles.
Terrain: Moderately rolling coastal and inland wilderness.
Food: The Farmer's Union General Store and the New Friendly Restaurant, both at about 16 miles.
Traffic/Safety: Narrow shoulders, but little traffic.

Miles and Directions

- 0.0 East on Rte. 86 from the Lincoln House Country Inn in Dennsyville, then turn left onto Rte. 1N.
- 5.8 Left off Rte. 1 just before the Crossroads Motel, then bear left again. You should soon pass a church on the left.
- 8.4 Right across bridge and bear left on the other side.
- 10.1 Right at the first crossroads.
- 15.8 Bear right.
- 16.4 Left at T onto Rte. 1N. You are in the town of Perry. The Farmer's Union General Store and Texaco station here make this a good place to break for a snack.
- 16.7 Turn right off Rte. 1 just in front of the Wigwam Store and across from the New Friendly Restaurant, a good lunch stop. This backroad will take you along the shore.
- 16.9 Stay left, going uphill, at the fork. A detour to the right will lead you to a small ocean beach at Gleeson Point.
- 18.0 Enjoy the views of New Brunswick, Canada, along with downhill stretch.
- 20.1 Turn right. A redemption center is just after the turn.
- 22.5 Cross Rte. 1.
- 26.1 Left at T. In a half mile, on Boyden Lake, there is a boat launch and swimming area.

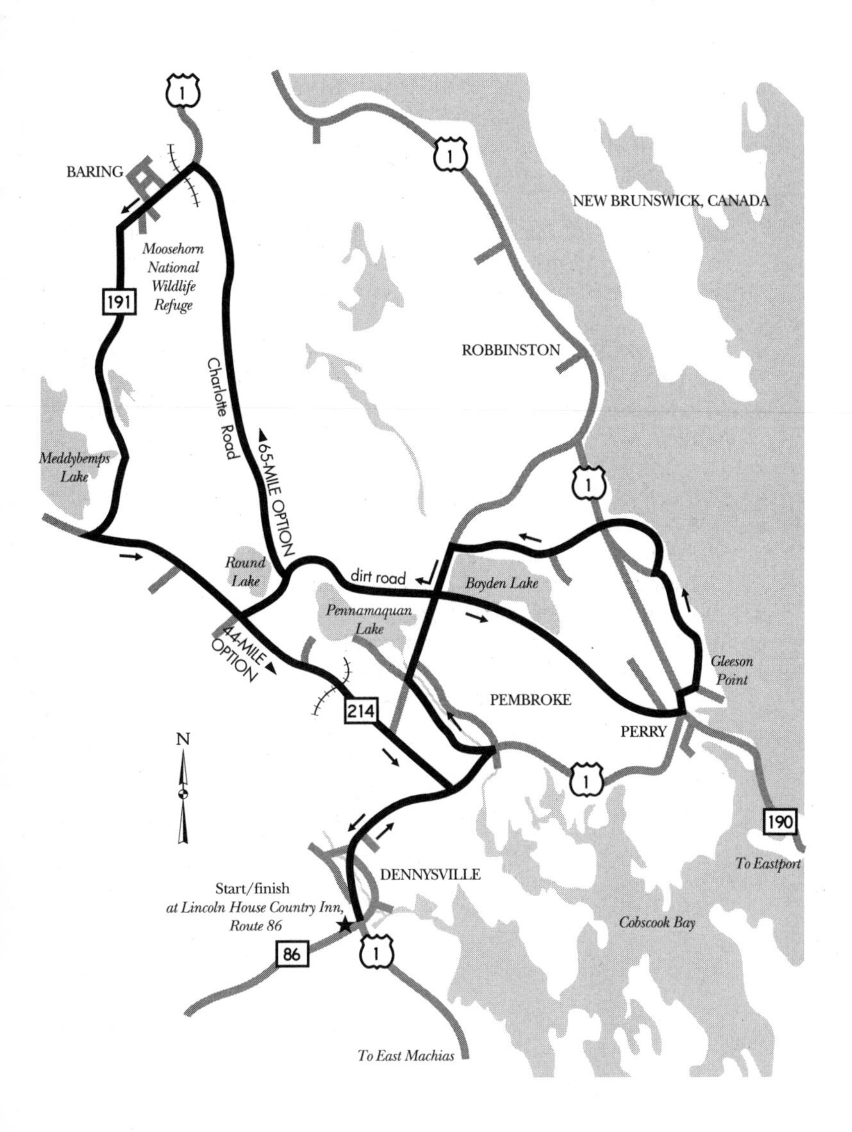
1
BARING
1
NEW BRUNSWICK, CANADA
Moosehorn
National
Wildlife
Refuge
191
Charlotte Road
ROBBINSTON
65-MILE OPTION
Meddybemps
Lake
1
Round
Lake
dirt road
Boyden Lake
Pennamaquan
Lake
44-MILE
OPTION
Gleeson
Point
214
PEMBROKE
PERRY
N
1
190
To Eastport
DENNYSVILLE
Start/finish
at Lincoln House Country Inn,
Route 86
Cobscook Bay
86
1
To East Machias

- 27.3 Right onto paved road (which turns to gravel for about a half mile) at same crossroads you approached from opposite direction at 10.1 miles.
- 31.4 Right at T toward Moosehorn National Wildlife Refuge.

You may cut off this ride's 23.1-mile northern loop by turning left here, turning left again onto Rte. 214 in 1.3 miles, then picking up the directions at mile 54.5.

- 32.1 Round Lake swimming beach—another spot for a dip along this ride.
- 38.7 Moosehorn National Wildlife Refuge headquarters. Clean public rest rooms.
- 41.1 Left at T onto Rte. 1N.
- 43.5 Left off Rte. 1 onto Rte. 191S toward Machias.
- 50.6 Left onto Rte. 214E at T.
- 54.5 Shortcut joins longer circuit at this crossroads, with the Charlotte Town Hall on the right soon after.
- 60.7 Right onto Rte. 1S at T.
- 65.2 Right onto Rte. 86 in Dennysville.
- 65.3 Arrive at Lincoln House Country Inn.

Massachusetts

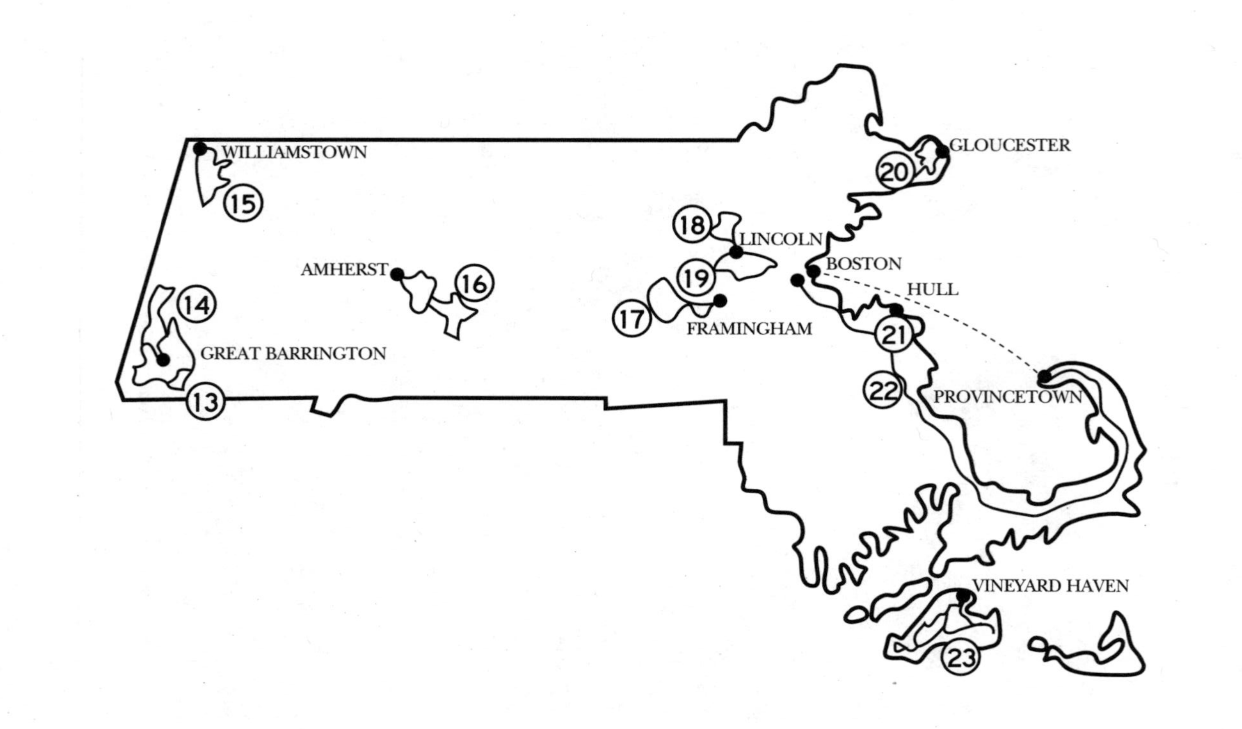
WILLIAMSTOWN
15
GLOUCESTER
20
18
LINCOLN
BOSTON
AMHERST
16
19
HULL
14
17
FRAMINGHAM
21
GREAT BARRINGTON
22
PROVINCETOWN
13
VINEYARD HAVEN
23

Massachusetts

13. Monument Valley Ramble 80
14. Great Barrington Cruise 85
15. Mount Greylock Classic 90
16. Five-College to Quabbin Reservoir Challenge 94
17. Sudbury Reservoir Ramble 100
18. Lincoln to Great Brook Farm Ramble 105
19. Walden Pond Cruise 110
20. Cape Ann Cruise 116
21. South Shore–Wompatuck State Park Ramble 122
22. Cape in a Day (or Two) Classic 129
23. Martha's Vineyard: Two Tours 134
The Vineyard: Gay Head Cruise 136
The Vineyard: Edgartown Ramble 140

13

Monument Valley Ramble

Great Barrington—South Egremont—Sheffield—Mill River—Monument Mountain—Great Barrington

The Monument Valley Ramble and the Great Barrington Cruise are companion rides; each starts and ends at the Chamber of Commerce information booth in Great Barrington. Ride one on Saturday and one on Sunday to experience a classic Berkshire countryside weekend. Or, if a longer route is preferred, connect the two to create one 60-mile figure-eight loop.

Both rides center on the Housatonic River Valley, winding across its plain and rolling along the foothills to either side. Once you climb the initial mile-long hill, the Monument Valley Ramble is virtually flat its entire first half. Passing country cottages and cornfields, the long stretch to Sheffield from the village of South Egremont, with the historic Egremont Inn at its center, is particularly pleasant cycling.

Sheffield provides a perfect setting for a leisurely midway stop. The first town chartered in the Berkshires, today Sheffield is the region's antiques trade center. Traffic on Route 7, Sheffield's Main Street, comes to a complete stop for almost an hour every Memorial Day, when the town celebrates with a local parade.

From Sheffield the ramble crosses the Housatonic. The concrete bridge, constructed in 1988, replaced a covered bridge ruined by an overloaded truck. While less charming, the new bridge affords a mid-river view down the valley.

Once across the river, you can choose either of two routes leading to the top of the valley's eastern ridge. The shorter option follows County Road, which climbs gradually alongside Ironwork Brook. The longer option adds 4.5 miles and climbs more steeply up a hillside rift cut by the Konkapot River. Both options then rejoin for a ridgeside roll along Lake Buel and Monument Valley roads back to Barrington.

Monument Mountain marks this tour's northern reach. The views of its pinkish rocky face from Monument Valley Road are a highlight of the tour. (Return for a hike to Monument Mountain's 1,700-foot peak, a longtime favorite local outing.) Ride the final stretch along Route 7 with caution as it descends steeply into Great Barrington.

Flat stretches across open farmland, a long but gradual climb, and gently rolling woodland roads combine to make the Monument Valley Ramble an ideal circuit for riders wanting to progress beyond 20-mile loops. More experienced riders will also find this a rewarding tour by tackling the hills aggressively and cranking on the flats.

The Basics

Start: Great Barrington, in the state's southwestern corner. Park in the center of town, along the main street or in the parking lot 2 blocks to the west. Distances are measured from the Chamber of Commerce information booth at the intersection of the town's main street, Routes 7 and 41 combined, and Taconic St.
Length: 36.2 or 31.8 miles.
Terrain: Rolling hills with only two climbs longer than a half mile. Moderately smooth road surface and primarily light traffic.
Food: Downtown Sheffield, along Rte. 7 at 12.5 miles, offers several options, including a small grocery store and a luncheonette.
Traffic/Safety: Watch for potentially heavy traffic along Rte. 7. Also, care should be taken when crossing the railroad tracks at the end of Sheffield–S. Egremont Rd. and at the intersection of Routes 7 and 41, just after crossing the Housatonic River.

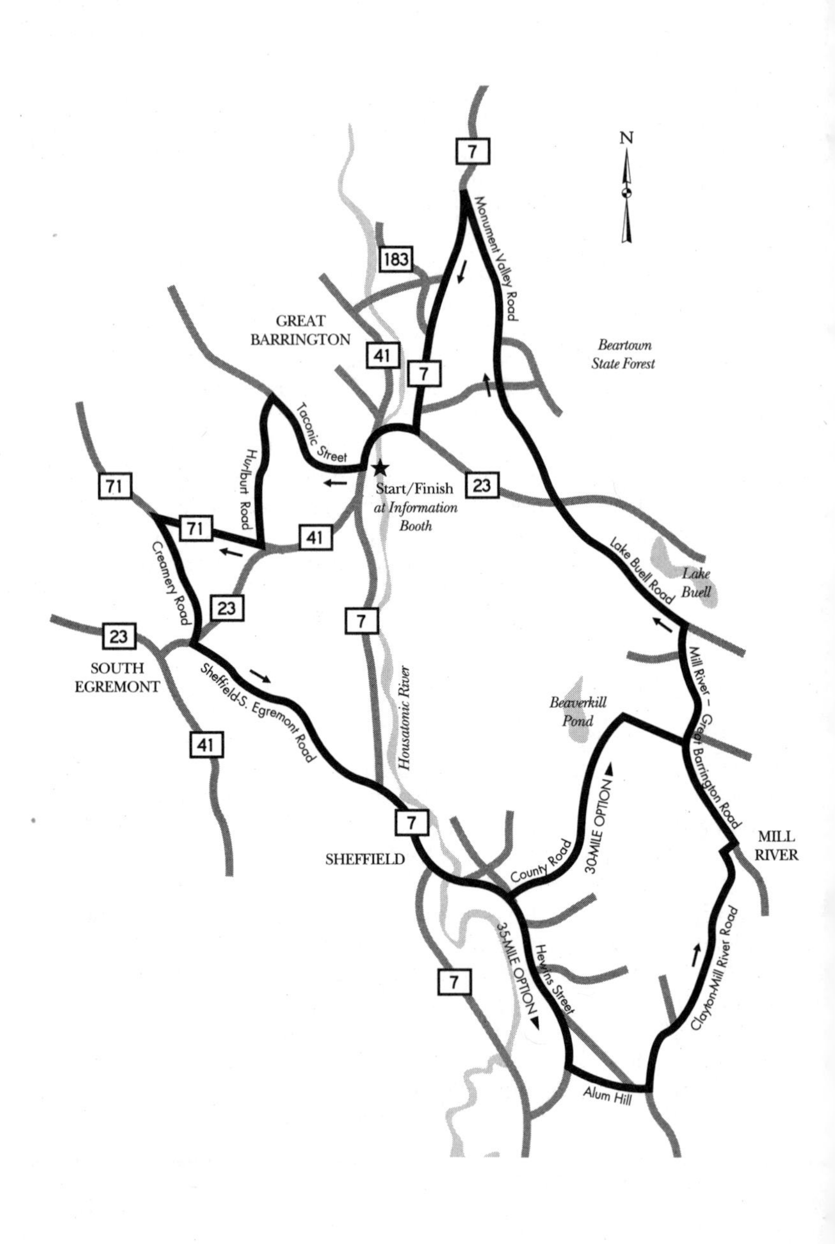
N
7
Monument Valley Road
183
GREAT
BARRINGTON
41
7
Beartown
State Forest
Taconic Street
Hurlburt Road
71
71
41
23
Start/Finish
at Information
Booth
Lake Buell Road
Lake
Buell
23
7
Creamery Road
23
SOUTH
EGREMONT
Mill River – Great Barrington Road
Beaverkill
Pond
Sheffield-S. Egremont Road
Housatonic River
41
30-MILE OPTION
7
SHEFFIELD
County Road
MILL
RIVER
35-MILE OPTION
Hewins Street
7
Clayton-Mill River Road
Alum Hill

Miles and Directions

- 0.0 From the Chamber of Commerce information booth, ride up Taconic St., following the signs toward Alford and Simon's Rock. Pass beneath a railway bridge as the road climbs, staying left at the first fork and following the first sign toward the local hospital.
- 0.4 Bear right with Taconic St. toward Simon's Rock as the road continues to climb. Taconic St. becomes Alford Rd.
- 0.9 Top of hill; begin descent.
- 1.7 Turn left onto Hurlburt at bottom of hill. Be sure you don't miss this turn.
- 3.9 Turn right on Rte. 71 at T intersection, soon passing a mid-cornfield airport on the right.
- 5.4 Make a sharp left onto Creamery Rd.
- 7.1 Bear right at stop sign onto Rte. 23 into South Egremont. Watch for the next left turn.
- 7.2 Turn left onto Button Ball Ln. immediately after passing the Weathervane Inn: This side road ends in 1 block at the Egremont Inn.
- 7.3 Turn left onto Sheffield–S. Agremont Rd. across from the Egremont Inn. With one small exception, this is a flat road for the next 3.6 miles.
- 10.9 Turn right onto Rte. 7 into Sheffield. In a few hundred yards, you can take a short detour to the left to see the oldest covered bridge in Massachusetts.
- 12.1 Turn left onto Maple Ave., which becomes County Rd. For a visit to Sheffield's grocery store and luncheonette on the right side of Rte. 7, continue straight for a short distance.
- 12.7 Cross concrete bridge over Housatonic River.
- 13.1 Bear left with County Rd. as Hewins St. forks right.

To ride the longer option, which adds 4.7 miles and a steeper climb, bear right here onto Hewins St. for 3.0 miles. Turn left onto Alum Hill Rd., which takes you over a short ridge, for 1.3 miles. Turn left onto Clayton–Mill River Rd. for 1.0 miles. After the tiered barn on your left, bear left, continuing on Clayton–Mill River Rd. for 2.9 miles. Turn right across bridge into the four corners town of Mill River, then make an immediate left turn up Mill River–Great Barrington Rd. for 1.7 miles. Then bear right, staying with Mill River–Great Barrington Rd. The shorter ride option joins from the left here, and you can continue with the directions below starting at 17.8 miles.

- 13.8 Continue straight on County Rd. as Home Rd. bears left. County Rd. climbs for the next 3.0 miles. Watch for rough pavement on some sections.
- 17.8 Bear left onto Mill River–Great Barrington Rd. at triangle. (Longer ride option joins here.)
- 19.7 Bear left onto Lake Buell Rd.
- 22.4 Cross Rte. 23 with caution and continue straight onto Monument Valley Rd. Look for views of Monument Mt.'s rocky outcroppings, to the left, in about 3.0 miles.
- 27.1 Turn left onto Rte. 7 toward Great Barrington at T. Ride with caution to the right. This road's broad shoulder narrows quickly for a portion. Be certain to stay to the right, especially on the steep descent midway back to town.
- 30.6 Bear right with Rte. 7 as Rte. 23 joins from the left.
- 31.1 Turn left with Rte. 7 after crossing the Housatonic River.
- 31.8 Arrive back at information booth at intersection of Rte. 7 and Taconic St.

14

Great Barrington Cruise

*Great Barrington—Alford—West Stockbridge—
Glendale—Housatonic—Great Barrington*

The Great Barrington Cruise is adapted from the Great Josh Billings RunAground, a bike-canoe-run triathalon that attracts nearly 2,000 entrants to the southwestern corner of Massachusetts every fall. This cruise follows the triathalon's cycling course almost to Stockbridge. It then turns south onto Route 183, a smooth backroad that rolls along the shaded banks of the Housatonic River, to complete a loop back to Great Barrington.

From the official triathalon starting line, at the intersection of Route 7 and Taconic Street in Great Barrington, the course heads uphill toward the town of Alford and Simon's Rock, an elite school. Taconic Street climbs for nearly a mile. Riding at your leisure, you will be able to enjoy some of the sights the racers barely have time to take in. Nineteenth-century summer homes and hillside farms line the backroads from Great Barrington to West Stockbridge. Descending along West Center and Maple Hill roads after 10 miles, the landscape opens up to offer fine views toward Monument Mountain, October Mountain State Forest (a favorite off-road cycling area), and the rest of the Berkshire range.

Crossing over the William River, the ride passes through West Stockbridge, humble cousin to Stockbridge, the aristocrat of Berkshire towns. Here racers would be gearing down in anticipation of the steep half-mile climb at the far end of this main-street stretch. You should gear down too, but you can stop as well for a rest and snack at the Village Variety store on the right.

Following the steep climb and long descent along Route 102E, you can easily detour into Stockbridge by passing the turnoff for Route 183S. In Stockbridge take a rest on the broad veranda of the historic Red Lion Inn. Illustrator Norman Rockwell, who moved here from Arlington, Vermont, in 1953, was a cycling enthusiast. Town historians report that he regularly led other bikers along his favorite roads. The Norman Rockwell Museum now sponsors short, leisurely rides re-creating his tour through town. Return along Route 102 to get back on course.

To take in some Berkshires culture on the way back to Great Barrington, pay a visit not only to the Norman Rockwell Museum but also to Chesterwood, in the town of Glendale, 18 miles into the ride. Chesterwood is the 1920s summer estate of Daniel Chester French, sculptor of Washington, D.C.'s Lincoln Memorial and Lexington's minuteman statue. His home, studio, and sculpture gallery and the surrounding grounds are open daily during the summer season.

The final miles parallel the cool and shaded banks of the Housatonic River. Note the turn-of-the-century railroad and mill buildings dotting the banks of the river below the town of Housatonic. The Rising Paper Company Mill, on the right at 23 miles, is a stunning example of Victorian factory construction.

The Great Josh Billings RunAground is held every September. For details and information on how to enter, contact the Arcadia Bike Shop in Lenox (413–637–3010). For a large, complimentary map of the area, stop at Apple Hill Realty at 297 Main Street in Great Barrington.

The Basics

Start: As with the Monument Valley Ramble, park in the center of Great Barrington, along the town's main street or in the public lot on its western end. Distances are measured from the traffic light at the intersection of the town's main street, Routes 7 and 41 combined, and Taconic St.
Length: 28.9 miles.

Terrain: Rolling hills, with only two climbs of more than a half mile in length. The first marks the very beginning of the tour; the second, its middle. Fairly smooth road surface and light traffic.
Food: The Village Variety store in West Stockbridge, at 14.7 miles, is a good midway snack stop.
Traffic/Safety: Watch for potentially heavy traffic on Rte. 7. Also, be careful at the 27-mile mark on Rte. 41, as the road narrows and winds beneath a railroad bridge.

Miles and Directions

- 0.0 From Great Barrington's main street, Routes 7 and 41 combined, turn west onto Taconic St., following signs toward Alford and Simon's Rock. Pass beneath a railway bridge as the road begins to climb, and stay left at the first fork, following the sign toward the local hospital.
- 0.3 Bear right on Taconic St. toward Simon's Rock as the road continues to climb. Taconic St. becomes Alford Rd.
- 0.9 Top of hill; begin descent.
- 4.2 Bear left onto West Rd. at the fork as you enter the small village of Alford. (East Rd. forks downhill to the right.)
- 9.0 Continue straight as dirt road intersects on your left.
- 9.6 Turn left at T onto West Center Rd. Look for beautiful northerly views up the Berkshire range for the next several miles.
- 13.1 Right onto Rte. 102E at T.
- 13.9 Rte. 102 crosses the Mass. Tpke. and descends toward West Stockbridge.
- 14.4 Right at flashing red light, onto combined Routes 102 and 41. Follow this road across the William River and bear right into West Stockbridge. The Village Variety store, on the right at 14.7 miles, is a snack stop.
- 15.0 Continue straight with Rte. 102E as Rte. 41 turns right toward Great Barrington.

To skip one long hill, turn right onto Rte. 41 and follow it all the way back to Great Barrington.

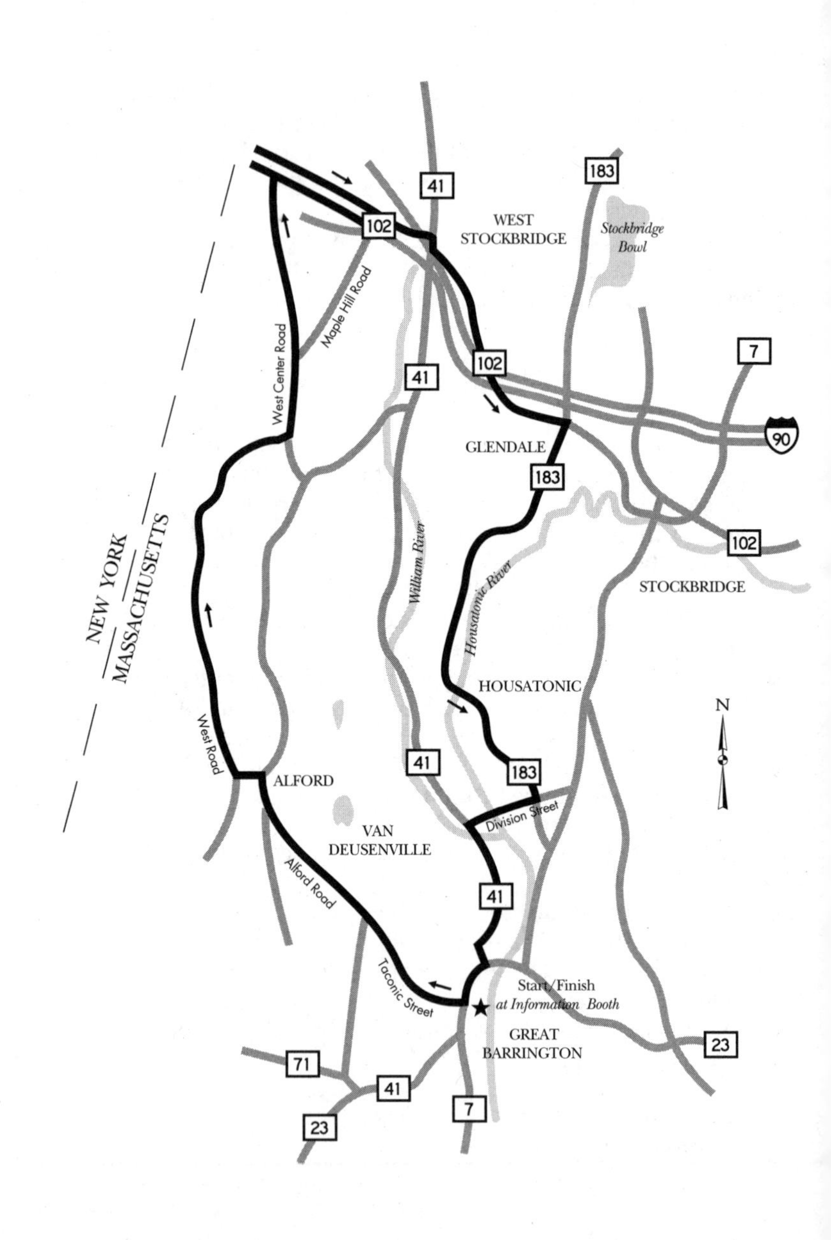

41
183
102
WEST
STOCKBRIDGE
Stockbridge
Bowl
Maple Hill Road
West Center Road
102
41
7
90
GLENDALE
183
NEW YORK
MASSACHUSETTS
William River
102
Housatonic River
STOCKBRIDGE
HOUSATONIC
N
West Road
41
183
ALFORD
Division Street
VAN
DEUSENVILLE
Alford Road
41
Taconic Street
Start/Finish
at Information Booth
GREAT
BARRINGTON
23
71
41
7
23

- 15.4 Begin one-half-mile climb. The climb is rewarded with an even longer downhill.
- 17.8 Turn right onto Rte. 183S at the flashing yellow light, following the sign toward Great Barrington. (Continue straight on Rte. 102 to detour into Stockbridge.)
- 18.5 Pass through Glendale. Both the Norman Rockwell Museum and Chesterwood, the 1920s summer estate of the sculptor of the Lincoln Memorial, are worth a detour.
- 19.4 Rte. 183 quickly descends to the bank of Housatonic River.
- 22.0 Staying with Rte. 183, turn left at stop sign opposite Pleasant St. Market in the town of Housatonic. Pass beneath railroad bridge, cross the river, and follow the road around to the right on the other side.
- 24.1 Turn right onto Division St. back across the Housatonic River into Van Deusenville.
- 25.1 Turn left onto Rte. 41S toward Great Barrington at blinking red light.
- 27.2 Continue straight as Rte. 7S merges into Rte. 41 from the left for the final mile into Great Barrington.
- 28.9 Ride ends back at intersection of combined Routes 7 and 41 with Taconic St.

15

Mount Greylock Classic

Williamstown—Mount Greylock Reservation—New Ashford—Williamstown

In the state's northwestern corner, 3,500-foot-high Mount Greylock rises over North Adams and Williamstown. It is a rarity among New England mountains in that a road crosses its highest point, making it possible to do a dramatic circuit ride. Just to the west the Taconic Trail section of Route 2 crosses the mountains that separate New York from Massachusetts. The Mount Greylock Classic will test your stamina while leading you through the scenic northern reaches of the Berkshire range.

The Mount Greylock State Reservation is a vast, 12,000-acre nature preserve that attracts hikers, campers, fishermen, mountain bikers, and hang gliders. The 37-mile ride features its ascent right at the start. The narrow Notch Road winds its way up Greylock's wooded northern flank, climbing 2,800 feet at an average grade of 6 percent in 8 tough miles to reach Mount Greylock at 3,491 feet. As you pedal through the shadows, it can be difficult to believe that these thousands of hillside acres were once mostly cleared by farming and lumbering.

From Notch Road, Summit Road leads to the Appalachian Mountain Club lodge on the mountain's windswept and often chilly summit. The 360-degree views here are magnificent (if it isn't cloudy). Climb the 92-foot tower, which marks the highest point in Massachusetts, for the ultimate view. The lodge snack bar and the grassy areas around the summit make this an ideal spot to stop for lunch and chat with the hikers and campers and those who have driven up for the view.

From Greylock's summit the classic loops downhill virtually all the way back to Williamstown, home of prestigious Williams College and the Clark Art Institute. Rockwell Road zips from the summit to Route 7 in a fast 10 miles. Route 7N carries a fair bit of traffic. It is scenic, though, and offers a broad paved shoulder for another 10 gradually downhill miles to the junction with Route 43. Also called Green River Road, this "low road" to Williamstown (Route 7 continuing into town is the high road) offers an ideal warm-down stretch. It follows the stream from which it takes its name for the final 5 miles to Main Street.

The climb up Mount Greylock is extremely difficult—so difficult that competitive athletes can't resist the challenge. Notch Road from North Adams to Greylock's summit is now the site of two annual races. The Mount Greylock Hill Climb bike race is held every September. Runners tackle the mountain in their annual Mount Greylock Road Race, normally held in August.

The Basics

Start: Williamstown, in the state's far northwestern corner, at the intersection of Routes 2 and 7. From Boston follow Rte. 2W through Greenfield and North Adams. From southern New England follow Rte. 7N through Pittsfield. Park in the public lot at the end of Spring St., the town's main shopping street, located directly opposite the Williams College campus.
Length: 37.2 miles.
Terrain: A challenging 7-mile climb. The rest of ride is mainly downhill.
Food: Appalachian Mountain Club lodge at peak of Mt. Greylock offers light snacks.
Traffic/Safety: In spring or fall the summit can be much colder and windier than the valley. Pack an extra layer of clothing—cycling tights and rain jacket would be perfect—for the summit and the fast descent. Watch out for occasional frost heaves on the descending road.

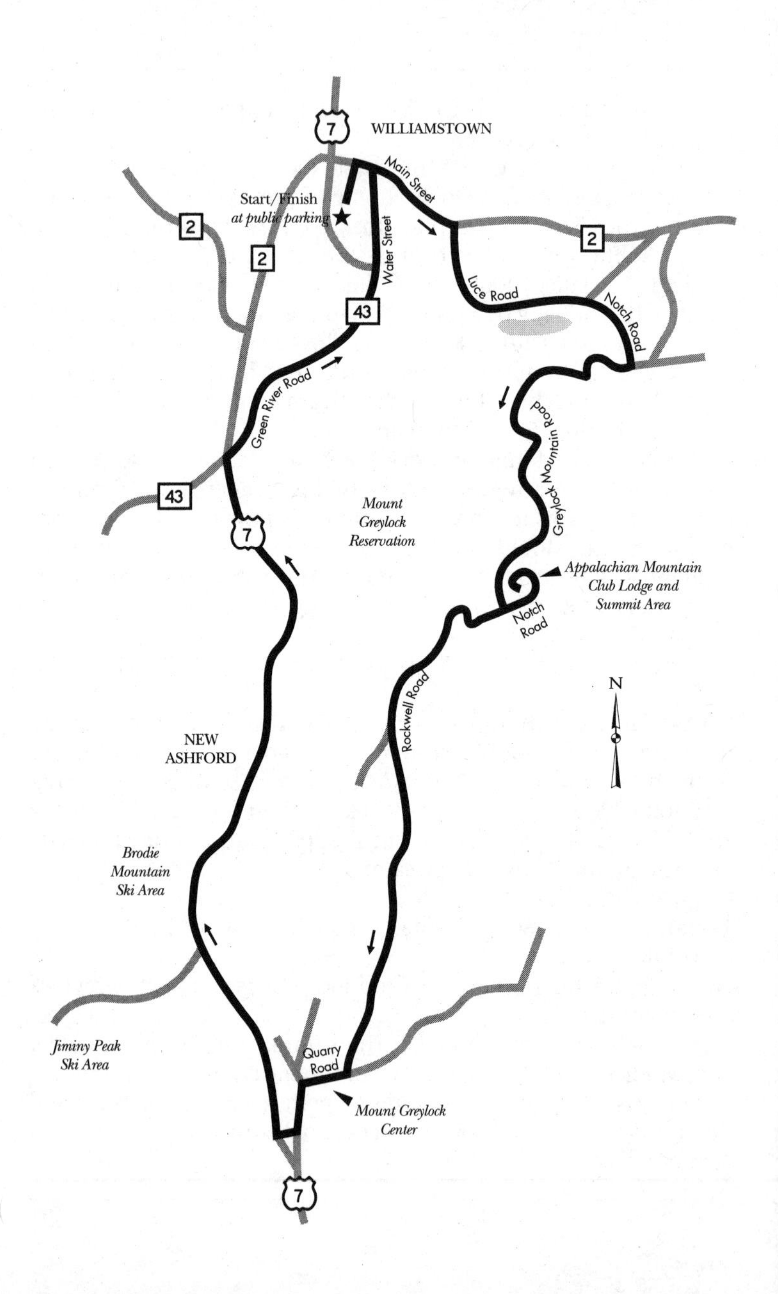

7
WILLIAMSTOWN
Main Street
Start/Finish
at public parking
2
2
2
Water Street
43
Luce Road
Notch Road
Green River Road
Greylock Mountain Road
43
7
Mount
Greylock
Reservation
Appalachian Mountain
Club Lodge and
Summit Area
Notch
Road
Rockwell Road
N
NEW
ASHFORD
Brodie
Mountain
Ski Area
Jiminy Peak
Ski Area
Quarry
Road
Mount Greylock
Center
7

Miles and Directions

- 0.0 From public parking at end of Spring St., pedal back up to Rte. 2 and turn right.
- 1.4 Turn right on Luce Rd., just after turn for Adams Rd.
- 2.1 Luce Rd. bears left and turns into countryside.
- 3.7 Pass reservoir on right, a good resting spot before climb.
- 4.2 Bear right at fork as Luce Rd. joins Notch Rd.
- 5.3 Turn right at fork, following sign into Mt. Greylock State Reservation. Climb steepens.
- 7.1 Cross Appalachian Trail. Watch out for hikers!
- 10.6 Cross Overlook Trail and begin to cross ridge. Look here for views down into "the Hopper," a bowl-shaped valley on the mountain's western flank.
- 11.4 Left at stop sign to summit and AMC lodge.
- 12.3 Arrive at AMC lodge parking lot.
- 13.3 Turning back downhill after a visit to the summit, stay left at intersection with Notch Rd. *Caution:* Be sure to maintain control of your bike throughout this descent.
- 19.8 Pass visitor center on left, continuing straight.
- 20.8 Stay left with main road.
- 21.6 Turn right on Rte. 7 toward Williamstown.
- 24.7 Begin gradual descent for next 7.7 miles to turnoff for Rte. 43.
- 32.4 Turn right onto Rte. 43N to Williamstown. (This is a more relaxing option than Rte. 7.)
- 37.0 Turn left on Rte. 2.
- 37.1 Turn left on Spring St.
- 37.2 Arrive at public parking.

16

Five-College to Quabbin Reservoir Challenge

Amherst—Belchertown—Bondsville—Ware—Quabbin Reservation—Belchertown—Pelham—Amherst

In the middle of Massachusetts, just east of the Connecticut River, lies the vast Quabbin Reservoir. Engineers created the reservoir in the 1930s by flooding the Swift River (and drowning the four towns along its course). Quabbin is now the centerpiece of a large wilderness area, and the more than fifty islands that stud its surface are home to wild turkey and deer. The observation tower on Quabbin Hill rivals the summit of Mount Greylock as a vantage point for the most panoramic view in the Commonwealth. Only the bald eagles that regularly soar above Quabbin's waters enjoy a better view.

Quabbin is a Native American word meaning "a lot of water." From the tower it is clear that this reservoir is aptly named. Its 412 billion gallons of water stretch as far as the eye can see. Quabbin Reservoir Park, which encompasses the reservoir's southern end, includes the observation tower, two huge dams, a visitor center, and miles of hiking trails. All are accessible from the 7-mile-long stretch of road that loops around the park's boundary. (The park closes at dusk.)

The Five-College to Quabbin Reservoir Challenge starts and ends at the Amherst town green, a focal point for the region's educational culture. The neighboring towns of Amherst, Northampton, and South Hadley are home to nearly 35,000 students of Amherst, Hampshire, Mount Holyoke, and Smith colleges and the University of Massachusetts. The Five-College to Quabbin Reservoir Challenge connects this community with the waterside wilderness of the Quabbin Reservoir Park.

The backroads in-between wend their way through farmland and woods, along rivers stocked with trout, and past small lakes lined with weekend cottages. You can shorten this 55-mile tour to 30 miles by starting in Belchertown and riding just the ride's southern loop. In Belchertown park along the town green on Route 202. Start out riding south along this road, picking up the directions at 14.5 miles on the full route. Then, heading west on Route 9 after a visit to the reservoir, turn left on Route 202 back into Belchertown rather than right toward Pelham and Amherst. Although 25 miles shorter, this loop includes most of the highlights of the longer ride.

The Basics

Start: Amherst, just east of Northampton. Follow I–91 north from Springfield and the Mass. Tpke. (I–90) or south from Greenfield and Rte. 2. From Northampton Rte. 9E to Amherst. Park around the Amherst town green, where Rte. 116 splits off to the south of Rte. 9.

Length: 55.0 or 30.0 miles.

Terrain: Mildly rolling hills and many long flat stretches. The longest climb is just under a mile, up Cold Spring Road, at 17 miles.

Food: Several choices in Belchertown, at 14.5 miles, and in Bondsville, at 21.9 miles. For a snack to fuel the final miles, try the Dairy Queen at 43.5 miles.

Traffic/Safety: There is little traffic on this ride, but watch out for faster traffic on Rte. 202 at about 43 miles.

Miles and Directions

- 0.0 From the Amherst town green, ride east on Rte. 9. You should shortly pass beneath a railroad bridge.
- 0.9 Right on South East St. at the first light. Enjoy the views to the left along this nice flat stretch—but ride single file.
- 3.0 Stay left at the fork.
- 3.3 Continue straight on S. East St.
- 5.2 Left onto Bay Rd. as S. East St. ends.
- 7.9 Right onto Stebbins Rd., clearly marked at the crest of a short hill.
- 9.7 Left onto Batchelor Rd. immediately after passing under the power lines.
- 10.0 Stay right at the fork.
- 10.6 Right at the T onto Boardman Rd.
- 11.1 Left onto Rte. 202, here named E. State St.
- 13.5 Continue straight as Rte. 21 joins from the right.
- 14.5 Right at the stoplight onto Rte. 181 toward Palmer and Bondsville. You are now in Belchertown, a nice spot for a snack. Detour farther to the left for a rest on the quarter-mile-long town green.

This ride's shorter, 30-mile option starts and ends here, at the Belchertown green. Follow directions below back to Belchertown.

- 14.8 Stay on Rte. 181S as it curves to the left for a nice downhill run. S. Main St. forks to the right toward Three Rivers. *Note:* The concrete bridge about 2.5 miles ahead is closed to motorized traffic but passable by bike or foot. If you want to detour around it, fork right onto S. Main St. and pick up the directions at 21.9 miles below.
- 16.9 Left onto Cold Spring Rd. at the crest of a short hill. This road begins to climb through a hillside orchard.
- 17.7 Stay left at the fork. You should now begin to descend through a thick woods, which is a wildlife management area.
- 19.0 Cross single-lane bridge over the Swift River. Approach the bridge slowly, as there are likely to be fishermen along its rails.

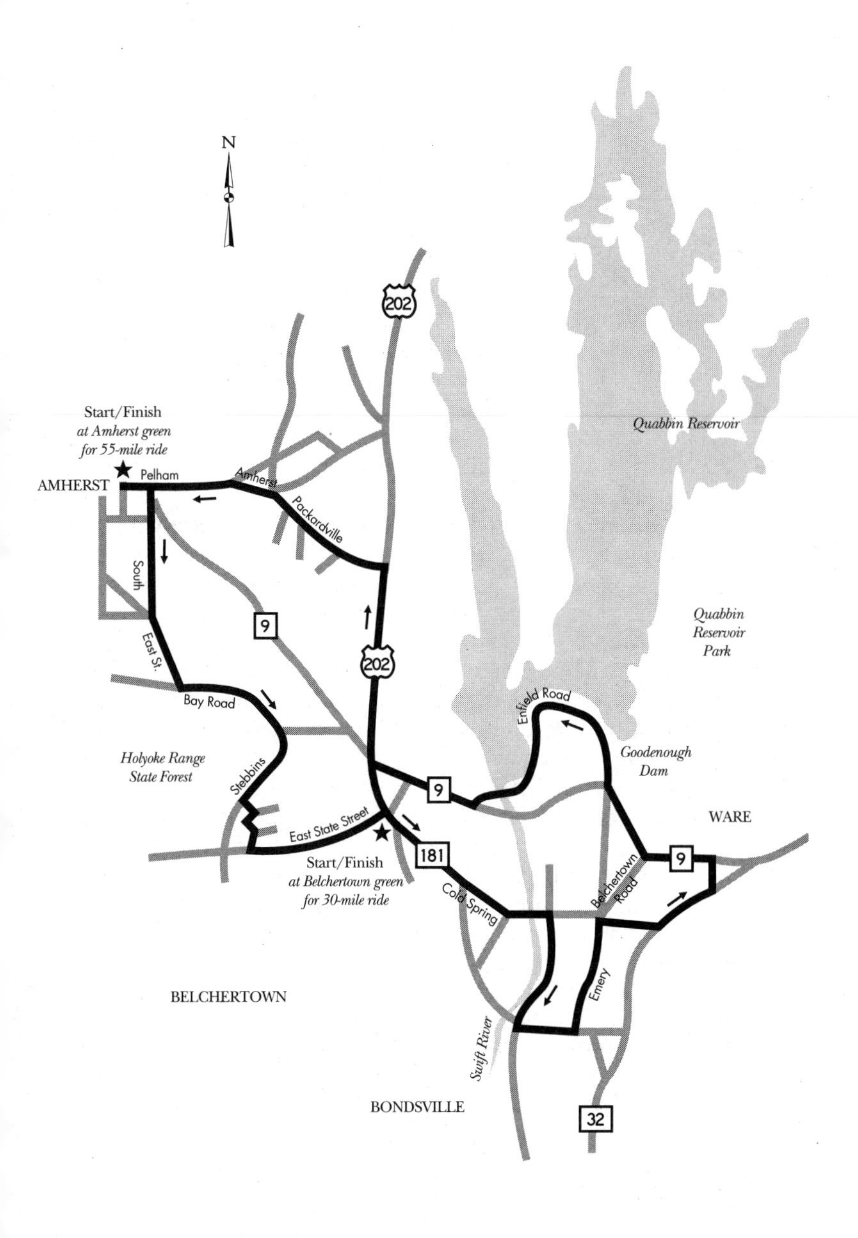
N
202
Start/Finish
at Amherst green
for 55-mile ride
AMHERST
Pelham
Amherst
Packardville
Quabbin Reservoir
South
9
East St.
202
Quabbin
Reservoir
Park
Bay Road
Enfield Road
Holyoke Range
State Forest
Goodenough
Dam
Stebbins
9
East State Street
WARE
181
9
Start/Finish
at Belchertown green
for 30-mile ride
Cold Spring
Belchertown
Road
Emery
BELCHERTOWN
Swift River
BONDSVILLE
32

Turn right on the far side, as another road continues straight and uphill. Follow this bumpy, unmarked road along the bank of the Swift River and then straight through the small town of Bondsville.

- 21.9 Left at the T as Rte. 181S bears right. There is a large white church directly at this intersection.
- 23.4 Left on Emery St. just after crossing railroad tracks. This left occurs just before the pond on the left.
- 24.6 Pass the tiny Palmer Metropolitan Airport on the right—and watch a small plane take off.
- 26.0 Right, downhill, onto Belchertown Rd.
- 26.6 Right on Beaver Lake Rd.
- 27.5 Left onto Vernon St. at end, onto Rte. 32N.
- 29.7 Left immediately after passing the McDonald's on the left. This road cuts over to Rte. 9W.
- 29.8 Left onto Rte. 9W toward Belchertown. Get ready for a series of climbs.
- 33.7 Right onto road leading into Quabbin Reservoir Park (between two stone pillars among the trees).
- 34.5 Continue straight past the turnoff for Goodenough Dam. Or you may detour for an approximately 4-mile trip to the dam and back. Continuing straight toward the Summit Rd. and Winsor Dam, be sure to stop for the views at the several parking areas along the way.
- 37.1 Ride through the rotary and onto the road toward the Summit Area parking lot. This is a short, steep climb.
- 37.5 Arrive at the summit overlook area. The observation tower here, open to the public, offers 360-degree views of the entire region. From the summit, coast back down to the rotary.
- 37.9 Ride around the rotary and exit onto the road descending toward the Winsor Dam.
- 39.3 Immediately after passing the Winsor Dam spillway, turn right toward and then across the dam.
- 40.4 Right onto Rte. 9.
- 43.5 Right at stoplight onto Rte. 202N toward Athol. *Caution:* Be careful on this higher-speed road.

Turn left here to return to Belchertown if you are riding this ride's shorter, 30-mile option.

- 46.9 ENTERING PELHAM sign.
- 48.0 Left on Packardville Rd. Although marked, this narrow turnoff is hard to spot. Look for the small PACKARDVILLE CORNER sign on the left. You should pass a small lake in just a half mile.
- 49.0 Stay right at this fork, toward Rte. 116 and Amherst, and stay right again at each of the two merges that follow in the next 2 miles.
- 51.2 Left at T onto Amherst Rd.
- 54.0 Continue straight through intersection with N. East St.
- 55.0 Arrive back at town green in the center of Amherst.

17

Sudbury Reservoir Ramble

Framingham—Ashland—
Southboro—Ashland—Framingham

The Sudbury Reservoir Ramble begins a trio of rides in the suburbs and countryside west of Boston. It's a more leisurely ride than either the Walden Pond Cruise or the Lincoln to Great Brook Farm Ramble. With a starting point 40 minutes from downtown Boston, this is a good half-day getaway tour.

The Sudbury Reservoir Ramble meanders through the best of Framingham's countryside. As one local rider describes it, "This is a neat ride with only two traffic lights. It passes by one farm with cattle and an orchard, two golf courses, another farm with horses, and both the Stearns and Sudbury reservoirs. It includes a stretch along a one-way countryside road that offers up some good views. It's mainly flat with a few rolling hills, and traffic is usually light."

With ingredients like that, it's clear that this is a convenient ride anyone can dig into.

The Basics

Start: At a town common located just north of Route 9 on Edgell Rd. in Framingham. You can reach the common by driving on Rte. 9 or the Mass. Tpke. (I–90). From exit 12 (Rte. 9) or the turnpike take exit 13 (Rte. 30–Natick/Framingham). From exit 13 take Rte. 30W toward Framingham. After about 2 miles you'll reach Rte. 9.

Turn right and take the first exit, which is Edgell Rd. Turn right on Edgell Rd. and soon reach the common with three churches on it. There is parking around the common.
Length: 24.8 miles.
Terrain: Rolling backroads with some short climbs and occasional soft shoulders.
Food: There's a grocery store at 7.0 miles in Southboro.
Traffic/Safety: There is traffic on some of these suburban roads. Always ride single file. Pay particular attention to oncoming traffic at the beginning of the ride (see below).

Miles and Directions

- 0.0 From the common ride south on Edgell Rd., crossing over Rte. 9.
- 0.1 *Caution:* This is the trickiest junction on the ride. Immediately after crossing Rte. 9, turn right onto High St. Almost immediately you will fork left, onto Salem End Rd. Use hand signals and watch for traffic exiting from Rte. 9 onto High St. on the right.
- 1.7 Bear right onto Gates St.
- 1.8 Left onto Parker Rd., passing by the Framingham Country Club golf course on your left. *Caution:* Watch for oncoming traffic from Gates St. onto Parker Rd.
- 3.0 Still on Parker Rd., enter Ashland.
- 3.2 Right at the second stop sign onto Oregon Rd.
- 4.0 Still on Oregon Rd., enter Southboro.
- 4.6 Right right with Oregon Rd.
- 4.8 Right at the stop sign onto Woodland Rd., immediately pass beneath the Mass. Pike (I–90).
- 4.9 Left onto Breakneck Hill Rd. immediately after passing beneath the Mass. Pike.
- 5.8 Stay right on Breakneck Hill Rd. as Mt. Vickery Rd. turns left.
- 5.9 Crossing Rte. 9, continue straight onto White Bagley Rd., which skirts the Sudbury Reservoir.

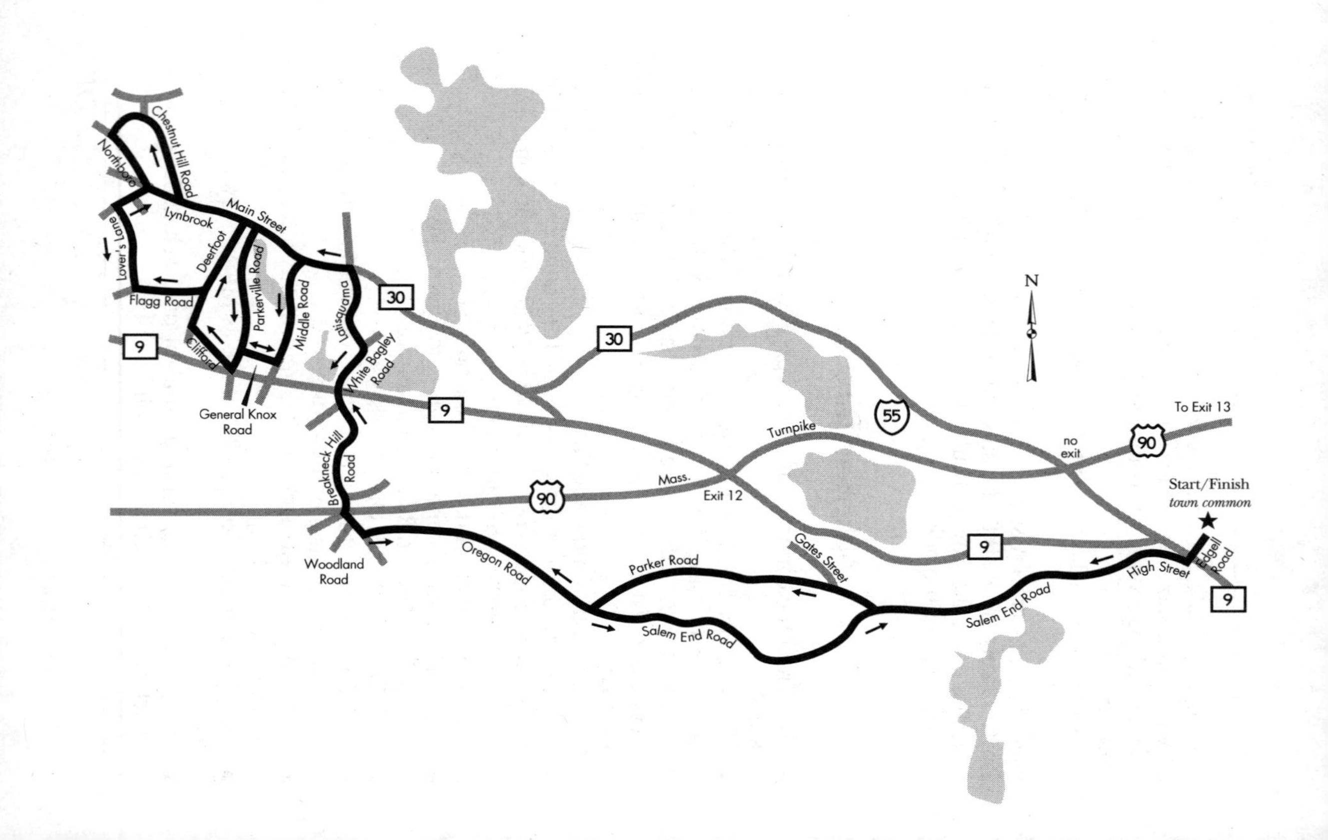

Chestnut Hill Road
Northboro
Lynbrook
Main Street
Lover's Lane
Deerfoot
Parkerville Road
Flagg Road
Middle Road
Latisquama
30
9
Clifford
White Bagley Road
General Knox Road
9
30
N
55
To Exit 13
Turnpike
no exit
90
Breakneck Hill Road
Mass.
Exit 12
90
Start/Finish
town common
Woodland Road
Oregon Road
Parker Road
Gates Street
9
Edgell Road
High Street
Salem End Road
Salem End Road
9

- 6.3 Left on Latisquama Rd., which soon passes another golf course on your left.
- 6.9 Left onto Rte. 30, here called Main St., at the stop sign in Southboro. Continue straight through town, crossing Rte. 85.
- 7.2 Left on Middle Rd., the first left after Rte. 85, which crosses the Sudbury Reservoir viaduct.
- 8.2 Take the next right, onto Gen. Henry Knox Rd.
- 8.5 At the T turn left onto Parkerville Rd.
- 8.6 Take the next right, onto Clifford St.
- 9.2 Bear right onto Deerfoot Rd.
- 9.3 Take the next left, onto Flagg Rd.
- 9.9 Right onto Lover's Lane, a patchy, unmarked road.
- 10.6 At the T, right onto Lynbrook Rd.
- 11.1 Right back onto Rte. 30 (Main St.).
- 11.2 Left onto Chestnut Hill Rd., a scenic one-way road that loops back toward Rte. 30, crossing the Sudbury River.
- 12.0 Left onto Northboro Rd.

You will come out on Rte. 30 again. You can take Rte. 30 to the left, to return to Framingham, or backtrack, by turning right on Rte. 30, left onto Lynbrook Rd., and then making these turns:

- 14.0 Left on Flagg Rd.
- 14.6 Left on Deerfoot Rd.
- 15.3 Right on Rte. 30 (Main St.).
- 15.4 Take the next right, onto Parkerville Rd., passing the Sudbury Reservoir on your left.
- 16.2 Left onto Gen. Henry Knox Rd.
- 16.5 Left at the T onto Middle Rd.
- 17.5 Right on Rte. 30 (Main St.).
- 17.7 Right on Latisquama Rd.
- 18.4 Bear right onto White Bagley Rd.
- 18.8 Cross Rte. 9 and continue straight onto Breakneck Hill Rd.
- 18.9 Stay left with Breakneck Hill Rd. as Vickery Rd. turns right.
- 19.9 Bear right onto Woodland Rd., cross under the Mass. Pike, and then make an immediate left turn onto Oregon Rd.
- 20.1 Bear left, staying with Oregon Rd.

- 21.8 Continue straight on Oregon Rd. as Parker Rd. turns left. Oregon Rd. becomes Salem End Rd.
- 24.5 Continue straight as Salem End Rd. becomes High St.
- 24.6 Left onto Edgell Rd., crossing over Rte. 9.
- 24.8 Arrive back at Framingham Centre.

18

Lincoln to Great Brook Farm Ramble

Lincoln—Concord—Carlisle—Concord—Lincoln

The Lincoln to Great Brook Farm Ramble is one of several rides recommended by the Lincoln Guide Service bike and cross-country ski shop in Lincoln. This full-service shop also rents road and mountain bikes. Owner Mike Farney is an accomplished veteran at selecting touring routes.

Lincoln, only a half hour from downtown Boston, is an ideal starting point for rides extending in every direction through a landscape of woods and fields, country cottages and estates. The Lincoln Guide Service has maps and directions for a dozen local rides.

You are likely to meet up with any number of other cyclists along these roads. Local clubs organize weekly rides for which Concord is a favorite destination.

The Lincoln to Great Brook Farm Ramble passes through a landscape rich with history. The first highlight is Walden Pond, where Henry David Thoreau took his retreat from civilization and wrote *Walden* from 1845 to 1847. Walden Pond is now a popular state park; its sandy swimming beach draws hundreds on summer weekends. It's a short hike off Route 126 to the original site of Thoreau's cabin. A mile beyond the Concord green on Monument Street are the Old North Bridge Historical Site and the Concord Battleground.

Here on the morning of April 19, 1775, a group of provincial minutemen met a column of British regulars. The redcoats had been dispatched from Concord to seize a stockpile of armaments and supplies that the provincials had stashed at the Barrett Farm (on the other side of the Concord River). A quick exchange of musket shot sent the British running back to town. Thus was "the shot heard round the world" fired, on a wooden bridge across a quiet river outside Concord. A visitor information center is located up a short road to the left as you cross the Concord River on Monument Street.

Today the countryside here is quiet, if not exactly undiscovered. There is always a new sight along the way—canoeists gliding down the Concord River, farmers planting crops on the river's plain as seen from high on Monument Street, newborn colts rolling in a pasture, Canada geese swooping through the trees to land with a splash on a pond.

At the midpoint of the ride sits Great Brook Farm State Park—935 acres of woods, fields, and wetlands, complete with 20 miles of trails open for mountain biking and cross-country skiing. And that's not all. You will skirt pastures, barns, a pond, and an ice cream stand that make up a working "interpretive" dairy farm right in the middle of the park. The 90-acre farm is leased from the Commonwealth by Mark and Tamma Duffy, who raise 120 cows on it. Expect a long line waiting for a scoop or two of homemade ice cream if you drop by the farm on a summer afternoon. The site also has a public parking lot, a grassy lawn, and a rest room. A couple of miles farther along the ride, on Curve Street, there's a large, sunken field on the right—it's the northernmost cranberry bog in the nation.

This ride can be linked with the Walden Pond Cruise.

The Basics

To reach the Lincoln Guide Service from Rte. 128, take exit 28 (Trapelo Rd.) toward Lincoln. (Note the paved bike path on the left side of Trapelo Rd. Lincoln is a bike friendly town.) After 2.5 miles turn left at a four-way intersection, onto Lincoln Rd. After another

1.3 miles, you'll reach the Lincoln Guide Service on the left. Park in its lot.

Many local cyclists also begin this ride in the center of Concord, at a stone water fountain just off Rte. 62.

Length: 30.2 miles, with a 20.5-mile option. If you begin in the center of Concord, either loop is 8.0 miles shorter.

Terrain: Rolling hills with no climbs longer than a half mile.

Food: A supermarket and a good deli are in the shopping center at the beginning of the ride. Several choices in Concord at 4.5 miles. If you are riding the longer route, Great Brook Farm sells ice cream and snacks during the summer season. On the shorter loop, Kendall's Ice Cream stand on Rte. 225 makes for an excellent midway stop; it is on the right at 10 miles.

Traffic/Safety: There's traffic on the roads in and out of tourist-filled Concord and on Rte. 126 past Walden Pond, especially on weekends in the summer and fall.

Miles and Directions

- 0.0 From Lincoln Guide Service turn left, crossing the railroad tracks, on Lincoln Road.
- 0.2 Take the first right, onto Codman Rd., passing the historic Codman House on the right.
- 0.9 Right onto Rte. 126.
- 2.5 Walden Pond—with several beaches, facilities, and a hiking trail around the pond—on the left. Continue on Rte. 126 across Rte. 2 at busy traffic light.
- 3.5 At bottom of small hill, fork right toward Concord as main road forks left.
- 4.1 Right onto Heywood St. after passing Concord fire station on the right.
- 4.3 Left onto Lexington Rd. at T, just after passing town information booth. There is a water fountain by the monument on the town green on the left.
- 4.6 Right onto Monument St. at far end of green. Continue on Monument St. past Old North Bridge and Concord Battle-

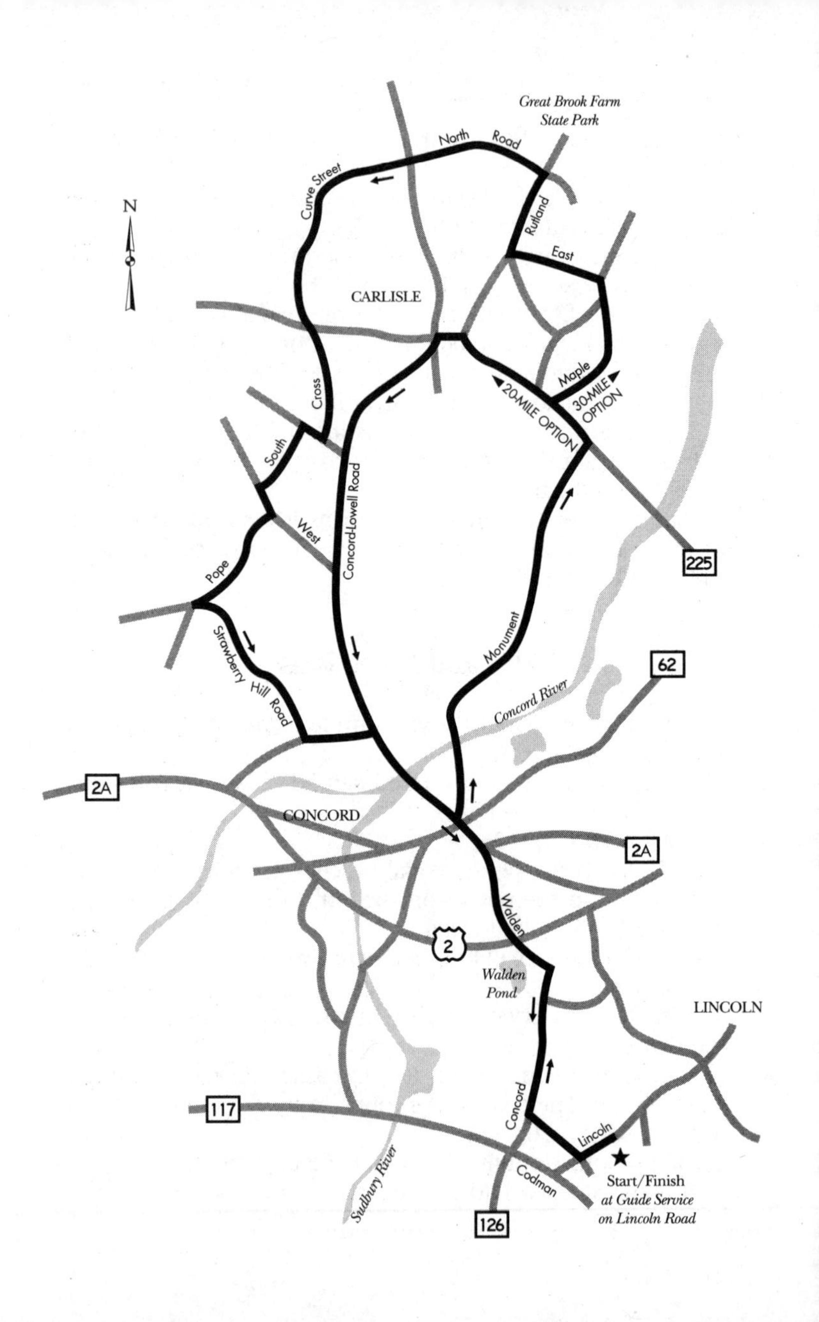

N
Great Brook Farm
State Park
North
Road
Curve Street
Rutland
East
CARLISLE
Maple
20-MILE OPTION
30-MILE OPTION
Cross
South
West
Concord-Lowell Road
Pope
225
Strawberry
Hill
Road
Monument
62
Concord River
2A
CONCORD
2A
Walden
2
Walden
Pond
LINCOLN
117
Concord
Lincoln
Codman
Sudbury River
126
Start/Finish
at Guide Service
on Lincoln Road

ground, across the Concord River, and past several fine old horse farms and Hutchins Farm, a popular organic farm stand.

- 9.0 Left on Rte. 225, here marked Bedford Rd.
- 9.2 Right onto Maple St., a narrow backroad, to continue with the longer, backroad route past Great Brook Farm.

If you are riding the shorter route, continue straight on Rte. 225 to the small rotary in Carlisle, then turn onto the Concord-Lowell Rd. back to Concord. From Concord backtrack to Lincoln, following the directions starting at 24.3 miles below.

- 10.6 Left onto East St., a more traveled road.
- 11.5 Right onto Rutland St. at stop sign, another backroad. You pass by a small herb farm.
- 12.5 Left onto North Rd. at the first four-way intersection.
- 13.7 Great Brook Farm State Park on the right. Stop for a tour through this working dairy farm or simply for a rest on the grassy lawn by the pond. Continue on North Rd.
- 14.1 Right onto Lowell Rd. and an immediate left onto Curve St. Watch for the cranberry bog on the right.
- 15.6 Bear left at the fork toward Rte. 225.
- 16.4 Left onto Rte. 225 for a short distance.
- 16.7 Right onto Cross St.
- 17.8 Right at stop sign onto South St., which is unmarked here.
- 18.8 Left onto West St. at stop sign.
- 18.9 Right onto Pope Rd.
- 20.1 Left onto Strawberry Hill Rd.
- 22.1 Left onto Barrett's Mill Rd. at the stop sign.
- 22.8 Right at the stop sign onto Lowell Rd. Continue back through Concord, straight through the intersection on the far side of the town green, with the water fountain on your left.
- 24.3 Right onto Heywood St., marked by the Concord information booth on the left, just after the turn.
- 24.4 Left onto Walden St., across Rte. 2, and onto Rte. 126 past Walden Pond.
- 27.3 Left onto Codman Rd. toward Lincoln.
- 30.0 Left onto Lincoln Rd.
- 30.2 Back at the Lincoln Guide Service.

19

Walden Pond Cruise

Belmont—Waltham—Lincoln—
Sudbury—Weston—Waltham—Belmont

"What's the best route to and from Walden Pond?" many a Boston cyclist has asked. Here's the answer. As it happens, this ride was also the favorite training route for John Allis, a three-time Olympian and respected dean of the local cycling scene. He rode the course twice daily to prepare for the 1968, 1972, and 1976 Olympic road races. Today it is also a favorite loop among recreational cyclists.

Allis first mapped the tour in 1972 by sitting down with a map and tracing what appeared to be the least trafficked roads leading west from Cambridge. The loop was originally 40 miles long, the distance he could ride in the two hours from his home in Cambridge.

Today the course starts at Belmont Wheelworks in Belmont. Alternate starting points include Cambridge and the green in Weston. Wherever you begin, though, you'll explore the near-rural suburbs of Lincoln, Sudbury, and Weston. These three towns are the center of the "green belt" west of Boston that offers excellent cycling surprisingly near a major urban center. This ride can be linked with the Lincoln to Great Brook Farm Ramble.

Since this loop passes many first-class attractions, you should do it at least once as a leisurely ride. Turn up the driveway of the DeCordova Museum in Lincoln, on Sandy Pond Road, for a quick tour of its sculpture gardens overlooking Sandy Pond. On a clear day New Hampshire's Mount Monadnock is visible on the horizon. Turning left onto Baker Bridge Road, stop at the Gropius House, an example of modern Bauhaus architecture. Or take a short side trip on Route 126 to historic Walden Pond—now a favorite swimming spot too. Stop on the wood plank bridge across the Sudbury River for the view to either side, where much of the shoreline is protected by the Great Meadows Wildlife Refuge. In Weston stop for a rest on the expansive green or at a nearby restaurant. Both are favorite meetings places for Sunday morning rides organized by the Charles River Wheelmen, the areas largest riding club (whose members include plenty of women).

This semiurban "escape route" offers a pleasant ride no matter what pace you keep.

The Basics

Start: You can begin riding from many different towns—Belmont, Waltham, Lincoln, Weston, or Sudbury. On the map the ride starts at Belmont Wheel Works bike shop in Belmont, at 480 Trapelo Rd., just east of Trapelo's intersection with Pleasant St. Belmont is located between Routes 2 and 20, on the inside of Boston's beltway, Rte. 128.
Length: 32.2, 27.0, or 13.0 miles.
Terrain: Rolling suburban and rural roads, with some extended climbs at the beginning in Belmont (which means "beautiful mountain").
Food: Many eateries and food stores along Trapelo Rd. in Belmont. A pizza place and convenience store are on the right at the intersection of Rte. 117 and Sudbury Rd. at 14.0 miles, and a restaurant in Weston is at 24.8 miles.
Traffic/Safety: There can be traffic at the beginning and end of the ride, on Trapelo Rd. and Pleasant St. (Rte. 60). In the middle watch out for some soft and sandy shoulders and sharper turns on narrower and windier roads.

Miles and Directions

- 0.0 From the Belmont Wheel Works, ride west on Trapelo Rd.
- 0.2 Turn sharp right, uphill, onto Pleasant St., Rte. 60.
- 1.3 Turn left onto Clifton St. at the second stoplight, opposite Leonard St.
- 1.6 Bear left through the rotary, continuing uphill on Prospect St.
- 2.0 Bear left at the next rotary, onto Marsh St., next to the Belmont Hill School.
- 3.1 Turn right at the T onto Concord Ave., just after crossing Winter St. Continue on Concord Ave. for almost 3 miles, crossing Waltham St. and then passing within sight of Rte. 2 on the right.
- 6.0 Turn left onto Spring St. When Concord Ave. ends.

For a 13.0-mile jaunt, continue across Trapelo Rd. onto Wyman Rd., which rolls for 1.2 miles, coming out at Totten Pond Rd. Turn left onto Totten Pond, and pick up the directions below at 29.3 miles.

- 6.5 Turn right onto Trapelo Rd. Follow Trapelo for almost 3 miles, crossing the Cambridge Reservoir, to its end in Lincoln center.
- 9.3 Trapelo ends at the intersection with Lincoln Rd. Cross this intersection onto Sandy Pond Rd. toward the DeCordova Museum. If you turn left onto Lincoln Rd., after 1.3 miles you will reach Lincoln Guide Service, a popular bike shop, and a shopping center with an excellent deli and modern art gallery.
- 10.0 Turn left onto Baker Bridge Rd. This is the first possible left turn after you pass the entrance to the DeCordova Museum on the right. Look for the modernistic Gropius House on the left on Baker Bridge Rd.
- 11.1 Left onto Rte. 126 at T. A right turn here would lead you to Walden Pond and Concord. Ride past the left turn for Codman Rd. and Codman House—another local attraction.
- 12.3 Turn right onto Rte. 117 at the stoplight.

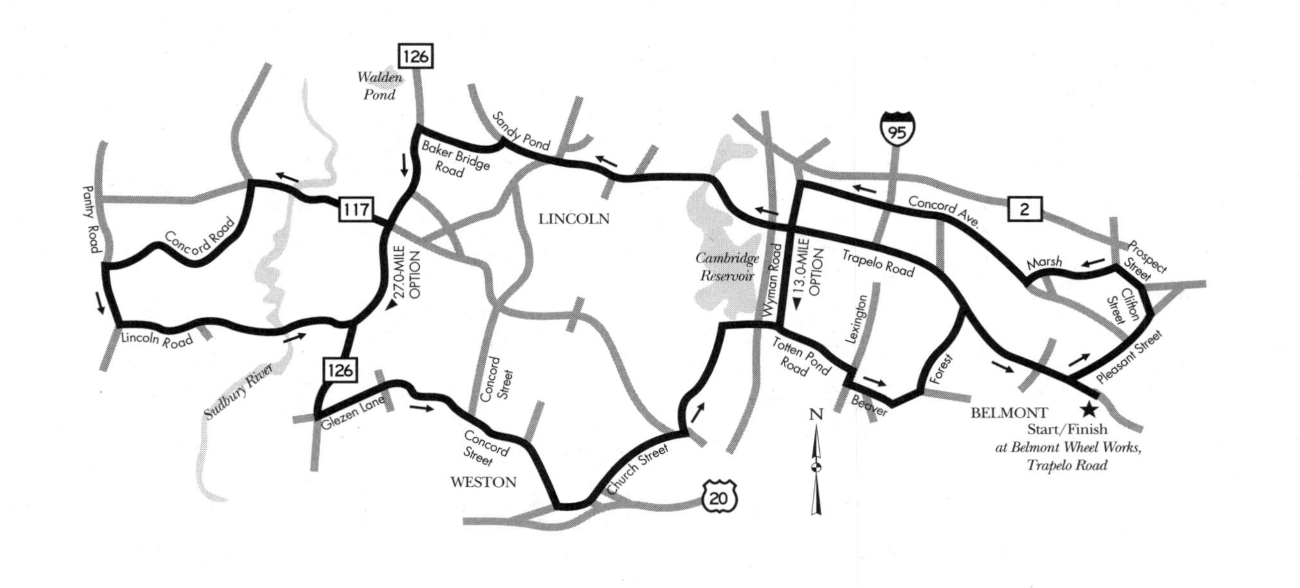

126
Walden Pond
95
Sandy Pond
Baker Bridge Road
LINCOLN
Concord Ave.
2
Pantry Road
117
Concord Road
Cambridge Reservoir
Wyman Road
13.0-MILE OPTION
Trapelo Road
Marsh
Prospect Street
27.0-MILE OPTION
Lexington
Clifton Street
Lincoln Road
126
Totten Pond Road
Forest
Pleasant Street
Sudbury River
Concord Street
Beaver
Glezen Lane
BELMONT
N
Concord Street
Church Street
Start/Finish
at Belmont Wheel Works,
Trapelo Road
WESTON
20

For a 27.0-mile ride, continue across Rte. 117 onto Rte. 126 (a designated "bike route"). Then pick up the directions at 19.9 miles. (Doing so, though, you will miss the most rural part of the ride.)

- 14.0 At the next stoplight turn left onto Concord Rd. Sudbury Rd. turns right. This is Concord Crossing. The pizza place and convenience store on the right are good for snacks.
- 16.3 Turn left onto Concord Rd. at the T as Pantry Rd. turns right.
- 17.1 Turn left onto Lincoln Rd. at Lincoln-Sudbury Regional High School, soon passing the Lincoln Meadow Conservation Land on the right, a hiking site.
- 19.2 Cross the wood plank bridge over the Sudbury River, pausing for the view, as Lincoln Rd. becomes Sherman Bridge Rd.
- 19.9 Turn right onto Rte. 126, keeping a sharp eye out for the next left turn.
- 21.0 Turn left onto Glezen Ln., a narrow, winding road. This becomes Sudbury Rd.
- 23.0 When you see the classical facade of the Campion Center, a former monastery, continue straight past it. You will have merged into Concord St., which then curves downhill to the right.
- 23.8 Bear right, staying on Concord St.
- 24.6 Turn left at the T, riding into the center of Weston.
- 24.9 After passing the town green, immediately turn left onto Church St. Follow Church St. as it winds downhill toward Rte. 117.
- 26.1 Right on Rte. 117, named North Ave. here, after crossing the commuter rail tracks at the Kendall Green Station.
- 26.3 Take first left, onto Lexington St. This becomes West St. Continue to the stoplight opposite the Cambridge Reservoir.
- 27.7 Turn right onto Winter St. at the reservoir. Winter St. becomes Totten Pond Rd. after crossing the overpass over Rte. 128. *Caution:* Watch for traffic around Rte. 128.
- 29.3 Turn right at the next stoplight, onto Lexington St., then bear left immediately with Lexington St., as Bacon St. continues straight.

- 29.5 Turn left on Beaver St. toward the Chapel High School.
- 29.9 Stay on Beaver St. through the traffic circle.
- 30.3 Bear left onto Forest St. at Bentley College.
- 31.5 Turn right onto Trapelo Rd.
- 33.0 Pass turnoff for Pleasant St. on left and continue on Trapelo back to Belmont.
- 33.2 Arrive at Belmont Wheel Works on the right.

20

Cape Ann Cruise

*Manchester—Magnolia—Gloucester—
East Gloucester—Rockport—Annisquam—
Gloucester—Manchester*

The Fisherman's Memorial on Gloucester's Pavilion Beach speaks for all of Cape Ann. Its rough-hewn mariner stands at his ship's wheel, gazing into a storm. He memorializes more than 10,000 lives lost at sea in Gloucester's 350-year history. He also symbolizes the rich heritage of the entire cape, where livelihoods are still extracted from the surrounding ocean.

The Cape Ann Cruise explores the best of Boston's North Shore. The 22-mile loop circles the rocky shores of Cape Ann, where fishermen's cottages and grand summer homes now share the ocean views. The route passes through the working waterfront of Gloucester and the harbor towns of East Gloucester, Rockport, and Annisquam, favorites of both artists and tourists.

The longer, 36-mile loop includes the coastal towns of Manchester and Magnolia, as well as the Hammond Castle Museum, a medieval-style castle built by John Hay Hammond, Jr., an accomplished inventor, in 1926–29. The Cape Ann Cruise can easily be extended to 40 to 50 miles by including the town of Beverly, to the southwest of Manchester.

The 36-mile loop starts in Manchester, not far from one of the area's best beaches. After your ride pay a visit to Singing Beach, so named for the sound its sand makes as the waves roll ashore. To get there follow Beach Street for a half mile away from the town center to its end. Walk or ride, as parking is extremely limited. The shorter option starts at the Fisherman's Memorial statue on Gloucester's Pavilion Beach.

From Gloucester both rides follow the same route around the cape. The opening miles pass through East Gloucester, with several scenic detour options to Hammond Castle Museum, Rocky Neck, and Eastern Point. Along Atlantic Road the pounding waves may send salt spray up to the road. Here you may want to stop for a rest on one of the many grassy spots above the rocks.

Rockport, midway on either ride, enjoys a varied and colorful history. This small town might have become a major east coast city, had a group of promoters a hundred years ago succeeded in making its harbor home to the U.S. North Atlantic Fleet. A crumbling breakwater off the shore is all that remains of their effort. If you spot a sea monster, you will not have been the first to do so. In the nineteenth century dozens of otherwise sober townspeople testified that they had spotted a 100-foot-long serpent in the local waters. You can learn more about the town's past at the Sandy Bay Historical Museum on King Street.

Halfway between Rockport and Annisquam, turn right off Route 127 for a detour to the rocky headland of Halibut Point State Park. This fifty-four-acre park is the site of a former granite quarry. Abandoned in 1929, the quarry is now filled with water. Pathways lead to a series of expansive granite shelves stepping down into the sea. This is a popular spot for walking, sunning, and picnicking. (There is a modest admission fee.)

The small, charming village of Annisquam is the last stop on the cape. The Annisquam River connects Ipswich Bay, on the cape's north side, to Gloucester Harbor, to the south. On a sunny day boats large and small parade through this waterway.

Although you'll undoubtedly encounter other cyclists along this route, bicycling must share with scuba diving the distinction of being Cape Ann's most popular recreational activity. On weekends divers splash around and crawl in and out of almost every protected cove around the cape.

The Cape Ann Cruise is particularly attractive in the spring and the fall, when weekend traffic subsides. In the summer try to get an early start, since the cape's cool ocean breezes, picturesque towns, and plentiful beaches bring out the crowds.

The Basics

Start: Manchester, off Rte. 128 near its northern end. For the 36-mile ride, park in the commuter rail parking lot on Beach St., just off Rte. 127, downtown. If this lot is full, try the high school parking lot less than a mile east on Rte. 127 on the left. Or park in Gloucester on Western Ave. for the 22-mile loop. The ride may be extended by starting in Beverly, Prides Crossing, or Beverly Farms and following Rte. 127E to Manchester.
Length: 36.4 or 22.5 miles (with optional extension to 40–50 miles).
Terrain: Flat to slightly rolling coastal route.
Food: Numerous eateries along the way in Gloucester, Rockport, and Annisquam provide fresh seafood and sandwiches.
Traffic/Safety: Sections of rough road, especially on the return from Rockport to Annisquam and Gloucester. Weekend summer traffic may be especially heavy. Also, use caution in the commercial district of Gloucester and at the rotary at Grant Circle at 28.6 miles (see optional bypass below).

Miles and Directions

- 0.0 From the commuter rail parking lot in downtown Manchester, turn right onto Beach St., crossing the railroad tracks; then immediately turn right onto Rte. 127 (Summer St.) toward Gloucester and Rockport.
- 1.6 Right onto Ocean St., a pretty seaside detour off Rte. 127.
- 2.5 Right onto Rte. 127 toward Gloucester.
- 2.9 Right on Raymond St. toward Magnolia and the Hammond Castle.
- 3.4 Straight through intersection. (Shore Dr., the sharp right turn, loops bumpily around a point of land that you might want to detour to explore.) Raymond St. becomes Norman Ave.

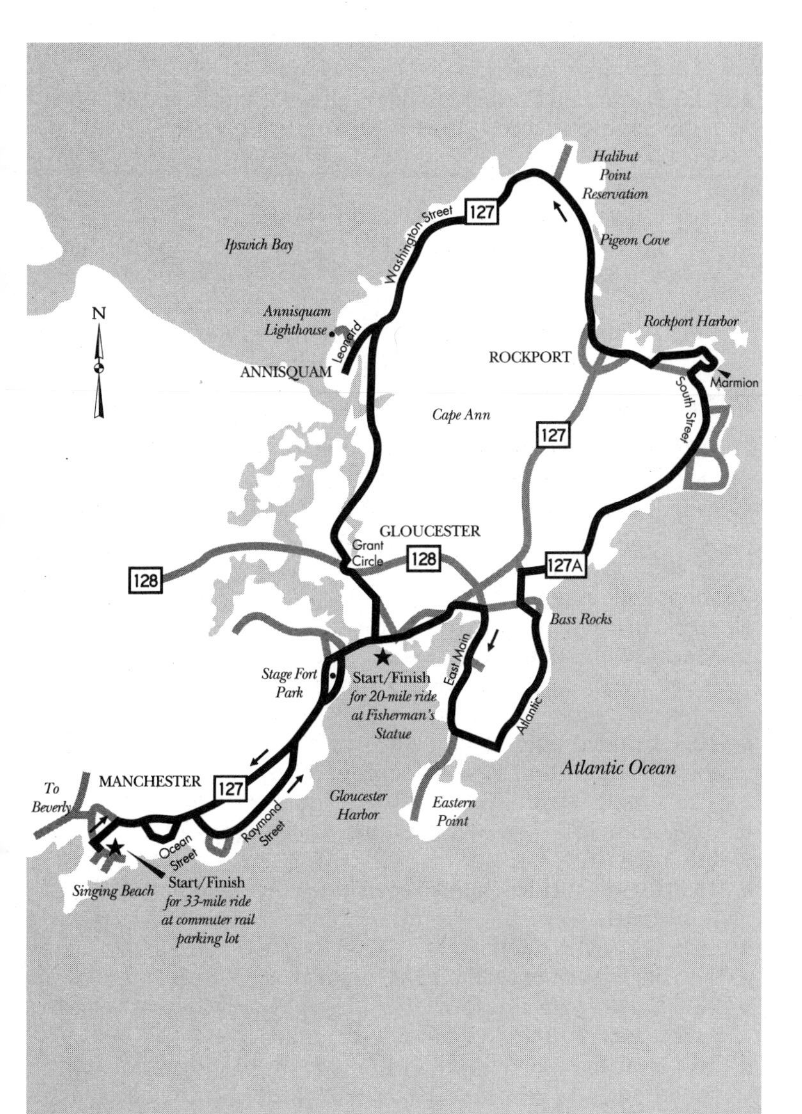
N
Halibut Point Reservation
127
Washington Street
Ipswich Bay
Pigeon Cove
Annisquam Lighthouse
Leonard
ANNISQUAM
ROCKPORT
Rockport Harbor
Marmion
South Street
Cape Ann
127
GLOUCESTER
Grant Circle
128
128
127A
Bass Rocks
East Main
Stage Fort Park
Start/Finish
for 20-mile ride
at Fisherman's
Statue
Atlantic
Atlantic Ocean
MANCHESTER
127
To Beverly
Gloucester Harbor
Eastern Point
Raymond Street
Ocean Street
Singing Beach
Start/Finish
for 33-mile ride
at commuter rail
parking lot

- 3.9 Continue straight onto Hesperus Ave.
- 4.8 Hammond Castle Museum on the right, with medieval interiors and artifacts. (There is an admission charge of about $6.00.)
- 5.4 Right onto Rte. 127.
- 6.9 *Caution:* Cross a short metal drawbridge.
- 7.1 Entering Gloucester on Rte. 127, pass the town's long Pavilion Beach and its Fisherman's Memorial statue. Stay on Rte. 127 as it turns left and then dips down to Gloucester's Inner Harbor and busy working waterfront. Ride carefully, as this is the most trafficked section of this tour.

The ride's shorter, 22.5-mile option starts here.

- 8.2 Bear right onto Main St.
- 8.3 Bear right at light onto. E. Main St. toward East Gloucester.
- 9.0 Bear right with E. Main St. at East Gloucester Square.
- 9.5 Pass turnoff for Rocky Neck on the right. The artist colony of Rocky Neck is an enjoyable detour, offering art galleries and shops and restaurants.
- 10.0 Turn left onto Farrington Ave. just after passing Niles Beach on the right. (For another scenic detour go straight between the stone posts, to do a 1.5-mile loop past many beautiful estates.)
- 10.5 Turn left onto Atlantic Rd., which passes along a dramatic, rocky coastline for the next couple of miles.
- 12.2 Turn left with Atlantic Rd. as it turns away from the water.
- 12.6 Cross Bass Ave. and continue straight onto Thatcher Rd., Rte. 127A.
- 16.3 Right onto Marmion Way shortly before entering Rockport center.
- 16.4 Bear right at fork.
- 17.5 Right back onto Rte. 127A, now called South St.
- 18.2 Downtown Rockport. To the right is Bearskin Neck, a tourist area of shops, restaurants, and galleries.
- 18.3 Bear right at the fork onto Beach St., staying next to the waterfront, toward Pigeon Cove. A park and bandstand on the left, opposite Rockport's Back Beach, provide a quiet rest stop.

- 18.7 Right at the stop sign onto Rte. 127 toward Pigeon Cove and Annisquam.
- 20.7 Pass entrance to Halibut Point State Park on right.
- 22.2 Bear right at Lane's Cove to stay on Rte. 127.
- 23.7 Right onto Leonard St. at Annisquam Village Church into Annisquam.
- 24.1 Bear left at fork.
- 24.3 Left on Bridgewater St., down a short hill, and right on River Rd. at the bottom, opposite the long wooden footbridge crossing Lobster Cove.
- 24.7 Turn right onto Leonard St. at end, bear right at fork, and backtrack to the Annisquam Village Church on Rte. 127. Or you may backtrack from the Lobster Cove Marina, turn right across Lobster Cove on the wooden footbridge, and turn right onto Rte. 127 farther south.
- 25.5 Right onto Rte. 127, here called Washington St., at the Village Church.
- 28.6 To avoid the busy Grant Circle rotary, take a left onto Poplar St., followed by a right onto Maplewood Ave. (under Rte. 128) and a right onto Grove St. Cross Washington St. onto Centennial Ave. Pick up directions below at 29.7 miles.
- 28.7 Ride halfway around Grant Circle, mindful of the traffic entering and exiting this rotary, and continue onto Rte. 127, Washington St., into the city of Gloucester.
- 29.2 Right onto Centennial Ave.
- 29.7 Right onto Rte. 127, now Western Ave., facing Western Harbor. Cross the short drawbridge spanning the canal that effectively makes Cape Ann an island.

The ride's shorter, 22.5-mile option ends here.

- 30.0 On your left is the Stage Fort Park waterfront, which you may want to explore.
- 30.4 Left on Rte. 127, back toward the commuter rail parking lot.
- 36.4 Commuter rail parking lot in downtown Manchester.

21

South Shore–Wompatuck State Park Ramble

Hull—Cohasset—Scituate—
Wompatuck State Park—Hingham—Hull

This ride begins at the most popular swimming beach near Boston, next to a musical amusement ride (an antique carousel). Then it explores four of the oldest and most scenic towns gracing the Atlantic Ocean: Hull, Cohasset, Scituate, and Hingham. Along the way the tour passes rocky cliffs, grassy wetlands, a half dozen beaches, several harbors full of sailboats, a historic lighthouse, and well-kept nineteenth-century homes and churches. Taking a break from the seashore, the ride heads inland, allowing you to sample a large state park that's popular among local cyclists for its miles of paved bike paths and mountain-biking trails. Not bad for a 26-mile jaunt.

Nantasket Beach in Hull, where the ride begins, looks like merely a summer hangout for the body-beautiful crowd, but it's also Nantasket Reservation, managed by the Metropolitan District Commission (MDC) of Boston. The beach was once also the home of an amusement park, Paragon Park, which has closed. Today the wide, long beach is enjoying a revival, though, as a bustling, casual site for sunbathing, people watching, and nighttime socializing.

The beach lies in the town of Hull, on a peninsula 25 miles south of Boston. Begun as a fishing village back in 1620, Hull now boasts 7 miles of swimming beaches, two historical museums, handsome New England–style churches, and an old fort on a hill with a panoramic view of Boston. It's worth doing the leisurely 10-mile "ride-within-a-ride" to explore Hull proper.

But first you're heading down a coastline that some cyclists have compared to places like Ireland. After cruising along a rugged shore, past spectacular mansions, the tour passes by more public beaches and tranquil wetlands, before arriving in historic Cohasset. First settled in 1670, Cohasset was a busy center of the fishing and shipping industry in the eighteenth and nineteenth centuries. Today its harbor is the home of mainly recreational sailing vessels, while the town has a classic New England common, ringed by grand nineteenth-century homes in Georgian, Federal, and Greek Revival architectural styles, as well as a historical museum and a maritime museum (open in the afternoon) and a dozen or so small stores. St. Stephen's Church on the common is famous for its (free) outdoor concerts every Sunday at 6:30 P.M. during the summer, performed on its fifty-four-bell carillon.

After cruising past more summer homes and beaches, you arrive at Lighthouse Point in Scituate, established in 1636. In 1810 the U.S. Congress allotted $4,000 to build a lighthouse in Scituate Harbor. Two years later the British appeared in the harbor during the War of 1812. Abigail and Rebecca Bates, the daughters of the lighthouse keeper, played a fife and beat a drum from the point—saving the town. Since then they've been called the "army of two."

Then it's inland, to explore a large state park (3,500 acres) on a quiet, 2.5-mile paved access road. Wompatuck State Park also boasts a 12-mile-long paved bike path and about 10 miles of mountain-biking trails, as well as 400 campsites and a freshwater spring, where people line up to fill plastic jugs.

One more town awaits. Hingham's history includes the Old Ship Church, now a National Historic Landmark, with a tall brick bell tower and a cemetery behind it. You pass right by it. The church, first built in 1681, is the oldest religious building in continuous use in the United States. Nestled behind it, watched over by large shade trees, lie many of those who first lived in the United States, 250 years ago, including Samuel Lincoln and his kinfolk, early ancestors of Abraham Lincoln.

The Basics

Start: Nantasket Beach in Hull. From the Boston area take Rte. 128S (I–95) and fork left onto I–93N (toward Braintree/Cape Cod). Then take exit 7/Rte. 3S (Cape Cod)—it's a major turnoff; just be in one of the two right lanes on I–93. (*Note:* Rte. 3 can be busy on Saturday mornings and Sunday evenings, as Bostonians head to and from Cape Cod.) Take exit 14/Rte. 228N (Rockland/Nantasket). (You will soon cross Rte. 53—a good place to rendezvous with other cyclists, since it has several eateries.) Pass through Hingham and continue on Rte. 228N. After a half mile fork left onto Kilby St. and then left onto Rockland St. At the next intersection turn right sharply onto George Washington Blvd., which heads into Hull. You will reach a long public beach on the right, with on-street parking, large parking lots ($2.00 all day), and an antique carousel on the left.

Length: 26.6 miles to do the inland loop, 24.0 miles if you retrace the coastal ride, and another 10.0 or so miles through Hull proper.

Terrain: Well-maintained paved roads, rolling gently along the coast and through several towns, suburban and rural landscapes, and a large park. Only a few short hills.

Food: In the four towns there are many convenience stores, restaurants, and bakeries. There's a good deli/bakery on S. Main St. in Cohasset, a famous ice cream/yogurt/slush stand (Dribbles) in Scituate, and eateries in Hingham.

Traffic/Safety: Always ride alertly and single file on the narrower roads along the coast. Also, watch for opening car doors in Hull, Cohasset, Scituate, and Hingham. The ride crosses two or three busy intersections (noted in Miles and Directions).

Miles and Directions

- 0.0 From Nantasket Beach ride southeast on Nantasket Ave.
- 0.5 Turn left onto Atlantic Ave., which is up a small hill. At 1.0 mile watch for a smaller public beach, Crescent Beach, on the left.

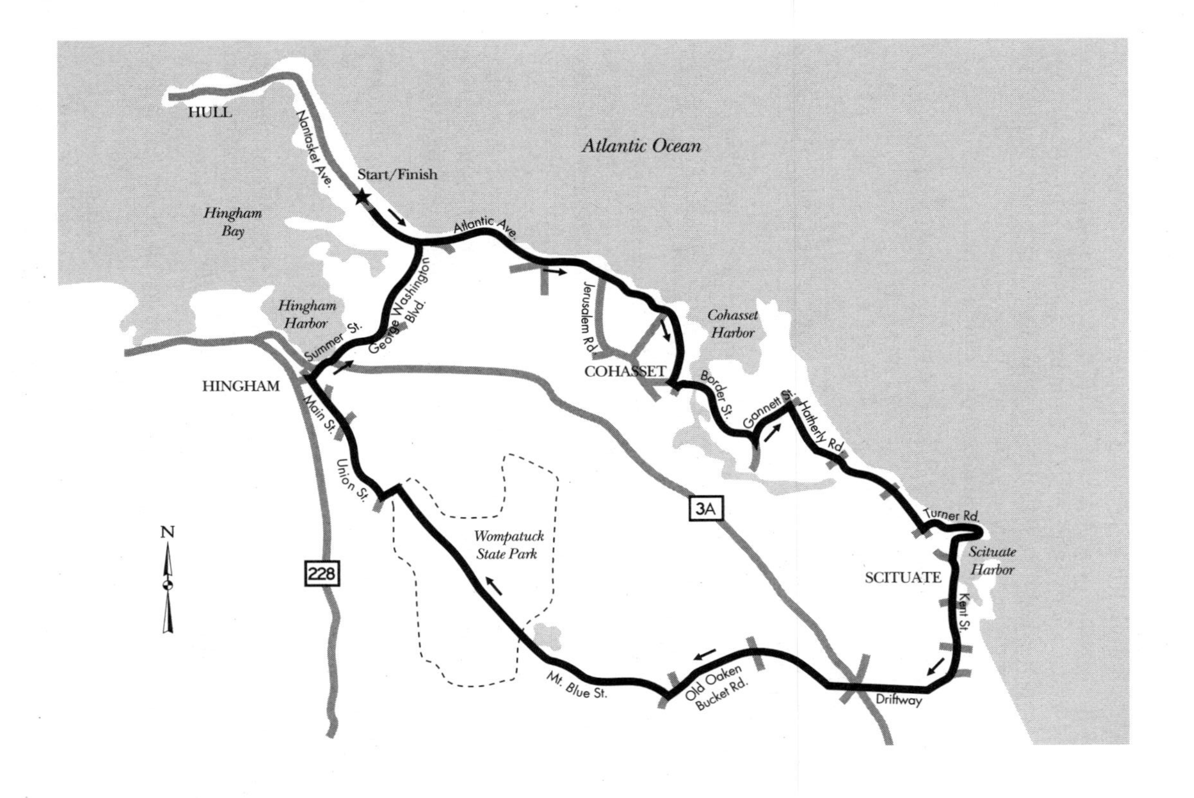

HULL
Nantasket Ave.
Start/Finish
Atlantic Ocean
Hingham Bay
Atlantic Ave.
George Washington Blvd.
Hingham Harbor
Summer St.
Jerusalem Rd.
Cohasset Harbor
COHASSET
HINGHAM
Main St.
Border St.
Gannett St.
Hatherly Rd.
Union St.
3A
Turner Rd.
N
Wompatuck State Park
Scituate Harbor
228
SCITUATE
Kent St.
Mt. Blue St.
Old Oaken Bucket Rd.
Driftway

- 1.8 Turn left, staying on Atlantic Ave. Now begins a spectacular stretch of road, with rocky cliffs and million-dollar mansions. After a mile or so, Jerusalem Rd. comes into Atlantic Ave. on the right. It's another scenic lane, which you might take from the other side on a return trip.
- 4.4 Arrive in Cohasset Harbor, veering right.

Before riding around Cohasset Harbor, you might want to turn left onto Elm St. and cruise into Cohasset proper. As you reach the center of town, you'll pass both the Maritime Museum and the Historical Society on the right. Next St. Stephen's Church appears on a hill on the right and then the common. There's a good deli/bakery a few blocks to the left on S. Main St.

- 4.6 Left onto Cove Rd., an immediate left onto Elm St., another left onto Border St., and soon cross a bridge.
- 6.3 Turn left at a T junction onto Gannett St. (unmarked).
- 6.9 Turn right onto Hatherly Rd. You can go straight at this junction to reach another good ocean view. On Hatherly Rd. you'll soon pass another beach, Egypt Beach. Notice the houses on pilings. This area has been flooded in the past during storms.
- 9.4 Turn left at a stoplight onto Turner Rd.
- 9.7 Right at a stop sign. Fork left at the next stop sign. Soon you'll reach a dead end at Lighthouse Point. Take the one-way street away from the lighthouse and continue hugging the coast.
- 10.9 Veer left at the stop sign and then keep veering left along boat-filled Scituate Harbor.
- 11.7 Turn left at the stop sign onto Beaver Dam Rd. and cruise into Scituate.
- 12.0 On the right watch for Dribbles, a refreshment stand famous among cyclists. Again, for more ocean views you can turn left on Foster St. at the intersection just after Dribbles.

You can retrace this coastal route back to Nantasket Beach, for a slightly shorter, 24-mile ride. If you do so, you might want to do a popular miniloop around Cohasset: Ride into the town of Cohasset and pick up Jerusalem Rd. off N. Main St. It rejoins Atlantic Ave.

- 12.1 Continue straight ahead, veering left on Front St., which becomes Kent St., then New Kent St., and finally Driftway, always curving right and inland.
- 14.3 Reach a rotary at busy Rte. 3A. *Caution:* Negotiating a rotary can be intimidating at first. Basically, you enter it counterclockwise, first yielding to any traffic already in the rotary and using hand signals. You're heading to the opposite side of the rotary, onto Old Oaken Bucket Rd., a small road with a sign on the left side of it that reads OLD SATUIT TRAIL.
- 17.0 Watch for the MT. BLUE ST. sign on the right. (This is the next right turn after Summer St.)
- 19.4 The road dead-ends at a metal gate with a paved road on the other side of it. This is the southern boundary of Wompatuck State Park. Ride around the gate and onto the paved road. After about a half mile, watch for a sign on the left, MT. BLUE SPRING. Stop for fresh springwater. At the northern end of the park, in a parking lot just across from the park headquarters, there's a new (1995) rental business, with snacks and bike tools available.
- 21.9 Veer right on Union St., just outside the park. Union St. becomes Middle St. and then Main St. as it enters Hingham.
- 22.9 At a stop sign go straight across onto the smaller road. You will soon pass the historic Old Ship Church on the right, with a cemetery behind it.
- 23.8 Turn right at a T junction onto North St. You will pass the Freewheeling Bike Shop. *Caution:* The rest of the ride into Hull uses wider, busier streets and passes through another rotary. Always make eye contact with motorists and use hand signals.
- 24.1 Turn right onto Summer St. (Rte. 3A) at Hingham Harbor. Go around the large rotary 180 degrees, following the signs for Nantasket/Hull.
- 25.0 Veer left onto George Washington Blvd. For those who prefer there's a paved bike path on the other side of the highway. (A side trip: You will pass Martin's Ln. on the left. It leads to World's End Reservation, a seacoast park with about 8 miles of unpaved carriage roads open for bicycling. There's a small charge to park a car and use the reservation.) The boulevard

takes you back into Hull and onto Nantasket Ave.

- 26.6 Arrive at the carousel on Nantasket Beach.

To do a 10-mile ride in and around Hull, just continue northward on Nantasket Ave., veering slightly left. After 2.7 miles you will reach the town of Hull. For a scenic loop keep veering left, hugging the shoreline and arriving at Windmill Point, affording an excellent view of Boston's skyline and a half-dozen Boston Harbor islands. Then loop back through town, following the signs to Fort Revere Tower or visiting the Lifesaving Museum (which has water and a rest room).

22

Cape in a Day (or Two) Classic

Boston—Milton—Brockton—Plymouth—Bourne—Yarmouth—Wellfleet—Provincetown

Many cyclists in New England dream about riding from Boston to Cape Cod—it's a fantasy trip, one they plan to do someday. For others, though, this tour is an annual event—thanks largely to the American Youth Hostels (AYH), which sponsors an annual 125-mile ride from Boston to Provincetown in late June.

For all but the most experienced cyclists, pedaling from Boston to Cape Cod is a challenge best done in a group. Nowadays there's also a fund-raising ride from Stockbridge in western Massachusetts to Provincetown, as well as a shorter, 85-mile ride from Plymouth to Provincetown the latter sponsored by the Appalachian Mountain Club (AMC).

To make any Boston to Cape Cod bike tour a little easier, in 1978 the Commonwealth of Massachusetts designated certain roads from the Charles River in Boston to Provincetown on the Cape as the official Boston–Cape Cod Bikeway route. Cyclists should, however, be aware that this "bikeway" uses active roads and is only partly marked with signs.

The AYH Cape in a Day (or Two) ride leaves from Boston College promptly at 6:00 A.M., after riders have sampled fruit, juice, bagels, and other munchies. The group splits up to spend Saturday night at two hostels on the outer Cape, in Eastham, 95 miles from

Boston, and in North Truro, at 115 miles. "The hostels hold a total of ninety-four people, but other cyclists come along just for a day, know friends on the Cape, make hotel reservations, or have their family follow them down," says Seth Davis, longtime leader of the AYH ride. The next day is reserved for exploring the National Seashore, with its dune-covered beaches; taking a leisurely ride into Provincetown for sightseeing and shopping; and catching the 4:30 P.M. ferry back to Boston. (Bring a sweater, since the ferry ride can be cool.)

The AYH ride includes a support van ("sag wagon") to assist with repairs and other breakdowns, meals, lodging at a hostel, and the ferry back to downtown Boston ($14.00 plus $2.00 for a bike). All for $70.00. No wonder it fills up in early May. Ride leaders recommend that anyone who wants to ride from Boston to Cape Cod have done at least a 60-mile ride, as well as regular shorter rides. To register for the AYH ride, contact Seth Davis at 186 Palmer Street, Arlington, MA 02174, or call the AYH office in Boston at (617) 731–5430.

Whatever group you join, pedaling from Boston to Provincetown will leave you with memories of an early morning passage through Boston's southern suburbs; a pit stop for food and juice or coffee in Plymouth; the first sight of the arching Sagamore Bridge, at 65 miles, marking the beginning of Cape Cod; the midday stretch through Sandwich, Barnstable, and Yarmouth; and turning up the Cape's hook for the final leg—and your legs' final push.

Once you're on the Cape, you can also explore the Cape Cod Rail Trail, a separate, 25-mile trail. It begins on Route 134 in Dennis (a half mile from exit 9 off Route 6). The rail trail winds through Dennis, Harwich, Orleans, and Eastham and into Wellfleet (its latest extension), ending at Lecounts Hollow Road near Route 6. There is access to the trail at many intersecting roads. The rail trail also passes Nickerson State Park in Orleans, where there's camping (508–896–3491), as well as unpaved trails for hiking and off-road cycling. (In addition, there's a more modest trail, the 3.6-mile Falmouth Shining Sea Trail, from Route 28 in Falmouth to Woods Hole.)

The Basics

Start: The AYH ride begins at Boston College in Newton (near Cleveland Circle). But, of course, you can begin anywhere that's convenient. (This author remembers fondly a three-person, 80-mile ride from Harvard Square in Cambridge to Woods Hole in Falmouth, then catching a ferry to Nantucket.) A useful map for maneuvering in and around Boston is Boston's Bikemap, which highlights the best cycling routes out to about Route 128. Most "escape routes" from the Boston area to Cape Cod follow the Emerald Necklace, a linear park with some bike paths that winds through Boston, Brookline, and Jamaica Plain and past the Arnold Arboretum. The Boston–Cape Cod Bikeway then passes through West Roxbury, before entering Milton, an attractive town just south of Boston. The AYH ride and the bikeway map follow different routes at several points along the way.

Length: From 115 to 135 miles, depending on where you begin in Boston and which route (the AYH or Boston–Cape Cod Bikeway) you take to Provincetown.

Terrain: Rolling, with some hills along the way. Both the AYH and the Boston–Cape Cod Bikeway routes follow low-volume roads once they're past Boston's more congested streets. But there's also some traffic on Cape Cod.

Food: Many convenience stores and eateries in towns along the way. The AYH ride stops for breakfast before Plymouth (20 to 30 miles) and for lunch at the Cape Cod Canal (65 miles).

Traffic/Safety: The Boston–Cape Cod Bikeway is not a separate bike path but connected, active roads, with some bikeway signs on them. The bikeway is meant for experienced cyclists who want to travel as safely as possible to and from Boston and Cape Cod. Traffic is always heavier from Boston to Provincetown in the summer and especially on weekends. This ride will regularly test your riding skills in a semiurban environment. It's for well-equipped cyclists in good shape.

Miles and Directions

Neither a map nor detailed directions are included for this ride. The AYH ride and the Boston–Cape Cod Bikeway route differ in at least a half dozen places throughout the 125-mile ride. The Boston–Cape Cod Bikeway map can be obtained from the AYH office at 1020 Commonwealth Ave., Boston, MA 02215 (617–731–5430). Send a self-addressed stamped envelope and $3.00, or drop in and buy one. This twelve-panel map highlights the roads for one possible route from the Charles River in Boston to Provincetown (with a spur to Woods Hole). The AYH might also send you a one-page cue sheet of its Cape in a Day (or Two) ride.

A useful map for cycling on Cape cod is the Cape Ann & North Shore/Cape Cod & the Islands Bicycle Map, found in many bike shops and bookstores or available from Rubel Bikemaps, P.O. Box 1035, Cambridge, MA 02140.

Here are a few highly approximate mileages and some suggested variations along the route:

- 0.0 Beacon St. in Newton.
- 4.0 Cross Rte. 1 in West Roxbury.
- 12.5 Cross I–95 on Rte. 138. The bikeway and AYH rides diverge at York St. off Randolph St., just before entering Canton.
- 20.0 The bikeway and AYH rides diverge on N. Quincy St., just before entering Brockton, taking different routes through Brockton. (Basically, the AYH ride uses Rte. 58, while the bikeway route takes other streets.)
- 45.0 Reach Plymouth.
- 62.0 The Sagamore Bridge in Bourne—the gateway to Cape Cod. (At this point you can take a spur route south toward Woods Hole in Falmouth, instead of toward Provincetown. To do so, turn right after crossing the bridge and pick up the bike path along the canal, then turn south on County Rd.)
- For the rest of the ride to Provincetown, you'll often have two (or even three) options. For instance, through Sandwich Route 6A is a scenic but busier road, while Service Rd. is less traveled but also less scenic.

- At 80 miles, in Dennis, you can take the Cape Cod Rail Trail, Rte. 6A, or Setucket Rd.
- From Eastham to Wellfleet the best choice is the extension of the Cape Cod Rail Trail.
- In Truro fork left off Rte. 6 onto Rte. 6A to reach Provincetown.

23

Martha's Vineyard: Two Tours

A springtime dawn breaks quietly over Martha's Vineyard. Mist rises from the lush fields, revealing deer that have come out to graze. Weathered shingle homes blend into the muted landscape. Rabbits disappear into the scrub oak woods at the sound of your tires humming down the road.

Martha's Vineyard remains a timeless paradise for beachgoers and cyclists alike. Its roads wind through woodland and farms, past miles of white sand beaches, around millponds, inlets, and creeks. This triangular-shaped island has served as an offshore vacation retreat since the last century. Today the Vineyard's population grows tenfold, from 12,000 to 120,000 residents, every summer. Although cycling here can be enjoyable at any time of year, the roads are quietest and the weather nicest in the spring and fall.

The first ride follows the rolling roads of the island's less populated western half. A 25-mile loop extends from the ferry landing in Vineyard Haven as far as the fishing village of Menemsha and the summer community of Chilmark. A 39-mile alternative follows the Vineyard's scenic roads all the way to Gay Head, where sunset-hued cliffs drop down to the sea. This hilly point of land features some of the island's most dramatic scenery.

The second day's ride is a 28-mile ramble that follows flat roads around the island's eastern half, exploring the historic and still busy beach communities of Edgartown and Oak Bluffs. The ride follows newly repaved bike paths through the island's state forest—which contains miles of unpaved roads—and along the oceanfront stretch from Edgartown to Oak Bluffs. An optional 3-mile detour crosses Edgartown Harbor by ferry to visit Chappaquiddick Island.

Each ride represents a day-long excursion, including beach and lunch stops. The easiest way to get to the island is to leave your car in Woods Hole, on the mainland side, and take only your bike across. You are likely to find yourself in the company of other cyclists for the trip. Youth hostel and student cycling groups are regular ferry passengers.

If you would like to start riding on reaching Cape Cod rather than waiting to arrive on Martha's Vineyard, consider following the Boston–Cape Cod Bikeway route from the Sagamore Bridge to the Woods Hole ferry. (See The Cape in a Day [or Two] Classic, Ride 22, for maps and other resources for doing so.) For the adventuresome the Vineyard offers more than 100 miles of paved and unpaved roads. A detailed road map of the Vineyard is available in many outlets on the island (published by J. Donovan).

The Woods Hole Steamship Authority runs daily ferries between Woods Hole and Vineyard Haven. The trip takes about forty-five minutes. Some ferries continue on to Oak Bluffs and Nantucket. Passengers traveling by bicycle or on foot do not need reservations. Call the Steamship Authority at (508) 548–3788 or 477–8600 for information on fares and schedules.

The Vineyard: Gay Head Cruise

Vineyard Haven—North Tisbury—Menemsha—Gay Head—Chilmark—West Tisbury—Vineyard Haven

The Basics

Start: The ferry terminal in Vineyard Haven. The several-times-a-day ferry from Woods Hole, at Cape Cod's southwestern tip, is the island's primary link with the mainland. Follow Rte. 28S from Buzzard's Bay to Woods Hole.
Length: 24.7 or 39.3 miles.
Terrain: Gently rolling, generally well-paved roads. No severe climbs—but some hills.
Food: Places to eat in West Tisbury, Gay Head, and Chilmark. (Some of them may be seasonal.) Stop in Gay Head, this tour's midway point, at 21 miles, for concession stands, a crab shack, and a restaurant as well as a picnic area and facilities. Alley's General Store in West Tisbury, at 32.9 miles, offers snacks, drinks, and a stoop to sit on.
Traffic/Safety: If you arrive in the summer, expect heavy, slow-moving traffic until you leave Vineyard Haven. And plan ahead for accommodations.

Miles and Directions

- 0.0 Coming off the Wood's Hole ferry, turn left onto Water St.
- 0.1 Right, following the sign toward West Tisbury, Chilmark, and Gay Head.

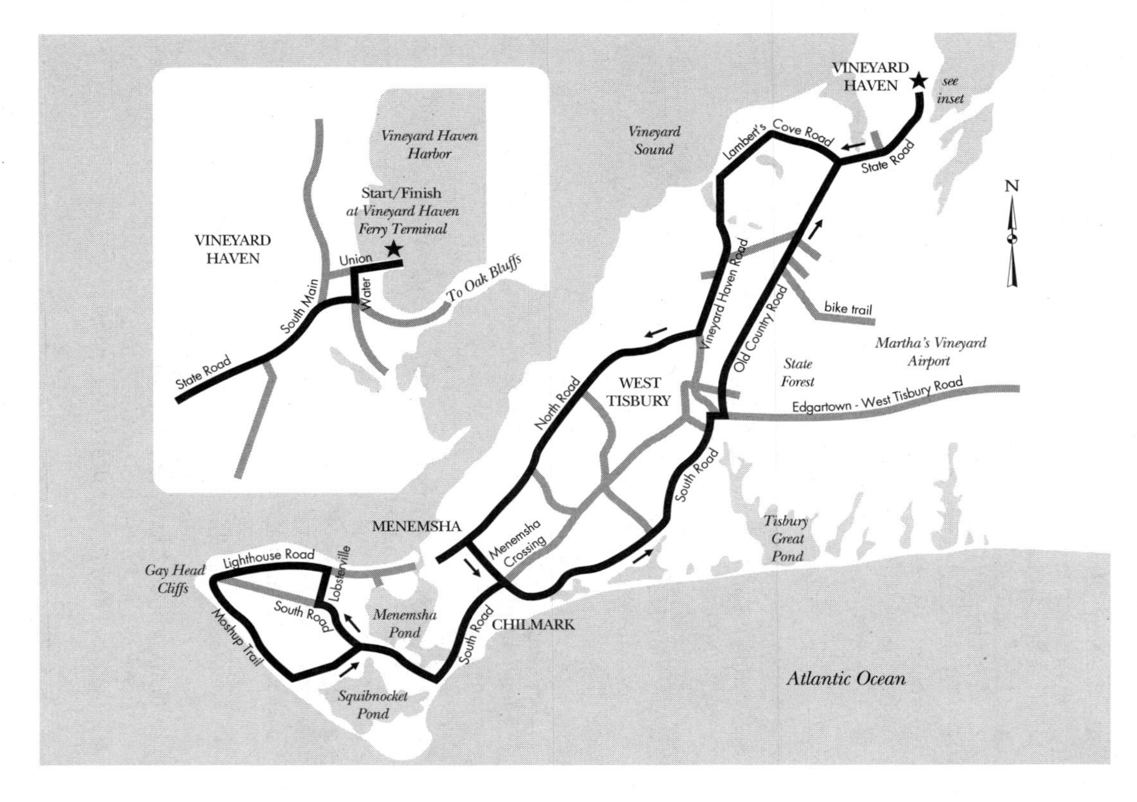

VINEYARD HAVEN
see inset
Vineyard Sound
Lambert's Cove Road
State Road
N
Vineyard Haven Road
Old Country Road
bike trail
Martha's Vineyard Airport
State Forest
WEST TISBURY
North Road
Edgartown - West Tisbury Road
South Road
Tisbury Great Pond
MENEMSHA
Menemsha Crossing
Lighthouse Road
Lobsterville
Gay Head Cliffs
South Road
Menemsha Pond
CHILMARK
Moshup Trail
Squibnocket Pond
Atlantic Ocean
Vineyard Haven Harbor
Start/Finish at Vineyard Haven Ferry Terminal
VINEYARD HAVEN
Union
Water
South Main
To Oak Bluffs
State Road

- 0.2 Stay left at the fork, merging into South Main St., which soon becomes State Rd.
- 1.4 Scenic turnoff on the right.
- 1.6 Right on Lambert's Cove Rd.
- 5.9 Right at T onto Vineyard Haven Rd.
- 7.1 Fork right onto North Rd. toward Menemsha. Look for the ancient oak tree in the clearing on your right just before this turn.
- 12.4 Left on Menemsha Crossing Rd. toward Chilmark and Gay Head.

You may detour into the small fishing village of Menemsha by simply continuing straight, downhill, for just under a mile. Double back to this intersection to continue.

- 13.3 At Beetlebung Corner turn right on South Rd. There's a general store with food here—open Memorial Day to Columbus Day.

If riding the shorter, 24.7-mile option, continue straight onto South Rd. toward West Tisbury, picking up the directions starting at 27.9 miles below.

- 16.4 Reach the ENTERING GAY HEAD sign. (Don't miss the views of Menemsha Pond on your right.)
- 16.8 Stay right on South Rd. as the Moshup Trail turns left.
- 18.0 Right on Lobsterville Rd. toward Lobsterville Town Beach for a downhill run.
- 18.8 Left, gradually uphill, onto Lighthouse Rd.

For a beachside detour follow Lobsterville Rd. around to the right as it traces the edge of the Menemsha Bight. This road follows the line of the beach for 2 miles to the narrow channel connecting Menemsha Pond to the Vineyard Sound. Continue the tour by retracing your route and then turning right onto Lighthouse Rd.

- 20.8 Right onto the short loop of road at Gay Head. Look for the lighthouse on your right. Leaving the road, walk your bike among the concession stands and up the short path to the Gay Head Cliffs viewing area.

- 21.2 Right at the end of the loop onto the Moshup Trail, which swoops downhill toward the open ocean. This road offers terrific views of the surf along Gay Head Town Beach for most of the next 2 miles.
- 24.4 Right back onto South Rd.
- 27.9 Returning to Beetlebung Corner, turn right with South Rd. toward West Tisbury.
- 32.9 Arriving in West Tisbury, you may want to stop for a snack and a sit on the front stoop of Alley's General Store on your left.
- 33.0 Continuing through West Tisbury, bear right onto Edgartown Rd. toward Katama and Edgartown.
- 33.3 Left onto Old County Rd., soon after passing the Old Millpond on the left.
- 36.4 Bear right onto State Rd. after the stop sign, returning to Vineyard Haven. *Caution:* Watch for traffic. Traffic laws are strictly enforced in Vineyard Haven—for cyclists too.
- 39.2 Turn left onto Water St.
- 39.3 Arrive back at the ferry terminal.

The Vineyard: Edgartown Ramble

Vineyard Haven—North Tisbury—Edgartown—Chappaquiddick—Edgartown—Oak Bluffs—Vineyard Haven

The Basics

Start: The ferry terminal in Vineyard Haven, the same starting point as for The Vineyard: Gay Head Cruise.
Length: 25.3 miles, or 28.3 with Chappaquiddick excursion.
Terrain: Flat coastal and woodland roads. Includes two long sections of well-maintained bike trail.
Food: Many selections for quick lunch stops at the Edgartown harborfront at 15.0 miles and in Oak Bluffs at 21.5 miles.
Traffic/Safety: In the summer even the bike paths can be crowded with cyclists, skaters, and walkers. Relax and enjoy.

Miles and Directions

- 0.0 Coming off the Wood's Hole ferry, turn left onto Water St.
- 0.1 Right, following the sign toward West Tisbury, Chilmark, and Gay Head.
- 0.2 Stay left at the fork, merging into S. Main St., which soon becomes State Rd.
- 1.4 Scenic turnoff on the right.
- 1.6 Continue straight onto County Rd. as Lambert's Cove Rd. turns right.

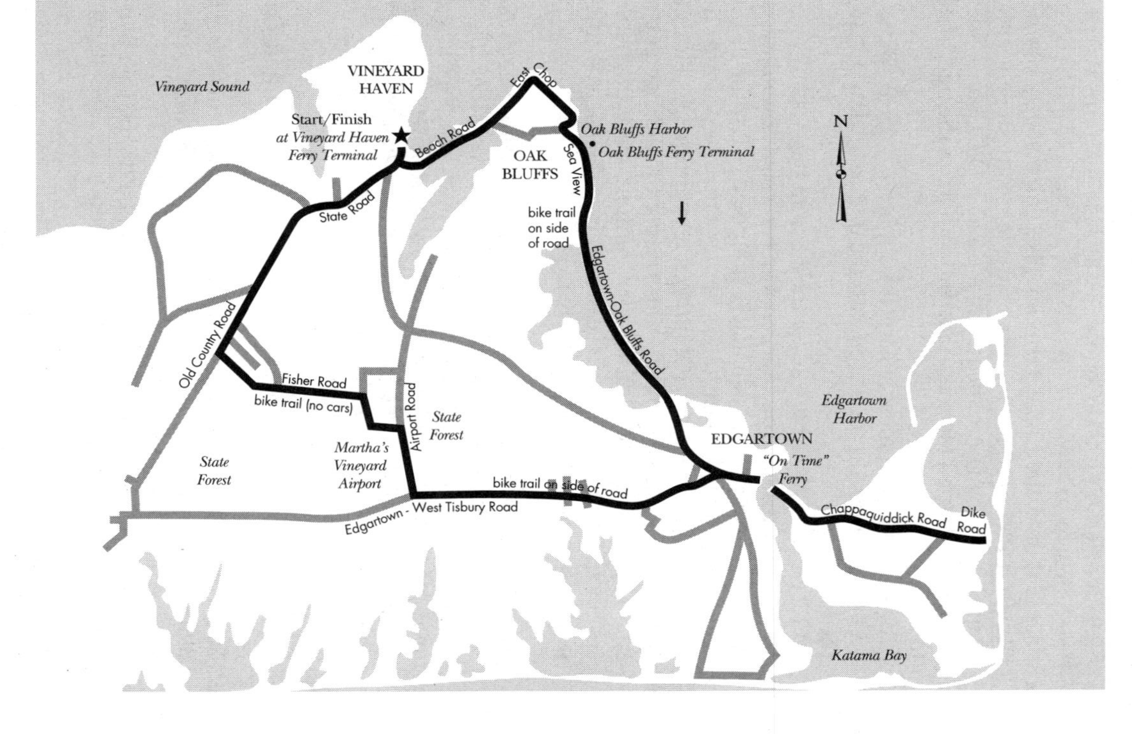

Vineyard Sound
VINEYARD HAVEN
Start/Finish at Vineyard Haven Ferry Terminal
East Chop
Beach Road
State Road
Oak Bluffs Harbor
Oak Bluffs Ferry Terminal
OAK BLUFFS
Sea View
N
bike trail on side of road
Edgartown-Oak Bluffs Road
Old Country Road
Fisher Road
bike trail (no cars)
Airport Road
State Forest
Martha's Vineyard Airport
State Forest
Edgartown Harbor
EDGARTOWN
"On Time" Ferry
bike trail on side of road
Edgartown - West Tisbury Road
Chappaquiddick Road
Dike Road
Katama Bay

- 2.9 Bear left onto Old County Rd. as State Rd. turns right toward Menemsha.
- 3.8 Left onto the Hopps Farm Rd. bike trail through Martha's Vineyard State Forest. As you enter the forest, go straight rather than turning right onto the trail that parallels Old County Rd.
- 6.3 Right, toward Martha's Vineyard Airport, as the trail comes to a T.
- 7.2 Left with the trail as it skirts the airport.
- 8.1 Right onto Airport Rd. or onto the trail paralleling it across the street.
- 10.1 Left onto W. Tisbury Rd. or the adjacent bike trail.
- 14.3 Right on Robinson Rd., following the sign toward Edgartown Center and Chappaquiddick. From here follow the bicycle route signs through Edgartown's narrow one-way streets to the "On Time" ferry terminal. (Or turn left to return to Oak Bluffs.)
- 15.0 Arrive at ferry terminal. After visiting Chappaquiddick Island or checking out Edgartown's waterfront, leave the harbor area by following Winter and Pease streets to the flagpole at the intersection of Pease and Main streets.

For the 5-mile round-trip excursion to Chappaquiddick Island, hop the ferry for the short trip across Edgartown Harbor. Follow the island's only paved road, Chappaquiddick Rd., past the beach club and up a small rise. In 2 miles the road turns sharply right. Continue straight onto Dike Rd., which is unpaved but smooth. It will lead you past a Japanese garden on the left to the Dike Bridge. Lock your bike for a walk onto expansive East Beach.

- 15.7 Right onto Main St. toward Vineyard Haven and Oak Bluffs.
- 16.3 Fork right onto Edgartown–Oak Bluffs Rd. toward Oak Bluffs. Hop onto the broad, smooth bike trail on the left just a short distance down the road.
- 21.3 Left onto Bluffs Ave. immediately opposite the Oak Bluffs ferry terminal. Then continue straight onto Lake Ave., skirting Oak Bluffs Harbor.
- 21.7 Right onto E. Chop Drive, also called Commercial Ave.,

continuing around the harbor. Follow E. Chop Dr., which turns into Highland Dr., around the waterfront.

- 22.7 East Chop lighthouse on the right.
- 23.4 Right on Temahigan Ave., toward Vineyard Haven, immediately after Highland Dr. turns sharply inland.
- 23.7 Right on Beach Rd. across the long causeway back to Vineyard Haven.
- 25.1 Right on Water St.
- 25.3 Right on Union St. at the Vineyard Haven ferry terminal.

New Hampshire

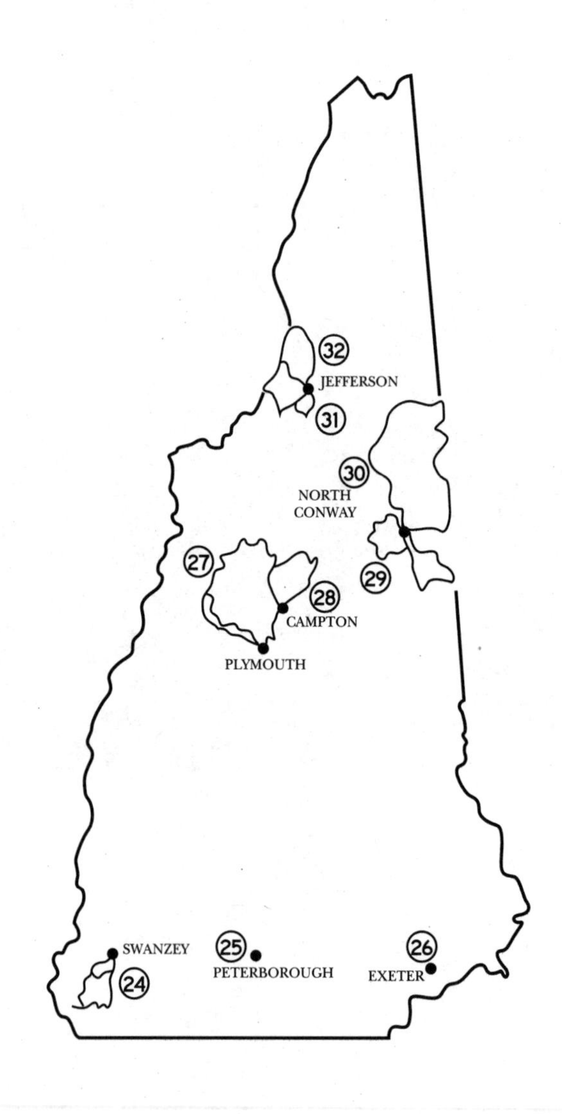
32
JEFFERSON
31
30
NORTH
CONWAY
27
29
28
CAMPTON
PLYMOUTH
SWANZEY
25
PETERBOROUGH
26
EXETER
24

New Hampshire

24. Covered Bridge Cruise 148
25. A Yankee Cruise 153
26. Town and Country Cruise 158
27. Kinsman Region Classic 163
28. Waterville Valley Challenge 168
29. Bear Notch Challenge 173
30. White Mountains Triple-Notch Classic 178
31. Cherry Mountain Ramble 184
32. North Country Challenge 187

24

Covered Bridge Cruise

Swanzey—Ashuelot—
Winchester—Richmond—Swanzey

Everybody loves a covered bridge (except, perhaps, the truck driver whose rig is too heavy to cross it). Cyclists feel a special attraction to these architectural monuments to New England's pioneer days. Covered bridges make one think of how the landscape looked before cars—before bicycles even—when horse-drawn coaches and ox carts provided the primary means of transportation. The tangible bequest of a simpler age, covered bridges give us a comforting sense of continuity with our past.

This 36-mile ride passes through four covered bridges as it parallels the Ashuelot River running south from Swanzey. The tour follows a triangular course, each leg of which has its own character. The first leg is flat. The second, crossing from Winchester to Richmond, features a difficult 2-mile climb. The third, from Richmond back to Swanzey, is rolling but mostly downhill. A shorter, 13-mile option skips the climb, but still includes four of the bridges.

The first bridge is just a mile north of the ride's Swanzey starting point. The next two bridges, both built in the early nineteenth century, cross the river within several miles of each other. Each bridge is different, varying according to its surrounding landscape and its builder.

At 8.5 miles, shortly after you cross the last of these three bridges, the loop turns left onto Old Westport Road. This beautiful, almost forgotten route runs along a fertile but narrow plain between the river and the Pisgah Mountains. Dozens of cows populate the pastures here.

Passing through Winchester, follow the river's elbow west toward the Connecticut River. Although one can continue straight onto the ride's second leg, the finest bridge of all is situated 3 miles downstream. The Winchester-Ashuelot bridge is neither the state's longest nor its oldest. But its open, unsheathed sides, its red roof, and its siting across a rocky stretch of the Ashuelot make it one of the most beautiful. There is a small grocery store here, as well as a pleasant spot to sit on the opposite side of the river.

Follow a dirt road along the riverbank back to Winchester, then climb eastward out of the Ashuelot River Valley. The climb is long and wearying, but it follows a smooth road and at the top offers a view toward famous, solitary Mount Monadnock.

The Basics

Start: Swanzey, in New Hampshire's southwestern corner, just below Keene. From the Boston area follow Rte. 119W to Richmond, then Rte. 32N to Swanzey. From central Massachusetts and southern New England, follow I–91N through Brattleboro, turn east on Rte. 9 to Keene, then go south on Routes 12 and 32 to Swanzey. Park in the lot of the Monadnock Regional High School, on Rte. 32 at its intersection with Sawyers Crossing Rd.
Length: 12.8 or 35.7 miles.
Terrain: A little bit of everything, including long flat stretches, some dirt road, and a 2-mile climb.
Food: There is a small grocery store at the covered bridge in Ashuelot, 17.2 miles into the ride, along with a place to stop for a rest on the bank of the river. There are also convenience stores in Winchester, at 15.0 miles, and at the main intersection in Richmond, at 26.2 miles.
Traffic/Safety: Watch for faster-moving traffic on the second half of the ride, on Routes 119 and 32.

Miles and Directions

- 0.0 From the parking lot of the school in Swanzey, ride west on Sawyers Crossing Rd. toward West Swanzey and Keene.
- 0.2 Stay with Sawyers Crossing Rd. as it turns right at the fork.
- 1.0 Pass through first covered bridge over the Ashuelot River and turn left on the other side.
- 1.5 Stay left as Ash Hill Rd. turns right.
- 2.9 Left onto Rte. 10S toward Winchester. (Don't let all the barking worry you. That's the Monadnock Regional Human Society across the street.)
- 3.4 Left at blinking light. This is the first possible left on Rte. 10.
- 3.9 Left at T and cross the 1832 Thompsen Covered Bridge, which crosses the Ashuelot River just above a small dam.
- 4.2 Right onto Homestead Ave., with a community church on the right.
- 5.6 Bear right at junction. Although unmarked, the road to the left is Swanzey Lake Rd.

For a short jaunt totaling 12.8 miles, turn left here and follow Swanzey Lake Rd. for 3.9 miles back to Rte. 32. Pass Swanzey Lake and the turnoff for Richardson Park on the left, or turn in there for a swim and continue to Rte. 32. Turn left on Rte. 32 back to Swanzey.

- 6.3 Left at stop sign, toward Winchester.
- 7.1 Left onto Rte. 10S, keeping an eye out for traffic. Ride slowly on Rte. 10, as you will be looking for the first right turn.
- 7.4 Right onto Coombs Bridge Rd., which turns downhill through a cluster of small roadside buildings. This is an easy road to miss, but there is a right turn sign preceding it.
- 7.6 Cross third covered bridge and turn left on the other side.
- 8.5 Sharp left at the intersection onto Old Westport Rd. The roads continuing straight and turning right are dirt. (These dirt roads lead into Pisgah State Park—a favorite local mountain-biking site.)
- 13.0 Bear left, staying by the river, as a dirt road joins in from the right.
- 13.5 Continue left on Old Westport Rd. Old Spofford Rd. enters

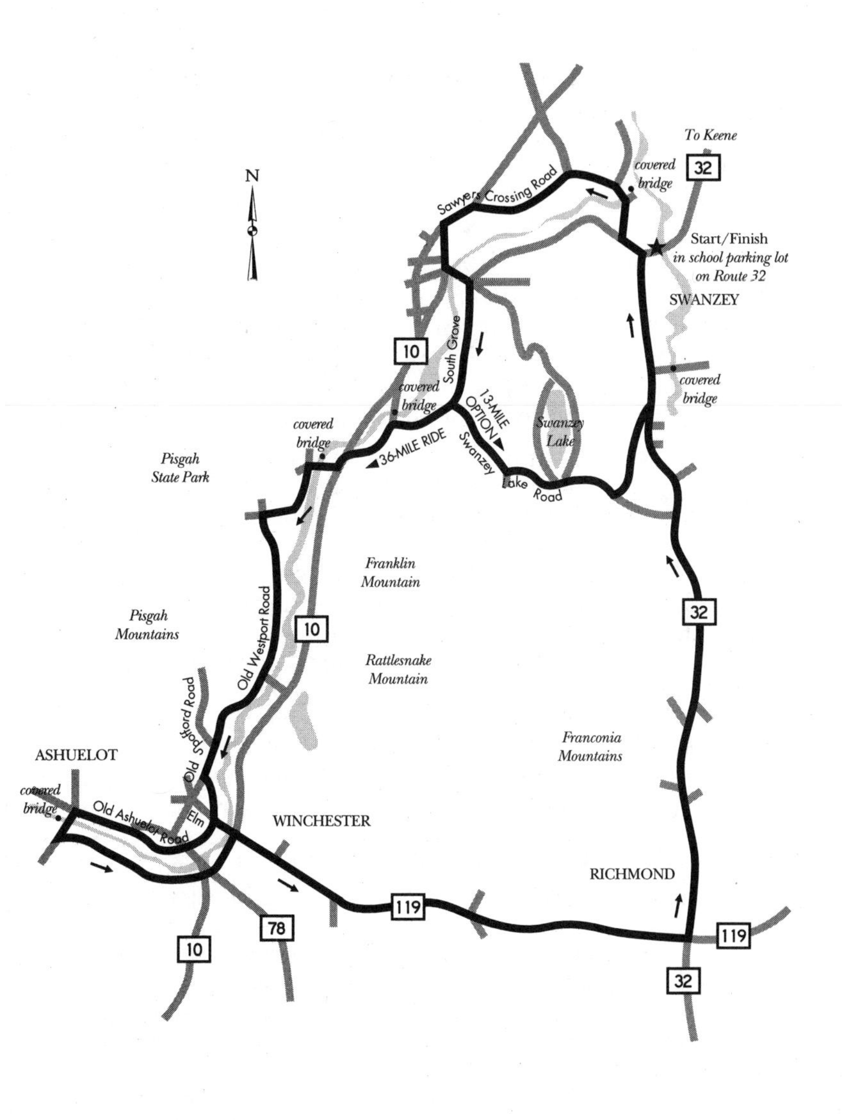
N
To Keene
32
covered bridge
Start/Finish
in school parking lot on Route 32
SWANZEY
Sawyers Crossing Road
10
South Grove
covered bridge
13-MILE OPTION
Swanzey Lake
Swanzey Lake Road
covered bridge
36-MILE RIDE
Pisgah State Park
Franklin Mountain
Pisgah Mountains
Old Westport Road
10
Rattlesnake Mountain
32
Old Spofford Road
Franconia Mountains
ASHUELOT
covered bridge
Old Ashuelot Road
Elm
WINCHESTER
RICHMOND
119
78
10
119
32

from the right. This junction is marked by a big red slate-roofed barn on the left.

- 13.8 Turn left onto an unmarked road at the intersection and continue downhill until the Elm St. bridge.
- 14.5 Right onto the narrow road immediately in front of the bridge. Do not cross the river here.

You could continue straight across the bridge here—if you wanted to shave 4.4 miles off the trip. Continuing straight, you would cross Rte. 10 in the center of Winchester, with the town hall on your right, and continue onto Rte. 119E toward Richmond. The miles you would miss, though, are among the most scenic of the trip, and the covered bridge at Ashuelot is the grandest along this route.

- 14.7 Bear right with the main road as it turns slightly uphill.
- 15.2 Ride directly across Rte. 119, onto Old Ashuelot Rd. This backroad will drop back down to the Ashuelot River.
- 16.5 Left onto Rte. 119W.
- 17.2 Left across the beautifully preserved Winchester-Ashuelot bridge as Rte. 119 veers right. After crossing bridge, bear left at Y intersection. This road is both paved and dirt.
- 20.1 Left onto Rte. 10N. Then continue through the light at the intersection. You should now be on combined Routes 10 and 119 leading back into Winchester. *Caution:* Rte. 119 has a narrow shoulder and traffic moves quickly.
- 20.5 Right onto Rte. 119 toward Richmond. This road will climb gradually alongside the appropriately named Roaring Brook. Once the stream and the road diverge, however, the road begins to climb more steeply. The final half mile is the steepest.
- 24.2 Reach top of climb, with a view of Mt. Monadnock straight ahead.
- 26.2 In Richmond, which is little more than a crossroads, turn left at the variety store onto Rte. 32N toward Swanzey. *Caution:* Rte. 32 is narrow and has no shoulder. The road features several steep drops for the first 5 miles, then it flattens out for the final run back into Swanzey.
- 35.7 Return to the Monadnock Regional High School at the junction of Rte. 32 and Sawyers Crossing Rd. in Swanzey.

25

A Yankee Cruise

Peterborough—Harrisville—Nelson—South Stoddard—Hancock—Peterborough

About the only attraction this part of New England doesn't offer cyclists is long steep hills. Otherwise it's got everything: scenic rural roads, well-preserved towns, pine and hardwood forests, farm fields, lakes, streams, a bog, and a lively assortment of summer arts and culture centers. Not to mention many secluded, unpaved roads, for those who also like mountain biking.

The Yankee Cruise begins in Peterborough, the hub of summer activity in southern New England. It's the home of the Folkway, a nationally known folk music club and restaurant; the Peterborough Players, a popular summer stock theater; a large, eclectic bookstore; and several good eateries. There's also a bike shop, Spokes and Slopes, on Grove Street, that sponsors weekly group rides; the headquarters retail outlet of Eastern Mountain Sports (EMS), just outside Peterborough on Route 202E; and the Sharon Arts Center, a large gallery just a few miles south of Peterborough on Route 123.

From bustling Peterborough the ride heads into the wooded countryside, reaching several smaller towns that embody concepts like Yankee ingenuity, Yankee individuality, and Yankee frugality. The revolutionary spirit that created our country may have begun 75 miles away in Boston, but it's kept alive in places like Hancock, Harrisville, and Dublin, with their simple lifestyles, open town meetings, and public greens.

The first town you reach, after 10 miles, Harrisville, has been called "one of the most perfectly preserved nineteenth-century New England mill towns and also one of the prettiest" by local author Linda Chestney. Its handsome brick mill buildings along a pond are a National Historic Landmark. Take a stroll around. A short side trip to the south will bring you to the neighboring town of Dublin, home of *Yankee Magazine* and the *Old Farmer's Almanac,* and Yankee Books, a large bookstore, as well as solitary, bald Mount Monadnock—the most climbed mountain in New England.

After passing several large lakes and small villages, you'll reach Hancock (named after John Hancock, signer of the Declaration of Independence and president of the Continental Congress). Hancock has kept its nineteenth-century appearance, with wood-framed buildings, picket fences, and a bandstand on the town green. But most of the ride cruises through a pastoral landscape of woods, bogs, lakes, summer homes, and fields. Needless to say, you can spend a day or more exploring the natural and historic sights in this convenient part of New England.

The Basics

Start: Center of Peterborough, at the intersection of Routes 101, 202, and 123. Park in a municipal parking lot just off Main St., near the river. Peterborough is 75 miles northwest of Boston.
Length: 36 or 16 miles, with a longer ride possible if you take a side trip into Dublin.
Terrain: Smoothly paved rural highways alternating with rougher, more secluded asphalt roads through a rolling countryside. Several modest climbs on the first half of the ride are followed by an extended descent almost all the way from Hancock to Peterborough.
Food: At 20 miles there's a small convenience store and deli, Stoddard Gas and Grocery, on Rte. 9, and at 29 miles there's a well-stocked grocery store, Hancock Market, open seven days a week, in the center of Hancock on Rte. 123. There is no food store (yet) in Harrisville.
Traffic/Safety: Most of this loop uses rural roads with light traffic and narrow shoulders. In the middle of the ride, there's a 3-mile stretch on a busier highway, Rte. 9. It was repaved in 1995 and has a wide shoulder.

Miles and Directions

- 0.0 Turn uphill on Main St. (away from the river). At the top of the hill, the street veers right and becomes Union St. You will pass a large playground and pool on the right.
- 1.6 Turn right onto Windy Row road, just before an Odd Fellow's Hall on the right.
- 2.8 Turn left onto Spring Rd. There's no street sign here, just small letters (SPRING ROAD) on an electrical box on a pole at the intersection. Go downhill, passing the West Peterborough Marsh on the right.
- 4.0 Turn right sharply at a stop sign, onto Rte. 137N.

For a shorter, 16-mile jaunt, keep going straight on Rte. 137 for 5.2 miles, arriving at the green in Hancock. Then pick up the ride directions below at 28.9 miles.

- 5.9 Turn left onto Sargent Camp Rd., a patchier surface. Keep following the asphalt road, with a brook on the right.
- 8.4 Veer right, as Bonds Corner Rd. blends into Hancock Rd. from the left. Soon pass a dam and a lake on the right, cross a bridge, pass some summer homes, and cruise next to long Skatutakee Lake on the left.
- 10.0 Turn right at a T junction with a stop sign at it. Climb a short steep hill to the historic town of Harrisville, with a cluster of handsome brick buildings on the right, and then Harrisville Pond on the right. (Stop in the Weaving Center building in the center of town for a walking map of Harrisville.)
- 10.7 Fork right onto Nelson Rd., skirting Harrisville Pond on the right. Keep following the paved road. You will pass Childs Bog on the left. And watch for some excellent views of nearby mountains.

To explore another historic town, turn left onto Silver Lake Rd. just after Childs Bog, and head south toward Rte. 101 and Dublin, which is the home of Yankee Magazine *and Yankee Books on Main St.*

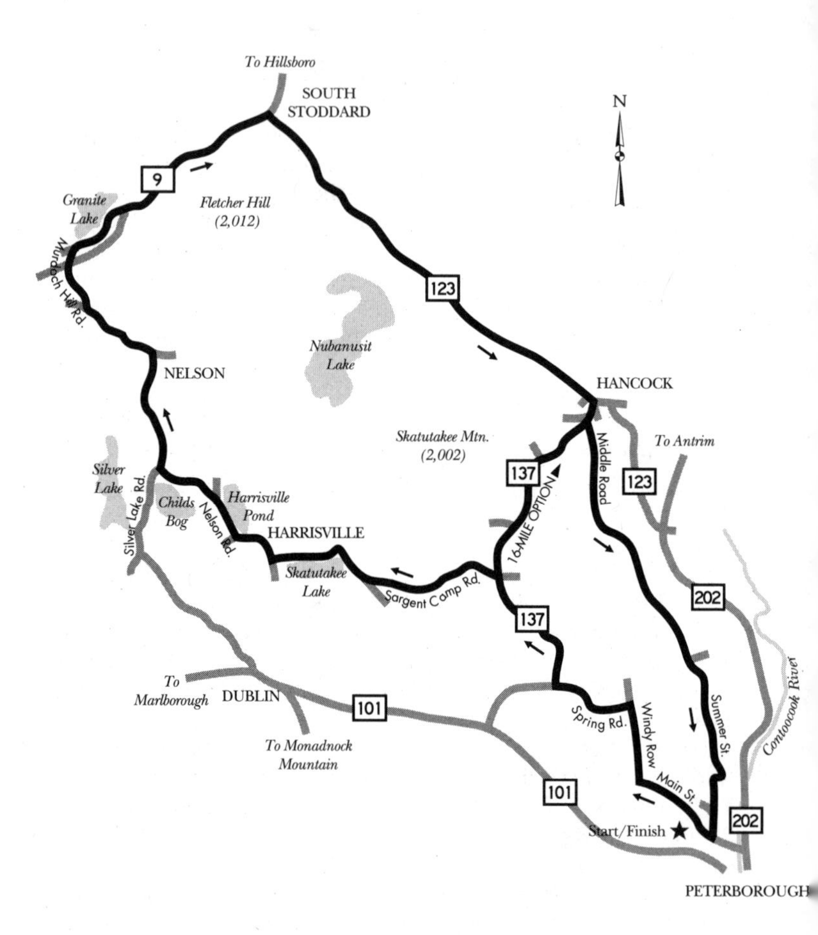
To Hillsboro
SOUTH STODDARD
N
9
Granite Lake
Fletcher Hill (2,012)
Murdoch Hill Rd.
123
Nubanusit Lake
NELSON
HANCOCK
Skatutakee Mtn. (2,002)
To Antrim
Silver Lake
Silver Lake Rd.
Childs Bog
Nelson Rd.
Harrisville Pond
137
16-MILE OPTION
Middle Road
123
HARRISVILLE
Skatutakee Lake
Sargent Camp Rd.
202
137
To Marlborough
DUBLIN
101
Spring Rd.
Windy Row
Summer St.
Contoocook River
To Monadnock Mountain
101
Main St.
202
Start/Finish
PETERBOROUGH

- At 14.4 miles you'll ride past a cluster of homes, the town of Nelson.
- 15.6 Turn right onto an unmarked road; there's a sign on it: NARROW BRIDGE. This is Murdoch Hill Rd. Soon you'll cross over a large highway, the Rte. 9 bypass.
- 17.0 Turn right at a stop sign, and ride along Granite Lake on the left.
- 18.4 Turn left at a stop sign, onto newly paved Rte. 9. *Caution:* Watch for fast-moving traffic as you enter Rte. 9. It may seem like a superhighway, but notice the MOOSE CROSSING/NEXT 10 MILES sign on it. After a couple of miles you'll pass Stoddard Gas and Grocery on the left.
- 21.4 Turn right onto Rte. 123.
- 28.9 Arrive at the town green in Hancock.

You can take either Middle Rd. or Routes 123 and 202 to return to Peterborough. If you prefer a faster, smoother, but busier highway, continue on Rte. 123S; after 2.5 miles you will reach Rte. 202, a larger highway that has a narrowing shoulder.

- 28.9 Turn right at the bandstand on the Hancock town green, onto Rte. 137, descending a short steep hill.
- 29.1 Fork left onto Middle Rd. (There's also a sign for BOSTON U. SARGENT CAMP to the left.) After about 4 miles, you'll pass a sign on the left for the Peterborough Players, a local theater company.
- 34.2 Fork to the left, staying on Middle Rd., which turns into Summer St.
- 36.0 Summer St. ends at Main St. in Peterborough, across from the municipal parking lot, on a corner with a golden-domed church.

26

Town and Country Cruise

Exeter—Newfields—Durham—
Lee—Nottingham—Exeter

Instead of large mountains and vast expanses of wilderness, this southeastern part of New Hampshire—barely an hour's drive from Boston—offers a pastoral landscape of fields, farmhouses, light woods, orchards, an ocean bay, and a half dozen small towns, two with major educational institutions.

The Town and Country Cruise begins in Exeter, the home of Phillips Exeter Academy, one of the nation's most prestigious preparatory schools. Found in 1781, Phillips Exeter has a beautiful, ivy-league-like campus that's worth a visit. (For instance, it's library was designed by the famous architect Louis Kahn.) The town of Exeter also has an attractive and quaint downtown, with a bandstand, a historical society, and the American Museum of Independence.

The first stretch of this ride follows the western shoreline of the Great Bay, a tranquil body of water that connects with the Atlantic Ocean. (The best route to the Atlantic Ocean itself is cycling due east of Exeter toward Rye.) Along the Great Bay lie two small, attractive towns, Newfields and Newmarket, and two rivers feeding into the bay, the Lamprey and Oyster. After 16 miles you will roll into Durham, a lively college town dominated by the large University of New Hampshire.

Then the ride turns inland, rolling through a landscape that alternates between open fields and woods, passing through another small town, Lee, then descending gently all the way back to Newfields, before doubling back to Exeter. Besides small bakeries and cafes in most of the towns along the way, late summer and fall bring many roadside stands selling fresh local fruits and vegetables.

The shorter, 31-mile option offers the same small-town and rural charms, winding along a scenic rural road for almost 5 miles. Either way, this is a cultivated and cultured tour.

The Basics

Start: Exeter, 4 or so miles west of I–95. Take exit 2 on I–95 (4 miles north of the Massachusetts border). From the west you can reach Exeter from Rte. 101. Take the Rte. 85S exit, turn right, and enter Exeter after 1.5 miles. There's parking in downtown Exeter, including a municipal lot behind the Academy Boathouse. For last-minute tune-ups, visit the Wheel Power bike shop downtown on Water St.
Length: 42.3 or 31.3 miles.
Terrain: Rolling, with no steep or long climbs—but plenty of short hills. The ride alternates between smoother, more trafficked roads and rougher, less busy ones. There's a 0.8-mile unpaved stretch at 28 miles that's hard-packed dirt (Poor Farm Rd.), with some loose stones. The return stretch on Rte. 87 is almost all downhill.
Food: Food stores come at convenient distances: the Newfields Country Store (on the left), at 4.0 miles; several bakeries and eateries in Newmarket, at 7.5 miles; in larger Durham, at 16.0 miles; and in tiny Lee, at 21.0 miles.
Traffic/Safety: Always ride single file on roads with narrow shoulders, particularly Routes 85 and 87. Be sure to cross railroad tracks at a perpendicular angle.

Miles and Directions

- 0.0 Distances here begin from the bandstand on Water St. in the center of downtown Exeter. Ride west on Water St.
- 0.1 Turn right onto Swasey Pkwy., which runs along the Squamscott River.

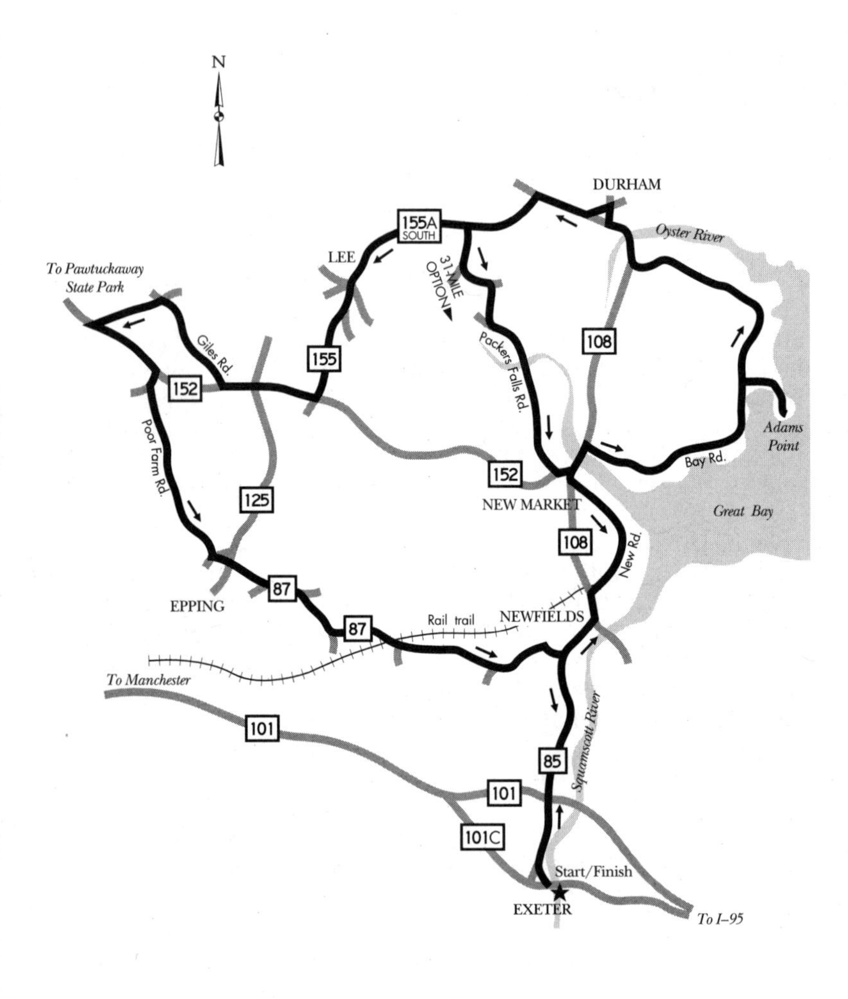
N
DURHAM
Oyster River
155A SOUTH
LEE
31-MILE OPTION
To Pawtuckaway State Park
Giles Rd.
155
Packers Falls Rd.
108
152
Poor Farm Rd.
125
Adams Point
Bay Rd.
152
NEW MARKET
Great Bay
108
New Rd.
EPPING
87
87
Rail trail
NEWFIELDS
To Manchester
101
Squamscott River
85
101
101C
Start/Finish
EXETER
To I–95

- 0.6 Veer right onto Rte. 85N. *Caution:* Watch for traffic as you pass underneath a narrow bridge at 1.2 miles.
- 3.9 Rte. 87 comes in from the left. This is where the longer loop will come out. Notice the large, classic New England homes on either side of Rte. 85.
- 4.7 At a T turn left onto Rte. 108N.
- 5.3 Watch for this one: a right turn just before a bridge, onto New Rd.

A note for off-road cyclists: If you turn left onto Ash Swamp Rd. at the bridge, you'll reach an abandoned railroad station. Behind it is the trailhead for an ultraflat rail trail (a former railroad bed with the ties removed) that runs for 25 miles, all the way to Massabesic Lake just east of Manchester. It crosses paved roads and highways along the way.

- 7.6 At a T turn right onto Rte. 108 again. Continue straight on Rte. 108 into Newmarket. (*Caution:* Always cross over railroad tracks perpendicular to the tracks.) Then slow down to sightsee the handsome brick buildings and quaint cafes in Newmarket.
- 8.2 Immediately after crossing the bridge in Newmarket, take a sharp right turn onto Bay Rd. *Caution:* Watch out for occasional potholes on this secluded road.
- 11.9 You will pass an unmarked road on the right with a gate and sign at it: AREA BEYOND GATE CLOSED 10 P.M.–4 A.M. You can take a 2-mile side trip by turning right onto this narrow road, to reach Adams Point, a state wildlife management area. There are a boat launch area and then a wooden lookout over the wetlands along the Great Bay. The lookout is part of an estuarine research center run by the University of New Hampshire.
- 15.6 At a T turn right onto Rte. 108 again, and soon cross the Oyster River.
- 16.0 Fork left, and head into the lively town of Durham.
- 16.2 Veer right, and then turn left twice, circling with traffic around the center of town, coming out on Rte. 155A heading west. Then ride past large university buildings and athletic fields.

- 17.4 Turn left onto Rte. 155A South.

  For the 31.3-mile ride, at 18.7 miles turn left onto Packers Falls Rd. (There's a sign at the junction, but otherwise the road is in the middle of farmland, so watch out for it.) Packers Falls Rd. winds for 4.7 miles, coming out at Rte. 152 in the middle of Newmarket. Turn left onto Rte. 152 and almost immediately right onto Rte. 108S. Retrace the route back to Exeter—watching out for New Rd. on the left soon after turning onto Rte. 108.

- 21.0 Pass through the town of Lee.
- 23.0 At a stop sign turn right onto Rte. 152. (If you take a left turn onto Rte. 152. you will reach Newmarket after 5 miles.)
- 24.0 Cross busy Rte. 125.
- 24.5 On a downhill watch for a right turn onto Giles Rd.
- 26.3 Turn left at a stop sign. This is unmarked McCrillis Rd. (Giles Rd. becomes unpaved ahead.)
- 27.5 Reach a T and take a sharp left onto Rte. 152.
- 28.6 Watch for a right turn at a small grassy island onto Berry Rd.
- 28.8 Fork left onto Poor Farm Rd. This becomes an unpaved, graded road for the next 0.8 miles.
- 30.4 Veer left at a stop sign, staying on the paved road, which is Old Nottingham Rd.
- 31.7 Veer left onto N. River Rd. and almost immediately right. You will come out after a few hundred feet at busy Rte. 125. Cross it and onto Rte. 87E. Newfields is 6 miles ahead.
- 38.3 At a T turn right onto Rte. 85.
- 42.3 Arrive back in Exeter.

27

Kinsman Region Classic

Plymouth—Campton—North Woodstock—Warren—The Rumneys—Plymouth

This challenging, 60-mile circuit traces a loop around the southwestern corner of New Hampshire's White Mountain National Forest. This is the park's Kinsman Region, named for the notch at its northern reach. It is dominated by four peaks—Cushman, Kineo, Carr, and Stinson—and bounded by the Pemigewasset and Baker rivers.

The circuit's greatest challenge is its 1,300-foot, 5.5-mile climb across the watershed between the two rivers. This ascent through dense and unspoiled forest with little traffic comes midway, following a long and rolling stretch from Plymouth to North Woodstock. Two parallel routes are available for the southward stretch home, both following the path of the Baker River along the forest's southwestern boundary.

Pedaling north from Plymouth, on a gradual ascent, you'll warm up as you pass the small farms and stands of pine along Route 175. Detour to view the covered bridge spanning the Pemigewasset River in the town of Blair, and keep an eye open for the deer that often come down to drink at this spot. Back on Rte. 175, you will soon start seeing beautiful mountain vistas. From Campton, the view up the Mad River toward Waterville Valley reveals the full mass of the surrounding mountains, their rocky peaks often fading into gray clouds. North of Campton, the hills begin to get longer, but the views are worth it. Five miles south of North Woodstock, the road crosses the Pemigewasset River and stays along its shore, providing several opportunities to rest (or soak tired feet).

Stop for a rest by the bandstand on North Woodstock's town green, as this route will soon begin a 5.5-mile-long climb toward Kinsman Notch. Be prepared for cooler weather at the top. It would not be unusual, even if you were basking in sunshine during the rest stop in North Woodstock, to find yourself ascending into a mist just a few miles away. In any conditions, the dense forest will soon blot out all sound but that of the brook hidden among the pines to your left. There are also several points along this road where you can dismount and rest. A sweeping 7-mile descent provides ample reward for the effort required by this long, steep climb.

In Warren, Route 118 joins Route 25, the valley's main road. In West Rumney, you can turn off Rte. 25 onto back roads for a slightly longer but more secluded return (see Option 2). This route traces the southern edge of the White Mountain National Forest as far as Rumney. It's not as flat as Route 25, but offers less traffic.

For a shorter ride, consider riding from Plymouth to Stinson Lake. You can do this option as a circuit (see map), but past the lake, the circuit will take you on some roller-coaster ups and downs: a 13% downhill that spins you right back up the next rise. This loop is another favorite of the Greasey Wheel bicycle shop in Plymouth. For the less adventurous, an out-and-back ride to Stinson Lake is quite enjoyable. The route is relatively easy, with gentle, rolling hills, and the lake is clear and placid, reflecting the beauty of the surrounding mountains. Either option is just about 30 miles. We recommend doing the route first, proceeding west from Plymouth into Rumney.

The Basics

Start: Plymouth. Take Exit 25 off I–93N and turn right on Rte. 175A into Plymouth. (From I–93S, take Exit 26.) Park around the town center's small common. To park outside the town, turn left off the exit and find a suitable spot near the intersection of Routes 175A and 175.
Length: 59.3 or 60.1 miles, or a 30-mile route (see text).
Terrain: Gently rolling hills with one important exception—a 5.5-

mile climb toward the White Mountain National Forest's Kinsman Notch.

Food: Several choices in North Woodstock, at 22.5 miles, or in Warren, at 39.0 miles. Plymouth also has many options.

Traffic/Safety: This route is mainly on secondary roads with little traffic, except for the return from Warren on Route 25 (there is also a small rotary). Where the traffic is heavier, the road is wider with a shoulder. Use caution on the steep descents and be prepared to stop.

Miles and Directions

- 0.0 From Plymouth, ride north on combined Routes 3 and 25 toward Rumney, Campton, and the White Mountains.
- 0.1 Right onto Rte. 175A toward Holderness.
- 1.0 Left onto Rte. 175N, just before top of hill, toward Campton and Waterville Valley.
- 4.8 Although the tour continues straight, a 1/2-mile detour to the left on Blair Rd. leads to a 300-foot wooden covered bridge across the Pemigewasset River.
- 6.1 Follow Rte. 175 through the small village of Campton Hollow, shortly after crossing Beebe River.
- 9.0 Cross Mad River and continue straight on Rte. 175 through Campton. Pass turnoff for Waterville Valley on right.
- 17.7 Left with Rte. 175 at stop sign following a short downhill. *Caution:* Route 173 is more heavily trafficked here.
- 21.9 Dismount to cross iron grate bridge across Pemigewasset River.
- 22.0 Right at T onto Rte. 3N toward North Woodstock.
- 22.5 Enter North Woodstock, with a view toward Franconia Notch straight ahead and the town green on the right. Turn left onto Rte. 112W toward Woodsville and Lost River. But first you may want to take in the sights and get a bite to eat. Continue straight on Rte. 3N (Main St.) for restaurants and the general store. 1.3 miles up Main St. brings you to Clark's Trading Post, where there is a covered railroad bridge, the last one of its kind still standing.

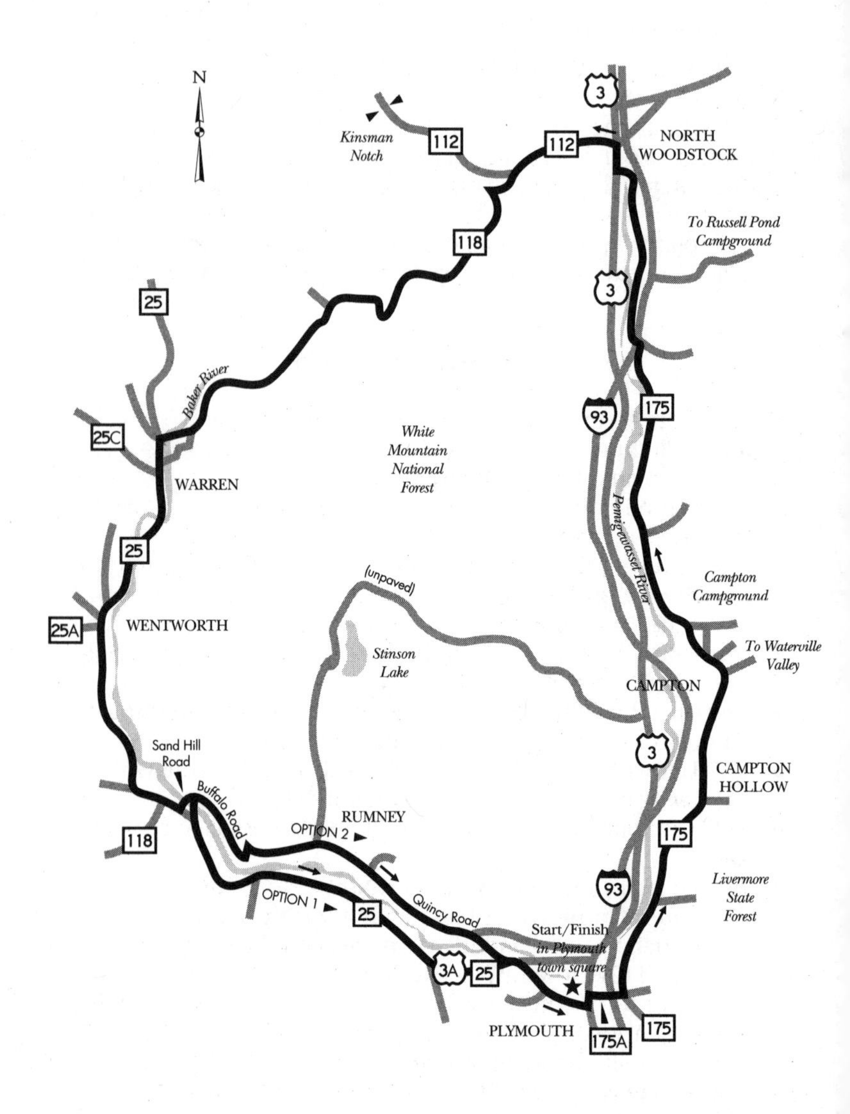
N
Kinsman
Notch
112
112
NORTH
WOODSTOCK
3
118
To Russell Pond
Campground
3
25
Baker River
93
175
25C
White
Mountain
National
Forest
WARREN
Pemigewasset River
25
(unpaved)
Campton
Campground
25A
WENTWORTH
To Waterville
Valley
Stinson
Lake
CAMPTON
3
Sand Hill
Road
CAMPTON
HOLLOW
Buffalo Road
RUMNEY
118
OPTION 2
175
Livermore
State
Forest
93
OPTION 1
25
Quincy Road
Start/Finish
in Plymouth
town square
3A
25
PLYMOUTH
175A
175

- 25.1 Left onto Rte. 118 toward Warren as Rte. 112 continues in the direction of Woodsville and Kinsman Notch.
- 25.2 Enter White Mountain National Forest and prepare for the climb to begin in earnest.
- 30.8 Top of climb. Sign warns of 7 percent grade for next 3 miles; prepare for total descent of over 7 miles.
- 38.2 Descent ends. Turn south toward Plymouth on combined Routes 25E and 118S. Continue straight through Warren.
- 43.1 Straight through town of Wentworth.
- 47.5 Stay straight on Rte. 25S as Rte. 118 turns to right in West Rumney.
- 48.4 Continue straight to stay on **Option 1.** Turn left onto Sand Hill Road for **Option 2** (see below).
- 51.7 Straight through blinking light in Rumney. A left here brings you to the Mary Baker Eddy historic house in Rumney.
- 55.0 Left into (small) rotary, following Route 25 toward Plymouth. Caution: Traffic in rotary has right of way. Use hand signals.
- 57.0 Right onto Highland Street, following sign to downtown Plymouth.
- 59.2 Arrive at Plymouth Common, at intersection of Routes 3 and 25.

Option 2

- 48.4 Turn left off Rte. 25 onto Sand Hill Road, about 1 mile after Rte. 118 turns off to the right.
- 48.6 Right onto Buffalo Road toward Rumney.
- 52.2 Straight as Buffalo Road becomes Quincy Road in Rumney. Turn left here for ½ mile to reach the house of Mary Baker Eddy, founder of the Christian Science Movement, and then a climb toward Stinson Lake.
- 56.4 Bear left onto Fairgrounds Road just past the Plymouth airport.
- 59.6 Right onto Rte. 3S into downtown Plymouth.
- 60.1 Arrive at Plymouth Common, at intersection of Routes 3 and 25.

28

Waterville Valley Challenge

Campton—Waterville Valley—
Thornton Gap—Woodstock—Campton

The Waterville Valley Challenge begins at an intersection southeast of Campton from which riders can savor a magnificent view of a bold ring of mountains framing an undisturbed foreground of pond, river, and pines. This gradual ascent leads into a round valley formed by nearly thirty peaks, belonging to the Squam Mountains to the south and the White Mountains to the north.

There are two options on this ride, both allowing you to savor the region's beauty and the uniqueness of Waterville Valley—which is now both a skiing and a mountain biking mecca. Option A is an up-and-back run from Campton to Waterville Valley. This route follows Route 49 for 9 miles into the valley, ascending gradually but relentlessly. Option B is a full circuit, proceeding north on Rte. 175 into Woodstock, then following Tripoli Road through Thornton Gap up into Waterville Valley. This route is somewhat steeper, and includes climbing on 5 miles of unpaved road. Fat tires are recommended for this option.

Narrow Tripoli Road leads from the shadowy interior of the forest to the open expanse of the valley. Passing through Thornton Gap, it crosses the watershed between the Mad and Pemigewasset rivers, following cascading feeder streams of each. There are a number of small campsites and trailheads along this passage. The East Pond and Mount Osceola trails, on the left, cross the Scar Ridge to the Kancamagus Highway. Back on pavement, the descent from Mt. Osceola trailhead into Waterville Valley is exhilarating. Use caution, however, and watch out for bumps in the road and rough pavement.

Many local riders insist that this is one of the best tours in the southern region of the White Mountain National Forest. The Greasey Gonzos, an informal club of the Greasey Wheel bicycle shop in nearby Plymouth, often ride this circuit on evening outings. It's also a favorite ride of employees at the Waterville Valley Base Camp in Waterville's town square.

A third option is simply to drive up to Waterville Valley and knock about on some mountain bikes, possibly including the climb to Thornton Gap in your explorations. Bring your own mountain bikes or rent from the Waterville Valley Base Camp, which also has maps of local offroad trails.

The Basics

Start: Campton, at the intersections of Routes 49 and 175. Take I–93 north to exit 28 for Campton and Waterville Valley. Turn right coming off the exit. Drive one and a half miles on Rte. 49 into town.
Length: 31.4 miles for the complete circuit; 27.7 miles for the up-and-back option.
Terrain: The climb from Campton to Waterville is gradual but long, along a smooth broad-shouldered road. On the circuit, Tripoli Road is steeper and more challenging, climbing up to Thornton Gap along a partially dirt road.
Food: Lunch and snacks are available in Campton or from stores and restaurants in the town of Waterville Valley.
Traffic/Safety: This route does not have much traffic, but use caution around intersections with Route 93 and on the steep descents. The descent from Thornton Gap to Waterville (on the full circuit) has no shoulder and the pavement can be bumpy.

Miles and Directions

Option A

- 0.0 On Rte. 49E in Campton point your bike toward Waterville

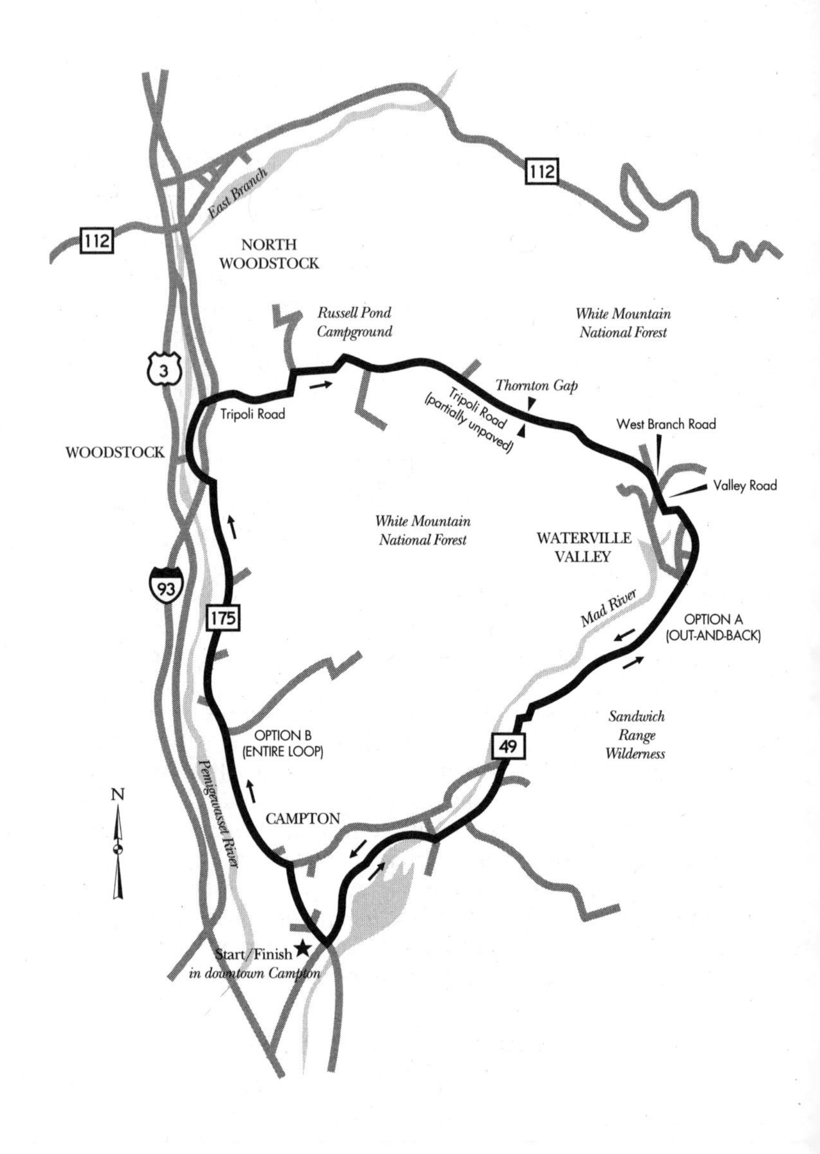
112
East Branch
112
NORTH
WOODSTOCK
Russell Pond
Campground
White Mountain
National Forest
3
Thornton Gap
Tripoli Road
(partially unpaved)
Tripoli Road
West Branch Road
WOODSTOCK
Valley Road
White Mountain
National Forest
WATERVILLE
VALLEY
93
Mad River
175
OPTION A
(OUT-AND-BACK)
Sandwich
Range
Wilderness
OPTION B
(ENTIRE LOOP)
49
N
Pemigewasset River
CAMPTON
Start/Finish
in downtown Campton

Valley. Ride toward the mountains along the Mad River, leaving the pond on your right. It's a gradual climb for the next 9 miles.

- 0.6 Enter the White Mountain National Forest.
- 2.6 Stay on Rte. 49 as it crosses the Mad River, following signs to Waterville Valley.
- 3.2 Pass Sandwich Notch Rd. as it spills down from the right.
- 9.4 Watch for the sign: WELCOME TO WATERVILLE VALLEY, INCORPORATED 1829, POPULATION 199. Stay on the main road, Rte. 49, as it becomes Valley Rd. and curves left.
- 10.3 Village Road. The main route continues straight, but turn left here to rest and visit the Town Square. Here you'll find the Waterville Valley Base Camp, Alpine Pizza, Jugtown Deli, Coffee Emporium and other eateries.
- 10.4 Right to stay on Valley Road and Route 49.
- 10.8 Left on West Branch Road just past the tennis courts. Notice Waterville's small Osceola Library on the corner.
- 11.6 West Branch Road ends in a T with Tripoli Rd., just after crossing a narrow wooden bridge. Turn left here to return to Waterville and back to Campton.
- 12.1 Straight at stop sign at entrance to Waterville Valley Ski Area. (If you haven't had enough climbing, turn right and climb 1.1 miles up Mt. Tecumseh to the ski area. This is a steep, tough climb—no gradual ascent here—but the summit is a terrific lookout, offering views of the area in all directions from different vantage points. This is an extremely exhilarating descent back to Tripoli Road, but keep your brakes on and watch for traffic on Tripoli Road as you rejoin it.)
- 13.3 You're back at the entrance to Waterville Valley. Turn right onto Rte. 49 for return trip to Campton.
- 22.7 Arrive back in Campton, at intersection of routes 175 and 49.

Option B

- 0.0 Proceed north on Rte. 175 through town of Campton, toward Thornton and Woodstock.
- 4.5 Stay straight on Rte. 175 toward N. Woodstock.
- 8.5 Turn left at stop sign at bottom of hill to stay on Rte. 175.

Caution: Watch for traffic on this busier section of Rte. 175.

- 10.5 Right on Tripoli Road at entrance to I–93 South. Prepare to climb as Mt. Osceola comes into full view in front of you. **Note:** Tripoli Road is closed to Waterville from November to May.
- 11.7 Enter White Mountain National Forest.
- 12.5 Pass the entrance to Russell Pond Campground.
- 12.6 Road narrows and becomes dirt.
- 17.1 Pass through Thornton Gap, 1,800 feet higher in elevation than Campton.
- 17.5 Dirt becomes pavement again at the Mt. Osceola trailhead. Prepare to descend.
- 20.8 Straight at stop sign at entrance to Waterville Valley Ski Area. (See Option A for a scenic climb in this area.)
- 22.0 Waterville Valley Township sign. A left turn here will bring you into Waterville's Town Square (see Option A). Turn right to begin 9.4 mile descent back to Campton.
- 31.4 Arrive back in Campton, at intersection of Routes 175 and 49.

29

Bear Notch Challenge

North Conway—Bartlett—Bear Notch—North Conway

With its two lanes arcing over the mountains, the Kancamagus Highway is considered by thousands of cyclists to be the ultimate road through the White Mountains. It stretches 34 miles from the Pemigewasset River at Lincoln to the Saco River at Conway, climbing to nearly 3,000 feet as it crosses the flank of Mount Kancamagus.

On a summer weekend afternoon, many cyclists and cars share the steep and twisting roadway. To catch some of the action—without being overcome by the crowds and cars—try this ride from North Conway through Bear Notch. The climb from Bartlett to Bear Notch is the route of a monthly 5-mile race sponsored by the local Red Jersey Cyclery bike shop. The racers can reach the summit at the notch in a little over twenty minutes. Since you're riding the course without worrying how you place, though, you can explore the many scenic areas along the way.

One challenging side trip is the steep climb to Cathedral Ledge (at 1.5 miles into the ride). There's a rewarding view back toward the Saco River plain from the top.

On the long gradual climb through Bear Notch, don't hesitate to pull off at the four scenic overlooks along the way. Bear Notch Road climbs from 600 to 2,000 feet in approximately 5 miles. Bear Mountain itself, to the left of the climb, is more than 3,200 feet tall.

Once you are on the Kancamagus Highway, if the ride through

Bear Notch hasn't tired you out you can detour to the west, uphill, to the Pemi and Kancamagus overlooks. Kancamagus Pass lies just over 8 miles distant and 1,500 feet up. On the return along route 112, stop at the Rocky Gorge Scenic Area and the Lower Falls swimming and picnic area to view the Swift River's rapids.

Don't forget to turn left through the covered bridge onto Dugway Road, following the signs to the Covered Bridge Campground. Dugway Road runs parallel to the Kancamagus until both end near the junction of the Swift and Saco rivers. From there West Side Road offers an attractive and completely flat alternative to Route 16 (North Conway's strip of factory outlet malls) for the ride back into town.

This is a tranquil and rewarding ride. It's challenging enough for the experienced cyclist, yet also suitable for those seeking a more leisurely tour.

The Basics

Start: In the center of North Conway at the Conway Scenic Railroad station, just behind Schouler Park in the center of town. During the crowded summer and fall seasons, you may find it easier to park on W. Side Rd., just over a mile into the ride. W. Side Rd. is also a scenic alternative to congested Rte. 16 for getting into town.
Length: 37.7 miles.
Terrain: Includes both quiet valley roads and a 1,400-foot climb in 5 miles through Bear Notch.
Food: Pack a snack to enjoy during a rest at any of several overlooks and picnic areas on Bear Notch Road and the Kancamagus Highway. There are several food stops on Rte. 302, before the climb through Bear Notch.
Traffic/Safety: Rte. 302 can be busy, but it has a decent shoulder. Pavement quality on the Kancamagus Hwy. varies, and summer traffic can include large recreational vehicles; use caution turning left to the covered bridge. Dugway Rd. is quiet but has rough pavement.

Miles and Directions

- 0.0 From the Conway Scenic Railroad Station in the center of North Conway, ride north on combined Routes 16 and 32, here named Main St.
- 0.4 Turn left onto River Rd., passing beneath the railroad bridge. Cross the Saco River and continue toward Echo Lake State Park and Cathedral Ledge.
- 1.4 Pass turnoff for W. Side Rd. South on left. River Rd. becomes W. Side Rd. North at this point.
- 1.9 Continue straight on W. Side Rd., passing entrance to Cathedral Ledge Park on left.
- 6.8 Left onto Rte. 302W, toward Attitash Ski Area and Bartlett. *Caution:* Railroad tracks at an angle just after Attitash.

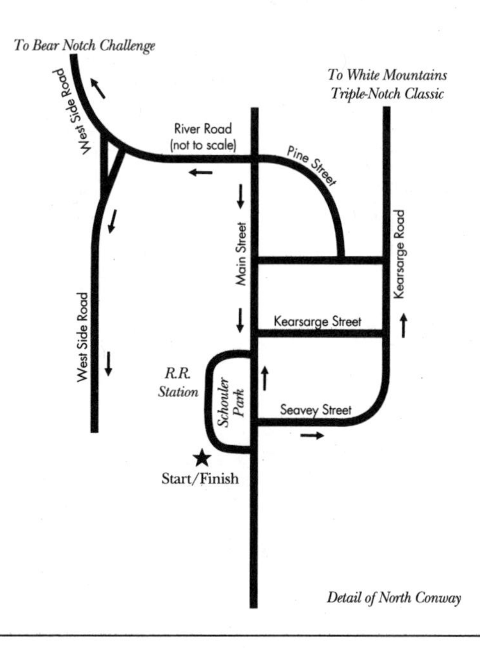

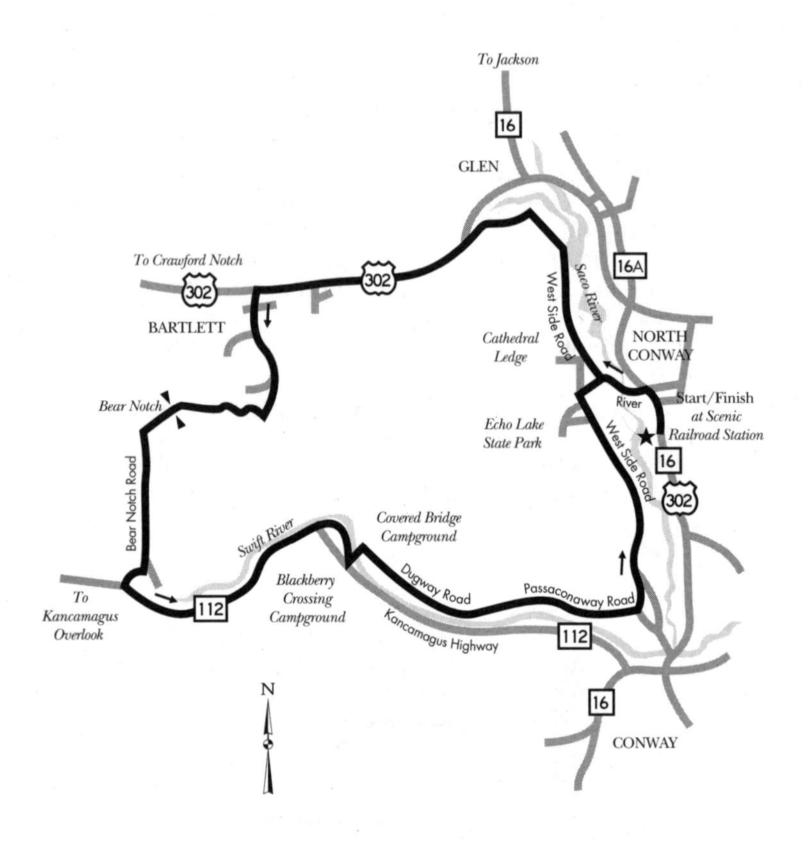

To Jackson
16
GLEN
16A
To Crawford Notch
302
302
BARTLETT
Saco River
West Side Road
Cathedral Ledge
NORTH CONWAY
Bear Notch
River
Start/Finish at Scenic Railroad Station
Echo Lake State Park
West Side Road
16
302
Bear Notch Road
Covered Bridge Campground
Swift River
Dugway Road
Passaconaway Road
To Kancamagus Overlook
112
Blackberry Crossing Campground
Kancamagus Highway
112
16
CONWAY
N

- 10.8 Left onto Bear Notch Rd. at the blinking yellow light in Bartlett and cross the Maine Central Railroad tracks.
- 11.4 Enter White Mountain National Forest, beginning climb toward Bear Notch.
- 15.5 Reach summit.
- 20.0 Left at the end of Bear Notch Rd. onto the Kancamagus Hwy., Rte. 112.
- 25.5 Left, crossing the covered bridge spanning the Swift River, and then right onto Dugway Rd.
- 31.3 Bear left onto Allen Siding Street.
- 31.6 Take the first left after crossing the railroad tracks.
- 31.9 Left onto W. Side Rd. back toward Echo Lake State Park and North Conway.
- 35.9 Pass the entrance to Echo Lake State Park on the left. The park staff may let you in without charging admission if you need to use the rest rooms or get water.
- 36.4 Right onto River Rd. back toward North Conway.
- 37.3 Right on Rte. 16 in North Conway center.
- 37.7 Arrive back at Schouler Park and railway station.

30

White Mountains Triple-Notch Classic

North Conway—South Chatham—Stow—Evans Notch—Gilead—Gorham—Pinkham Notch—Glen—North Conway

New Hampshire's White Mountain National Forest is an experienced cyclist's dream come true. Here smooth highways run through mountain passes and wind along unspoiled rural valleys, revealing new vistas at every turn. Hikers, campers, rock climbers, river runners, and cyclists all consider this a recreational paradise. The national forest's 750,000 acres afford room for everybody—even if it may not seem that way in downtown North Conway, the region's gateway town, during the summer season.

The Triple-Notch Classic will lead you deep into cool conifer forests, far from the factor outlet stores in North Conway. The tour circles past and through some of the most notable landmarks in the White Mountain region: Hurricane Mountain, Evans and Pinkham notches, the Great Gulf Wilderness area, Mount Washington, and the village of Jackson, with its humble covered bridge.

This 74-mile circuit should be tackled by experienced cyclists only. It is a favorite of the Granite State Wheelmen (GSW), New Hampshire's largest cycling club. GSW club members meet in North Conway in the late summer to ride this and other tours.

They stay in the Cranmore Mountain Lodge, although Conway and the surrounding villages also abound with small inns and B&Bs catering to an outdoor crowd. Plan a weekend of your own, mix cycling with hiking, swimming, or just lying about, which is all you may feel like doing after conquering this tour.

The three climbs of the Triple-Notch Classic are Hurricane Mountain and the more gradual and smooth Evans and Pinkham notches. If you feel like limiting your day's cycling to two climbs, you can avoid the wildly beautiful but extremely severe climb up Hurricane Mountain Road by circling to the south. A triple chainring is recommended for Hurricane Mountain. Directions for an alternate starting route, around Hurricane and neighboring Black Cap mountains, are presented below.

Once over or around Hurricane Mountain, the ride rolls gently along the border with Maine toward Evans Notch. After passing the Cold River Campground, you will climb steadily through a white birch forest. Four miles later, stop at the Evans Notch Overlook to count the peaks around you. The next 8 miles pass through a winding canyon to the Androscoggin River below.

Pedal slowly through Pinkham Notch, since there is much to see. Pull off the road at the scenic turnout for the Great Gulf Wilderness Area. A sign here names the peaks of the Presidential Range before you.

The classic passes by the entrance to the Mount Washington Auto Road. This toll road is open to bicycles one day every year for the Mount Washington Hillclimb, a fierce race to its peak. The road ascends 4,000 feet in 8 twisting miles. Much of it is unpaved. The weather near the summit is notoriously unpredictable and harsh—in 1934 instruments on the summit recorded the greatest wind speed ever documented on the planet, 231 miles per hour.

Rather than climb this hill, stop at the Appalachian Mountain Club (AMC) lodge in Pinkham Notch. There is a small cafe, as well as a large lounge area and a bookstore with dozens of volumes about the surrounding wilderness. The ride's remaining 19 miles are virtually all downhill or flat, passing from wilderness into civilization, with a scenic stop in the village of Jackson.

The Basics

Start: In the center of North Conway, at the junction of combined Routes 16 and 302 with Seavey St. (See the Bear Notch Challenge for map detail of downtown North Conway.) This intersection is opposite the Conway Scenic Railroad Station and just 2 blocks south of the Joe Jones bicycle, ski, and outdoor equipment shop.
Length: 74.5 miles or, with the route around Hurricane Mountain, 81.1 miles.
Terrain: Three major climbs—Hurricane Mountain and Evans and Pinkham notches—each with elevation gains of more than 1,200 feet. You will also enjoy two 8-mile-long descents. The alternate route avoids the hardest climb up Hurricane Mountain and offers a more gentle warm-up to the ride.
Food: Small grocery stores on the route in Stow and Gorham. Mt. Washington Cafeteria or AMC lodge, in Pinkham Notch, two-thirds of the way into the ride.
Traffic/Safety: Use extreme caution descending Hurricane Mountain Rd. (17 percent grade for 1.5 mile), since the pavement is bumpy. The road through Evans Notch is narrow and winding; you may have to pull off the pavement if there are big vehicles passing, but traffic is generally light. The road through Pinkham Notch is popular with motorists, but there is an ample shoulder. As you descend into Jackson, the wind can be a factor, and the shoulder narrows.

Miles and Directions

- 0.0 To bypass Hurricane Mountain, see "Alternate Starting Route" on page 183.) From Rte. 16 in North Conway, ride east on Seavey St. toward the Cranmore Mt. ski area.
- 0.5 Turn left with Seavey St., continuing past the Sunnyside Inn and toward Cranmore Mt. Seavey St. becomes Kearsarge Rd.
- 2.0 Right onto Hurricane Mt. Rd. at the end of Kearsarge Rd., soon after passing the Cranmore Mt. Lodge on the right. Severe climb over Hurricane Mt., beginning in just under 1 mile.

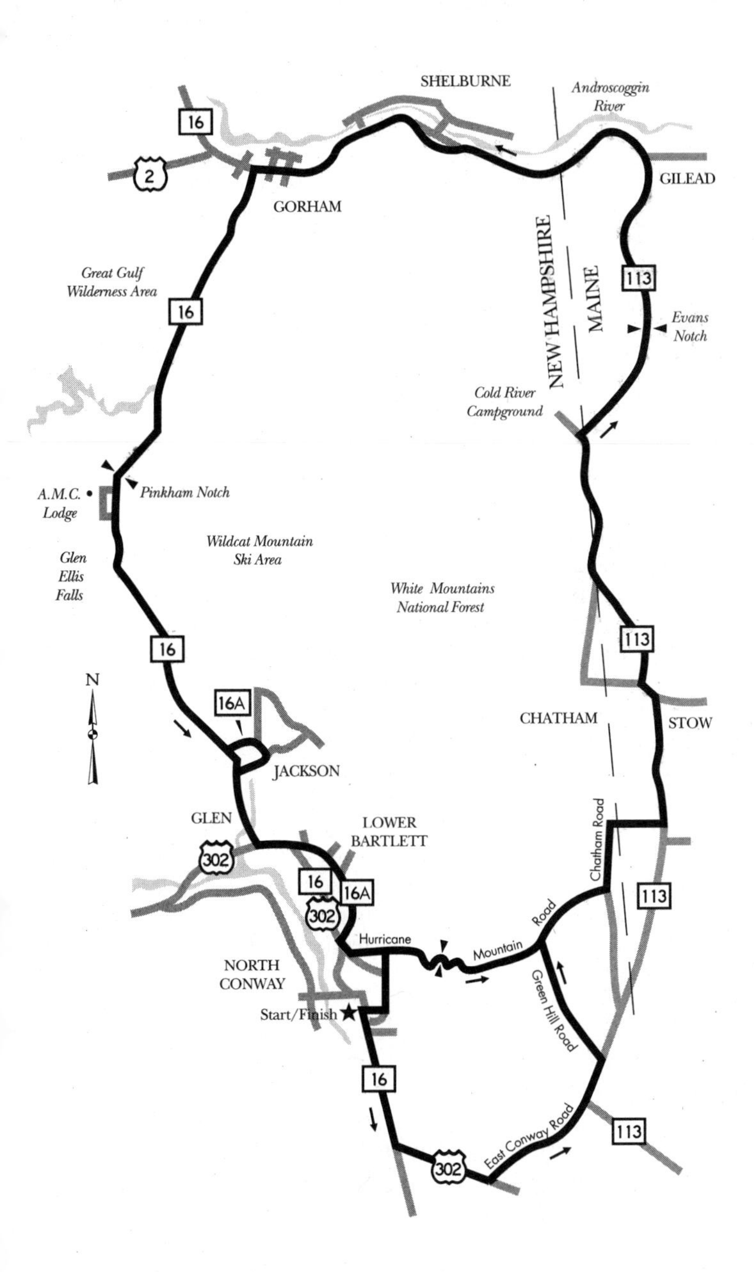
SHELBURNE
Androscoggin River
16
2
GORHAM
GILEAD
Great Gulf Wilderness Area
16
NEW HAMPSHIRE
MAINE
113
Evans Notch
Cold River Campground
A.M.C. Lodge
Pinkham Notch
Wildcat Mountain Ski Area
Glen Ellis Falls
White Mountains National Forest
16
113
N
16A
CHATHAM
STOW
JACKSON
GLEN
LOWER BARTLETT
Chatham Road
302
16
16A
113
302
Hurricane
Mountain
Road
NORTH CONWAY
Green Hill Road
Start/Finish
16
East Conway Road
113
302

- 6.8 Hurricane Mt. Rd. bottoms out at Chatham Rd. Turn left.
- 12.1 Chatham Rd. ends at T in North Fryeburg, Maine. Turn left on Rte. 113N toward Chatham and North Chatham.
- 14.8 Right with Rte. 113N toward North Chatham and Gilead at Stow Corner Store on left.
- 17.9 Continue straight, crossing into New Hampshire, as Rte. 113B merges in from left.
- 22.4 Enter White Mt. National Forest. Begin climb to Evans Notch shortly after passing into Maine again.
- 24.7 Cold River Overlook on the right.
- 25.1 Climb ends at Evans Notch Overlook. Begin 8.2-mile descent.
- 33.3 Descent ends. Turn left at stop onto Rte. 2W toward Gorham.
- 39.6 Rest area. Information, water, and rest rooms.
- 44.4 *Caution:* Railroad tracks at angle as you enter Gorham. In Gorham turn left on Rte. 16S toward Conway and Mt. Washington Auto Rd. Climb to Pinkham Notch begins gradually.
- 52.2 Reach Great Gulf Wilderness Area scenic overlook on right. Mt. Washington Stage office, gift shop, and cafeteria are across road on left.
- 54.8 End of climb. AMC lodge on right. Prepare for 10-mile descent to Jackson village and Glen; 9 percent grade for next 3 miles.
- 64.1 Pass the turnoff to the left for Rte. 16A. For a scenic 1-mile detour, turn left here (Rte. 16A is also Jackson Village Rd.). Follow this road as it curves to the right through Jackson Village and the Jackson covered bridge, before rejoining Rte. 16S.
- 66.1 Left at stop sign at T intersection in Glen, continuing on Rte. 16S.
- 67.3 Left, crossing busy Rte. 16, onto Rte. 16A, to avoid the busy main road into town.
- 70.3 Turn left as Rte. 16A merges back into Rte. 16.
- 70.5 Left onto Hurricane Mt. Rd.
- 71.5 Right onto Kearsarge Rd., toward the Cranmore Mt. Lodge. Follow Kearsarge Rd. back to Rte. 16 in North Conway center.
- 73.5 Arrive at combined Routes 16 and 302 in North Conway.

Alternate Starting Route

This alternate route avoids Hurricane Mt., adding 7.1 flat miles. First you must ride through North Conway's strip of factory outlet malls along Rte. 16, which is choked with traffic during most weekends. Ride cautiously, keeping a sharp eye out for drivers turning in and out of the parking lots on either side. Within 5 miles you will enter the rural farmscape of the Saco River plain.

- 0.0 Ride south on combined Routes 16 and 302 from the junction with Seavey St. in North Conway.
- 2.4 Left onto Rte. 302E toward Center Conway, East Conway, and Fryeburg, Maine. Rte. 16 continues straight here.
- 4.0 Left onto E. Conway Rd., toward East Conway and Chatham, Maine.
- 9.6 Stay left at junction. A granite pillar in the intersection here indicates that this is East Conway. The road to the right leads to Fryeburg, Maine.
- 10.5 Straight onto Green Hill Rd., leaving Rte. 113 as it curves right toward West Fryeburg.
- 13.9 Continue straight through intersection onto Chatham Rd. as Hurricane Mt. Rd. comes down from the left. You have now completed the detour around Hurricane Mt. Pick up the directions above at 6.8 miles.

31

Cherry Mountain Ramble

Jefferson—Jefferson Highland—Meadows—Whitefield—Jefferson

The Cherry Mountain Ramble explores the pocket of land that lies between the Pilot Region, a small mountain range, and the main body of the White Mountain National Forest. This rolling terrain is laced by the streams that run off the mountains to the west—Haystack Mountain, Mounts Starr and Waumbeck, Mount Martha, Cherry Mountain, and Beech Hill—on their way to the Connecticut River. The opening miles offer terrific views of this entire range.

This 28-mile tour is intended as a companion ride to the North Country Challenge. It is perfect for working the kinks out of your legs in anticipation of the next day's big ride. In fact, you could shave off a few miles and make this an even more relaxing outing by pedaling directly south from Jefferson on less busy, scenic Route 115A and joining Route 115 at Jefferson Station.

The Cherry Mountain Ramble is short enough to allow time to enjoy the vistas on the first half of the ride. Jefferson does have two "attractions," although they're strictly for kids. Santa's Village, near the intersection of Routes 2 and 116 in Jefferson, is where St. Nick and his entourage of reindeer and helpers spend their summers. Six Gun City, at the junction of Routes 2 and 115, is an out-of-place replica of a small western town. If you're tired of pedaling, you can take a stagecoach ride past the blockhouse, jail, and saloon. Both sites are open only during the summer.

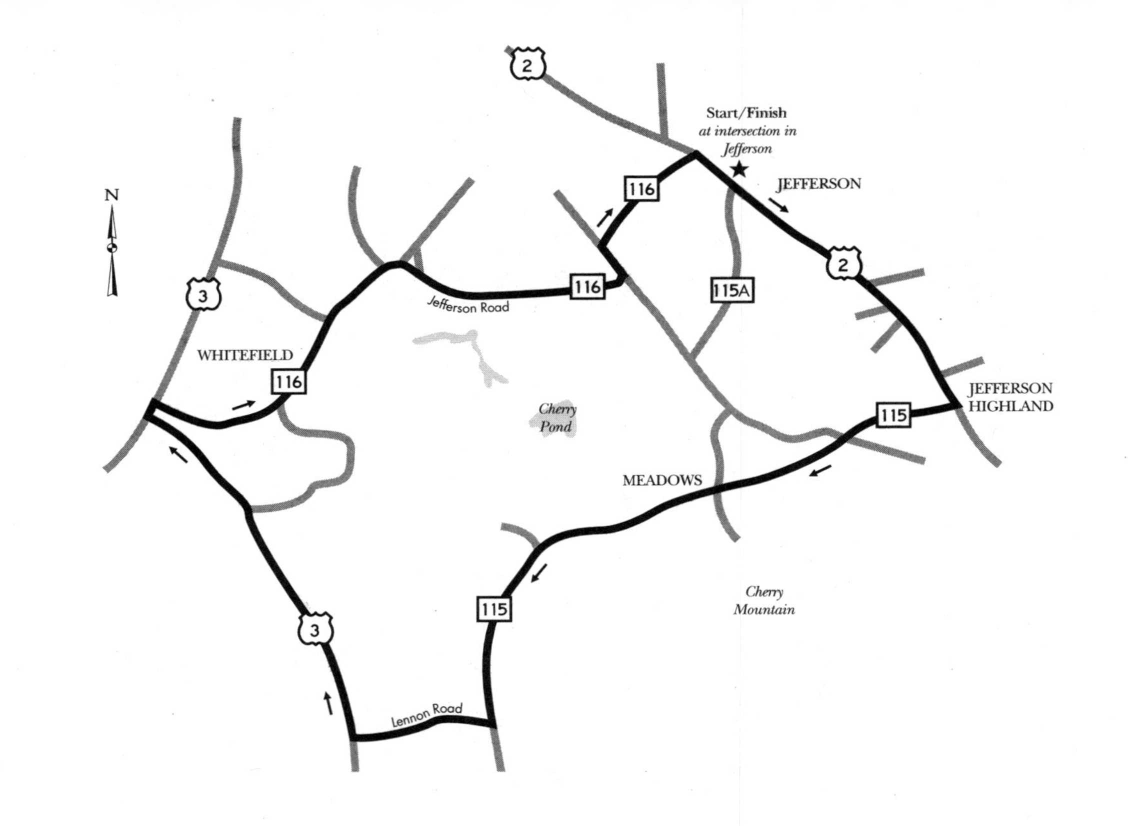

2
Start/Finish
at intersection in
Jefferson
JEFFERSON
N
116
2
3
Jefferson Road
116
115A
WHITEFIELD
116
Cherry
Pond
JEFFERSON
HIGHLAND
115
MEADOWS
115
Cherry
Mountain
3
Lennon Road

The Basics

Start: Jefferson, located at intersection of Routes 2 and 115A, just southeast of Lancaster. Follow either I–91N along the Vermont–New Hampshire border or I–93N through New Hampshire. From I–91 turn south onto I–93 in St. Johnsbury, cross into New Hampshire, then take Rte. 116N to Jefferson. Driving north on I–93, follow Rte. 116N to Jefferson.
Length: 28.8 miles.
Terrain: Rolling foothills of the White Mountains.
Food: Pack your own, or stop for a snack in Whitefield.
Traffic/Safety: Watch out for the occasional logging truck on Rte. 2, and *always* ride single file on the narrower rural roads.

Miles and Directions

- 0.0 From the center of Jefferson, at the intersection of Routes 2 and 115A, ride east on Rte. 2. *For a more leisurely, less traveled ride, avoiding Rte. 2, head directly south on Rte. 115A, through Jefferson Station, to Rte. 115S.*
- 3.9 Turn right onto Rte. 115S toward Meadows and Jefferson Station, circling the western base of Cherry Mt. At 9.8 miles there's a parking area with a good westerly view.
- 11.8 Cut over to Rte. 3 by turning right onto Lennon Rd. before reaching the junction of Routes 115 and 3 in Carroll. Enjoy the long coasting stretch!
- 13.6 Turn right onto Rte. 3 toward Whitefield.
- 18.4 In Whitefield, immediately after crossing a bridge, take two successive right turns to get onto Rte. 116N, Jefferson Rd., to Jefferson. Stay with Rte. 116 all the way to Rte. 2.
- 28.5 Turn right onto Rte. 2E.
- 28.8 Arrive in Jefferson.

32

North Country Challenge

Jefferson—Grange—Groveton—Stark—Groveton—Guildhall—Lunenburg—Whitefield—Jefferson

The North Country Challenge can be a companion ride to the shorter Cherry Hill Ramble for a weekend of cycling through New Hampshire's north country. This challenge qualifies as a metric century ride, one that covers 100 kilometers, or 62 miles.

Both of these rides come from Adolphe Bernotas, who organized the first ride to Canada for his club, the Granite State Wheelmen, in 1979. Since then little about this countryside has changed. Jefferson and the surrounding region have avoided the development that has brought both prosperity and traffic to the state's southern half.

This is the ultimate ride from Jefferson. It combines covered bridges, sensational downhills, flat stretches along the Connecticut River, and quaint Yankee villages with open views, vistas, and panoramas in abundance. In short, you will see much of the best of New England within a manageable 64 miles. For instance, there's the village of Stark, west of Groveton on the Ammonoosuc River, where a covered bridge and a traditional New England church nestle side by side in the shadow of sheer granite cliffs.

The Basics

Start: Jefferson, located on Rte. 2, just southeast of Lancaster and

southwest of the White Mt. National Forest's Pilot Region. Follow either I–91N along the Vermont–New Hampshire border or I–93N through New Hampshire. From I–91 turn south onto I–93 in St. Johnsbury, cross into New Hampshire, then take Rte. 116N to Jefferson. Driving north on I–93, follow Rte. 116N to Jefferson.
Length: 64 miles.
Terrain: Rolling landscape of hills and valleys, with many long flat stretches. This is a good ride for those who have never done a 50-plus-mile ride before.
Food: Your choice of general stores in Stark, Groveton, Lancaster, Whitefield, and Jefferson. If you are packing a lunch, the Guildhall green at 34.3 miles is a good midway point to stop for a picnic.
Traffic/Safety: Only the normal precautions are necessary on these rural roads with narrow shoulders.

Miles and Directions

- 0.0 From the center of Jefferson, at the intersection of Routes 2 and 115A, ride west on Rte. 2 toward Lancaster.
- 0.8 Right onto North Rd.
- 3.1 Stay left at fork, as Gore Rd. turns right.
- 5.9 Right on Grange Rd., at the H (hospital) sign toward Grange, Lost Nation, and Groveton. You have missed this turn if you enter Lancaster. Follow Grange Rd. all the way to Groveton.
- 17.1 In Groveton turn right onto Rte. 110 at stop sign, passing between the Canadian National Railway line and the Ammonoosuc River on the way to Stark.
- 19.6 Pass turnoff for Emerson Rd. on left. Continue straight on Rte. 110.
- 23.9 In Stark turn left through the covered bridge, then immediately left again onto N. Side Rd., the backroad to Groveton.
- 24.5 Road turns to dirt for 0.7 mile.
- 27.5 Fork right onto well-maintained dirt road, passing the N. Side Deli. Nash Stream Rd. curves to the left across river here.
- 30.9 Pavement resumes.

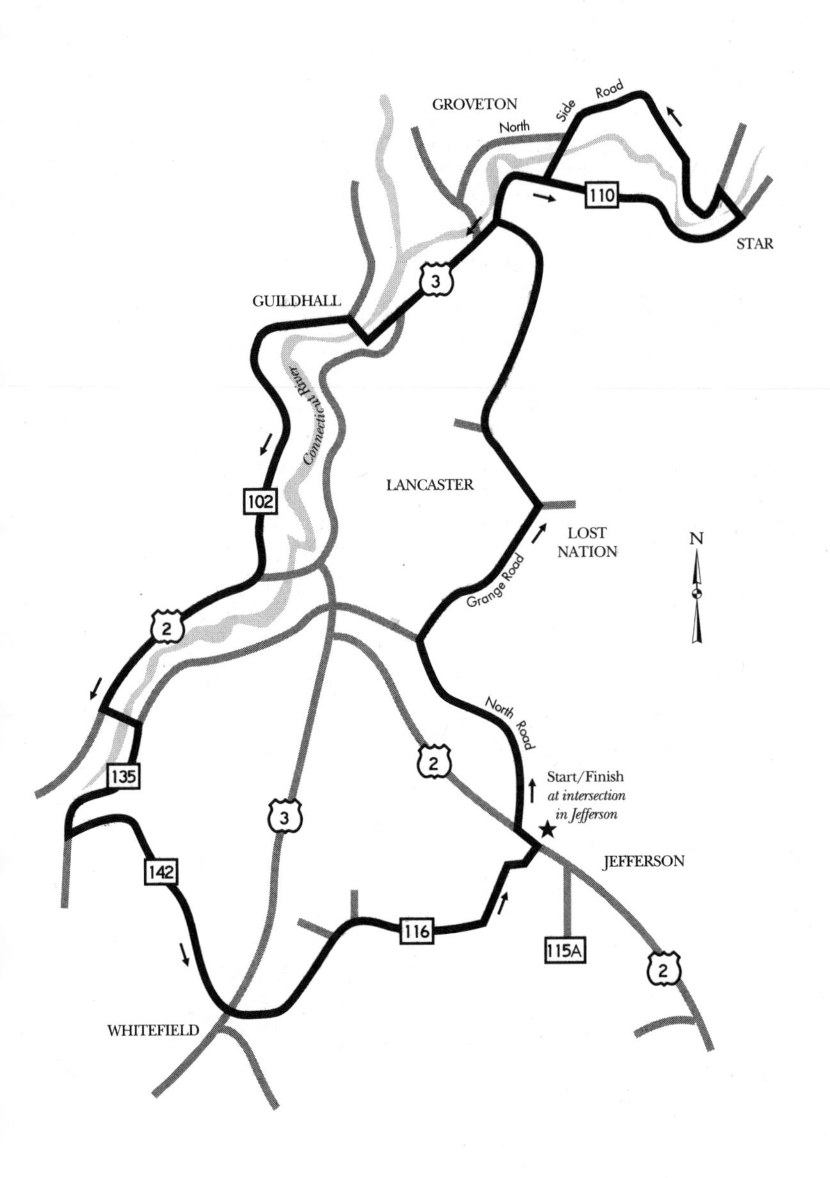
GROVETON
North Side Road
110
STAR
3
GUILDHALL
Connecticut River
102
LANCASTER
LOST NATION
Grange Road
N
2
North Road
135
Start/Finish
at intersection
in Jefferson
JEFFERSON
3
142
116
115A
WHITEFIELD

- 31.4 At stop sign in Groveton, go straight, joining Rte. 3.
- 31.7 Recross Ammonoosuc River. Pass junction with Rte. 110 on left, staying on Rte. 3.
- 34.6 Bear right before the shopping center, following the signs to Vermont, as you enter the small town of Northumberland.
- 35.3 Sharp right across the bridge into Guildhall, Vermont.
- 35.4 Left onto Rte. 102S coming off the bridge.
- 42.7 Continue straight along western side of Connecticut River as Rte. 102 merges into Rte. 2.
- 46.7 Left at fork, staying by the river, as Rte. 2 turns inland toward Lunenburg. Watch for this turn; it's easy to miss.
- 47.1 Cross the Connecticut River into New Hampshire through the covered bridge.
- 47.2 Right onto Rte. 135S, Elm St., coming off the bridge.
- 50.0 Left onto Rte. 142S toward Whitefield. This is the first clear left turn since you turned south on Rte. 135. It comes immediately before Rte. 135 crosses a set of railroad tracks.
- 55.9 In Whitefield turn left at the first stop sign. At the second stop cross Rte. 3 and follow Rte. 116N, Jefferson Rd., to Jefferson. Stay with Rte. 116 all the way to Rte. 2.
- 64.9 Right onto Rte. 2E at stop sign.
- 65.5 Arrive in Jefferson proper.

Rhode Island

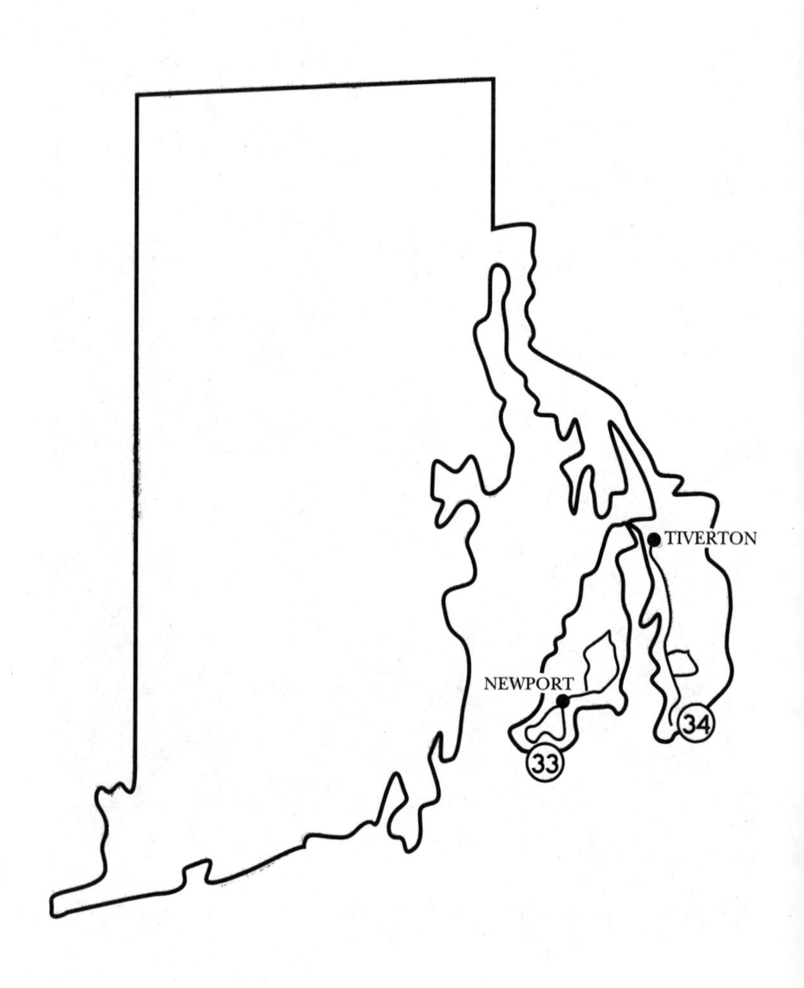
TIVERTON
NEWPORT
33
34

Rhode Island

33. Newport (and Beyond) Ramble 194
34. Sakonnet Point Ramble 199

33

Newport (and Beyond) Ramble

Newport Harbor—Brenton Point—
Middletown—Newport Harbor

This ramble draws a figure-eight loop around Newport and Middletown. The first half follows Ocean Drive along the magnificent shoreline jutting out from Newport. The second half passes from Newport's splendor and bustle into the quieter countryside and charm of the island's southwestern end. The two loops, measuring 8.5 and 17.2 miles, respectively, may be ridden separately or together.

Because Newport is a summer resort, it often has heavy traffic from June through August. You might consider doing this ride in the spring or fall. In the off-season you will be able to find a parking spot at King Park, which lines Newport Harbor's southern edge along Wellington Avenue. From there ride away from town. To complete the first, 10-mile loop, follow the general rule of staying on the principal roads closest to the shore, until you arrive at Bellevue Avenue, which leads back into town.

Turn to the right in the first 2 miles for a side trip to Fort Adams State Park. This granite-walled fort was originally constructed to guard the entrance to Narragansett Bay. Sited on a point of land jutting northward into the water, the fort offers good views of Newport Harbor. Continuing south toward Brenton Point, the ride passes Hammersmith Farm, where Jacqueline and John F. Kennedy spent numerous summer vacations. Its shingle-style mansion and bayside gardens were designed by Frederick Law Olmsted. Canada geese flock on this old farm's broad pastures every fall.

From the U.S. Coast Guard station at Castle Hill, the ride turns south toward the open sea. Follow Ocean Drive along the rocky shoreline for the next 4 miles. Take the time to explore the many grassy areas, boulders, and tidal pools to the right. If you have packed something to eat, stop along this stretch for a roadside picnic. If the wind is blowing from the south, you are likely to feel some of the salt spray sent flying by waves crashing against the rocks.

Bellevue Avenue is the chain along which Newport's jewels are strung. Many of the town's most famous mansions (once called "cottages")—Belcourt Castle, Marble Head, Beechwood, Chateau-sur-Mer, and the Elms—line either side. Glancing through the gates as you ride by will help you decide which to tour.

The longer of the two loops along this route explores the quieter countryside northwest of Newport. Tidy shingled homes, small farms, and large fields line the backroads between Newport and Middletown. The road through sandy Easton and Sachuest points offers views back to Newport, where the most famous of the town's mansions, the Breakers, is visible above the cliff. Back lanes follow the Sakonnet River's western shore, opposite terrain covered by the Sakonnet Point Ramble, before turning back to Newport on busier Route 138.

The Basics

Start: King Park, on the southern side of Newport Harbor. (You might want to pick up a map of Newport beforehand.) From I–195 out of Providence, follow Rte. 138 into Newport; from the Boston area follow Rte. 128 to Rte. 24 to Rte. 79 to Rte. 138. To reach the park, drive (or ride) down the harborfront (Thames St.), then turn right on Wellington Ave. King Park will be on the right.
Length: 25.7 miles for the full two-part loop 8.5 or 17.2 miles for either half.

Terrain: Flat coastal roads, with a few gentle rises. Heavy traffic in summer.
Food: There are no commercial areas along this oceanside route. Pack a snack to enjoy along the shore.
Traffic/Safety: The return section on the longer ride has a 2.5-mile stretch on Rte. 138, a busy, four-lane road. Riders not comfortable on a highway might prefer to turn around and retrace the route.

Miles and Directions

- 0.0 From King Park ride westward, away from town, along Wellington Ave.
- 0.5 Left with Wellington Ave. as it becomes Halidon Ave.
- 0.8 Right onto Harrison Ave.
- 1.2 Bear right with Harrison Ave.
- 1.7 Pass entrance on right to Ford Adams State Park. The fort guards the mouth of Newport Harbor. It is worth a quick side trip to view Newport from across the water.
- 2.1 Bear right onto Ridge Rd. as Harrison Ave. bears left.
- 2.8 Right onto Ocean Ave., at T, after passing Castle Hill Coast Guard Station. Ride past Brenton Point State Park.
- 4.8 Stay straight on Ocean Ave. where Brenton Rd. forks left.
- 6.5 Right at the T, then turn left almost immediately onto Bellevue Ave.
- 8.0 Right onto Narragansett Ave. to begin the second loop of this figure-eight route.

To complete the 8.5-mile option, turn left onto Narragansett Ave. and then right onto Marchant St. in 3 blocks. Marchant St. will end at Bellevue Ave. across from King Park.

- 8.3 Left on Annandale Rd.
- 8.9 Right on Memorial Blvd., Rte. 138A. *Caution:* There can be a lot of traffic here in the summer.
- 9.9 Stay right at fork on Purgatory Rd., toward East Point, after passing Newport Beach on the right. (Rte. 138 goes left.)

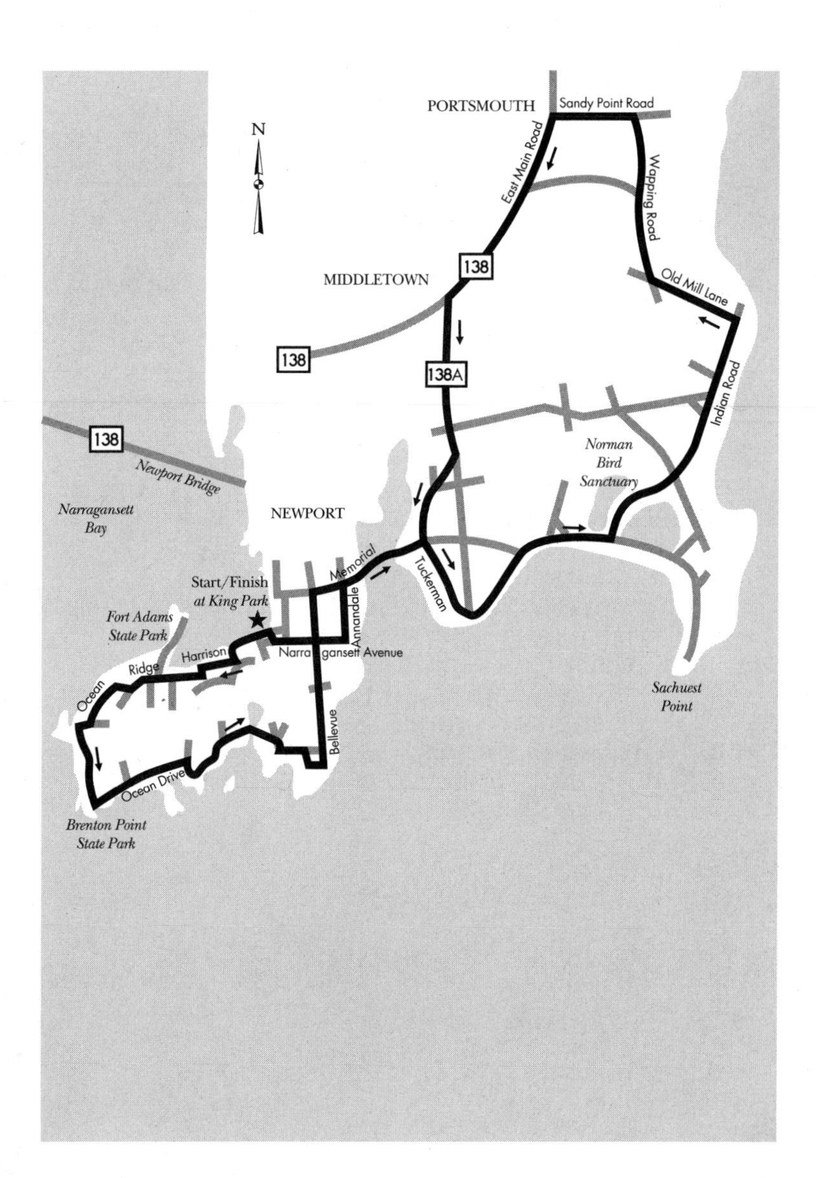

PORTSMOUTH
Sandy Point Road
N
East Main Road
Wapping Road
138
MIDDLETOWN
Old Mill Lane
138
138A
Indian Road
138
Newport Bridge
Norman
Bird
Sanctuary
Narragansett
Bay
NEWPORT
Memorial
Tuckerman
Start/Finish
at King Park
Fort Adams
State Park
Annandale
Harrison
Narragansett Avenue
Ridge
Ocean
Bellevue
Sachuest
Point
Ocean Drive
Brenton Point
State Park

- 10.3 Right on Tuckerman.
- 11.6 Bear right toward the Norman Bird Sanctuary.
- 11.9 Bear left at fork toward the bird sanctuary. You may want to detour to the right for a visit to Sachuest Point, a peninsula of sandy beach marking the mouth of the Sakonnet River.
- 13.2 Cross Third Beach Rd., continuing straight on Indian Road.
- 15.1 Left onto Old Mill Ln., where a sign indicates that the road you are on is coming to a dead end.
- 15.8 Right at the T onto Wapping Rd.
- 16.8 Stay straight on Wapping Rd. at fork.
- 17.8 Left at T onto Sandy Point Rd. Sign points left toward Rte. 138. Pass a horse farm on the right.
- 18.3 Left onto Rte. 138 at the stoplight. *Caution:* Rte. 138 has a lot of traffic and only a scant shoulder. If you're not comfortable riding on a highway, simply turn around and double back.
- 20.9 Left onto Rte. 138A, Aquidneck Ave., following the sign for Newport Beach.
- 23.0 Stay with Rte. 138A as it turns left, at a stoplight, and then right, immediately thereafter, toward Newport Beach.
- 24.7 Returning to Newport, turn left off Rte. 138A, Memorial Blvd., onto Bellevue Ave.
- 25.2 Right on Narragansett Ave.
- 25.6 Turn right on Marchant St.
- 25.7 Arrive back at Wellington Ave. and King Park.

34

Sakonnet Point Ramble

Tiverton—Little Compton—
Sakonnet Point—Tiverton

In southeastern Rhode Island country lanes lace the 4-mile-wide strip of salt marshes, farms, and woods lying between the broad Sakonnet River and the Massachusetts border. This is Rhode Island's flatter self; the barely rolling landscape contrasts with the wooded hill and valley country west of Narragansett Bay. This ramble hugs the Sakonnet River's eastern shore from the town of Tiverton to Sakonnet Point, an undeveloped, scenic spot that juts out into the sea. The route turns inland just long enough to pass through the village of Little Compton—by most accounts, the prettiest in the state.

Pedaling past expansive wetlands and pastures, one would never know that this is the nation's smallest and most densely populated state. The ramble starts just off Route 77, a mile south of Tiverton, where a small bridge crosses the neck of Nannaquaket Pond. Fishermen often drop their lines here, where the currents carry their hoped-for prey through a narrow channel out to the river. From here Nannaquaket Road leads past gracious homes situated on a ridge between the pond and the Sakonnet River.

Following a short stretch along Route 77, the ride turns back toward the river, passing through the Seapowet Wildlife Management Area. Great blue herons are often spotted feeding in these wetlands. The well-paved course crosses a one-lane wooden bridge over one of the Sakonnet River's many tidal inlets. The open landscape has broad views south toward the mouth of the Sakonnet, where it empties into Rhode Island Sound.

Little Compton has a white frame church at one end of its traditional New England green. The green, the general store, and a neighboring restaurant are the focus of the town's day-to-day activity. You'll also pass the Sakonnet Vineyards in Little Compton on Route 77. It offers public tours (401–635–8486).

The route continues on Route 77S to its end at Sakonnet Point. Stop to take in the ocean views on three sides; then return along Route 77 and Neck and Nannaquaket roads to Tiverton.

The Basics

Start: Tiverton, located just south of Fall River, Massachusetts. From I–195 between Providence and New Bedford, Massachusetts, turn onto Rte. 24S to Tiverton. Off Rte. 77 just a mile south of town, take a right onto Nannaquaket Rd. Just over the short bridge on the right side is a small unpaved parking area that you'll share with local fishermen.
Length: 28.7 or 12.3 miles.
Terrain: Gently rolling coastal roads.
Food: Olga's Cup and Saucer Bakery at Walker's Roadside Stand between Tiverton and Little Compton at 8.4 miles. General store in Little Compton at 10.8 miles. Near the end of the ride, at 20.6 miles, Tiverton Four Corners consists of little else but Gray's Ice Cream and the general store. There is no food at Sakonnet Point.
Traffic/Safety: This is a highly safe ride. The only trafficked merge is onto Rte. 77 south of Little Compton.

Miles and Directions

- 0.0 From bridge and pond ride away from Rte. 77, on Nannaquaket Rd.
- 1.5 Merge back into Rte. 77S, keeping an eye out for the next right turn.

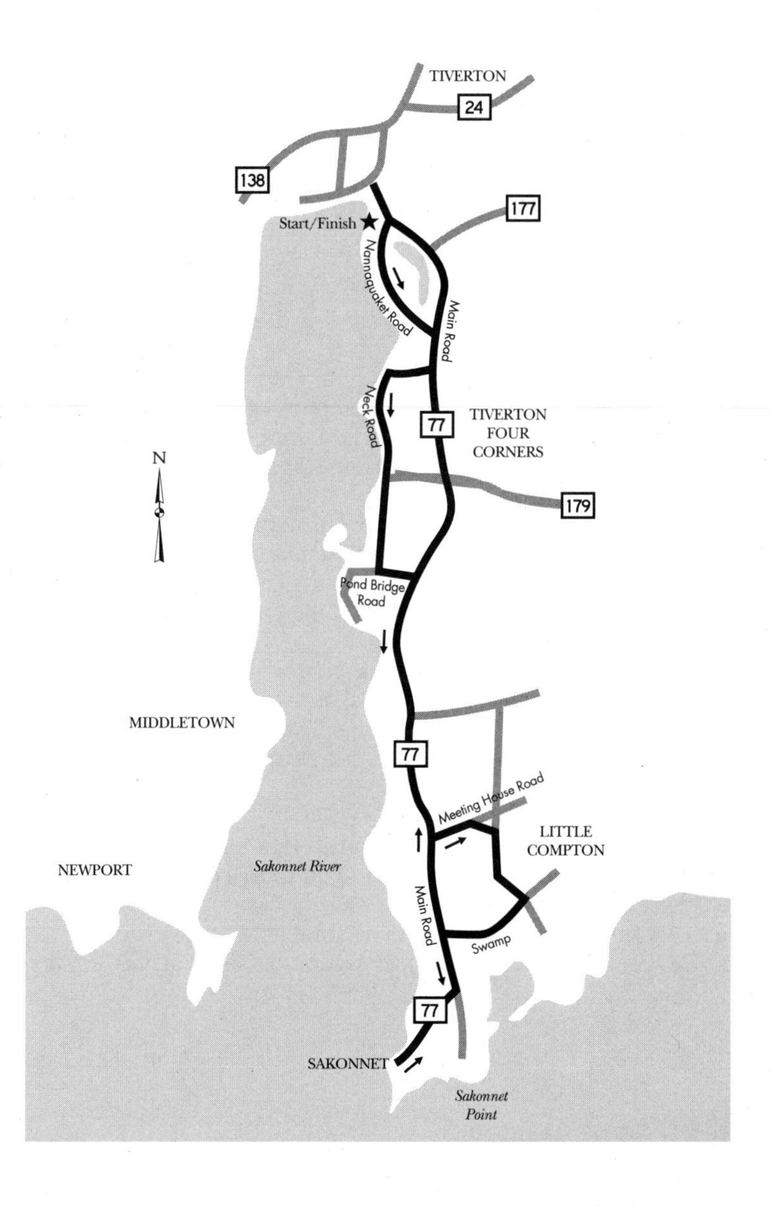
TIVERTON
24
138
177
Start/Finish
Nannaquaket Road
Main Road
Neck Road
77
TIVERTON
FOUR
CORNERS
N
179
Pond Bridge
Road
MIDDLETOWN
77
Meeting House Road
LITTLE
COMPTON
NEWPORT
Sakonnet River
Main Road
Swamp
77
SAKONNET
Sakonnet
Point

- 2.0 Turn right onto Seapowet Rd.
- 3.4 Cross paved bridge through the wetlands of the Seapowet Wildlife Management Area.
- 4.2 Seapowet Rd. becomes Neck Rd.
- 5.5 Turn left onto Pond Bridge Rd. Pass dam and fish ladder at bottom of hill.
- 6.1 Turn right, again, onto Rte. 77S.

For a short, 12-mile loop, turn left here to return to Tiverton along Rte. 77N.

- 8.0 Watch for sign for Little Compton. Stop at Olga's Cup and Saucer, on the right, for a snack and some local conversation.
- 9.6 Turn left onto Meeting House Rd., following the sign toward the Commons.
- 10.1 At fork veer right and arrive in Little Compton. Potential snack stops are the Common's Restaurant and the Wilbur General Merchandise Store across from the church on the green.
- 10.4 Turn right on the far side of the green (with a church on your left).
- 11.6 Turn right onto Swamp Rd.
- 12.8 Turn left onto Rte. 77S to Sakonnet Point.
- 15.3 Arrive at Sakonnet Point. Take a break to enjoy the panoramic views of the river, the ocean, and Newport. From here start back along Rte. 77N.
- 22.8 Left back onto Pond Bridge Rd.
- 22.6 Right onto Neck Rd., which becomes Seapowet Rd.
- 26.7 Left onto Rte. 77. *Caution:* You must cross lanes to make this and the next turn.
- 27.1 Left onto Nannaquaket Rd. (third left).
- 28.7 Return to start, near intersection of Nannaquaket Rd. and Rte. 77.

Vermont

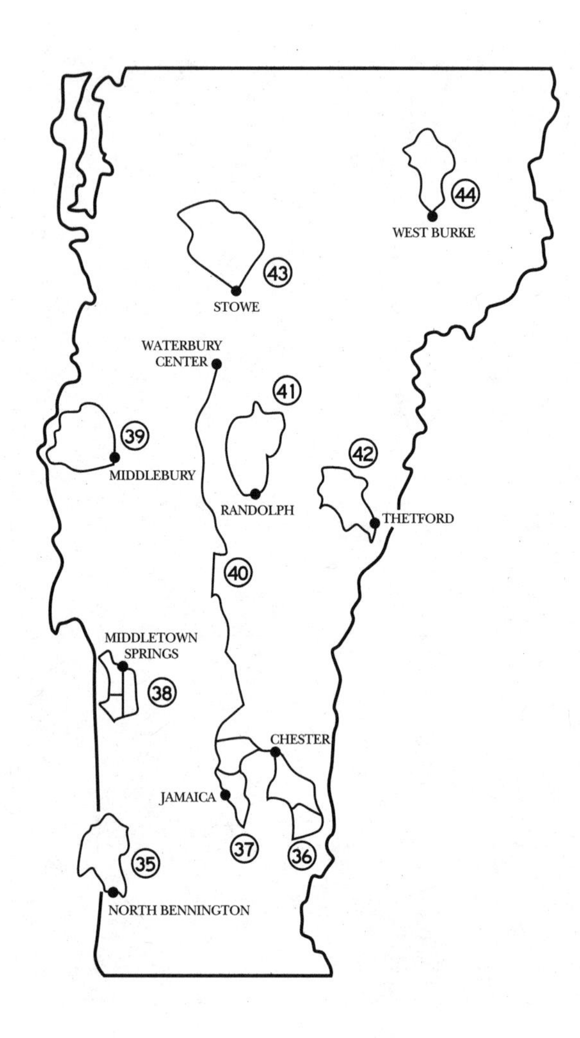

44
WEST BURKE
43
STOWE
WATERBURY
CENTER
41
39
MIDDLEBURY
42
RANDOLPH
THETFORD
40
MIDDLETOWN
SPRINGS
38
CHESTER
JAMAICA
37
36
35
NORTH BENNINGTON

Vermont

35. Bennington to Battenkill River Challenge 206
36. Chester Country Weekend: Saxtons River Cruise 212
37. Chester Country Weekend: West River Challenge 217
38. Middletown Springs Cruise 222
39. Champlain Valley Cruise 227
40. Tour of Scenic Rural Vermont Classic 231
41. Randolph Challenge 235
42. Orange County Challenge 239
43. Smuggler's Notch Challenge 243
44. Northeast Kingdom Challenge 248

35

Bennington to Battenkill River Challenge

North Bennington—White Creek—Cambridge—Arlington—South Shaftsbury—North Bennington

In the Vermont valley the early hours of a Saturday in June belong to grazing cows and casting fly fishermen. The Bennington to Battenkill River Challenge lets you in on their secret. This southwestern corner of Vermont, bounded by the Battenkill and Waloomsac rivers, hides some of the most pastoral land in New England.

The ride roughly follows the course of these two rivers as they wind their way through a landscape of rolling green hills just west of the Green Mountains. Although both rivers flow all the way to the Hudson, the challenge ventures only briefly into New York, before turning back into Vermont.

North Bennington, an old-time country town refreshingly free of glitz and boutiques, provides a hospitable starting point for this 41-mile tour. Park in the lot of the restored, Victorian-style train station, which looks just as it did when built in 1890. Down the block, clustered south of the Main and Bank streets junction, the Main Street Cafe and Power's Market dispense early morning breakfasts and snacks for the road.

Route 67A, the ride's initial leg, passes into open farmland in just half a mile. Also named White Creek Road, this 9-mile stretch offers a chance to warm up along a scarcely traveled road that is far preferable to the more trafficked Route 67 just to the south. On crossing into New York, the tour follows Route 22N, a busy but broad-shouldered road, for a fast 3-mile leg to Cambridge.

Running east from Cambridge, Route 313 unfolds as a highlight of the tour. Nearing the Vermont border, the road begins to run parallel to and often within sight of the Battenkill River, recognized as one of New England's best wild trout streams. Several shaded parking areas with river access allow cyclists to pull over and watch anglers land fighting brown, rainbow, and brook trout.

On a summer weekend you are likely to come across an inn-to-inn touring group or other cycling club along these 15 miles of road between Cambridge and Arlington. A favorite resting spot is the riverbank by the Bridge at the Green, a covered bridge built in 1852. It spans the Battenkill fully within sight of Route 313 halfway into the ride, a mile or two after you cross back into Vermont.

If this tour through trout-fishing country has you intrigued, consider renting a canoe or a tube for a closer look on a float downstream. Or detour north from Arlington on Route 7A for a visit to Manchester's American Museum of Fly Fishing and its neighbor, the venerable Orvis Company. Orvis has been outfitting sportfishermen since 1856. The company offers tours of its factory, where it manufactures bamboo rods, trout flies, and other fishing and outdoor equipment. Passersby are welcome as well in its retail store, which some consider the Abercrombie and Fitch of the Green Mountain State.

Arlington vies with Stockbridge, Massachusetts, for the distinction of being illustrator Norman Rockwell's hometown. Both claims are just, as Rockwell lived here from 1939 to 1953, before moving south to the Berkshire town.

The challenge enters its toughest stretch as it turns a back south from Arlington. Bypassing busy Route 7A, it picks up a network of unpaved roads bordering the Green Mountain National Forest. As you turn left on Maple Hill Road, gear down and prepare for a long gradual climb along nearly 5 miles of maintained dirt road—which may not be appropriate for thin tires. Ride easily here and enjoy the intimate feel of a slow cruise through a forest. You will pass the renovated Peter Matteson Tavern Museum on the left. From there the road climbs more gently and then becomes paved.

These backroad efforts pay off once you turn right onto Buck Hill Road, which descends almost 500 feet in 2 miles of fun, swooping turns. Enjoy the downhill run, but don't miss some of the ride's best views along the way. Then cool off along the final 2 flat miles back to North Bennington.

The Basics

Start: Park at the restored Victorian train station in North Bennington. Following Rte. 7N through Bennington, turn west onto Rte. 67A toward Bennington College. Continue past the college into North Bennington. The station is located straight ahead on Rte. 67, here N. Main St., opposite the post office.
Length: 43.1 miles.
Terrain: Rolling farmland and river valley. One gradual 2-mile climb on 5-mile packed dirt road. This road may not be appropriate for all thin-tired bikes.
Food: Several parking and picnic areas along Rte. 313 on the Battenkill River invite you to stop for a picnic and rest. The first of these is located at the entrance to the Battenkill Special Trout Fishing Area, at 20.2 miles. There are eateries at 12.5 miles, and the Wayside Country Store, at 25.5 miles, features a pleasant front stoop.
Traffic/Safety: Traffic is fast on Rte. 22N, but the highway has a good shoulder. Also, the downhill stretch into Vermont has a narrow shoulder.

Miles and Directions

- 0.0 From the intersection of Routes 67 and 67A in the center of North Bennington, ride west, passing the Merchants Bank building on your right.
- 0.2 Fork right onto Rte. 68, White Creek Rd., at a store.

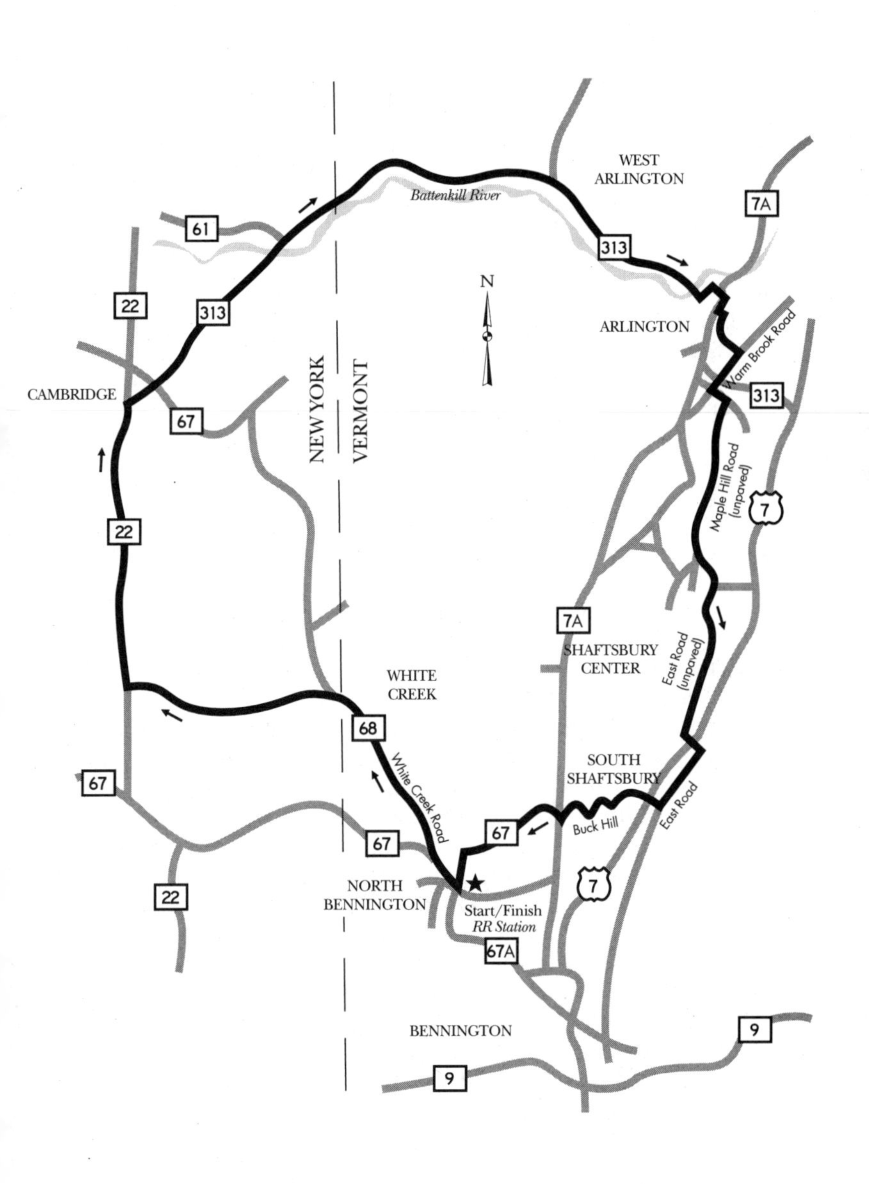

WEST
ARLINGTON
Battenkill River
7A
61
313
N
22
313
ARLINGTON
Warm Brook Road
CAMBRIDGE
313
67
NEW YORK
VERMONT
Maple Hill Road
(unpaved)
7
22
7A
SHAFTSBURY
CENTER
East Road
(unpaved)
WHITE
CREEK
68
SOUTH
SHAFTSBURY
White Creek Road
67
East Road
67
Buck Hill
67
NORTH
BENNINGTON
7
22
Start/Finish
RR Station
67A
BENNINGTON
9
9

- 2.9 Enter town of White Creek, marked only by a sign and a cow pasture.
- 3.8 Stay left with Rte. 68 toward Cambridge and Eagle Brook. Follow this route, ignoring all secondary turnoffs, to its intersection with Rte. 22.
- 9.3 Right onto Rte. 22N toward Cambridge. This is a fast road; ride well over to the right on the broad, paved shoulder.
- 12.9 Right onto Rte. 313E, here named Gilbert St., toward Arlington. Downtown Cambridge is straight ahead.
- 18.6 Continue straight as a road to the left detours to the Eagleville covered bridge. You may detour as well, if you wish, for a first glimpse of the Battenkill.
- 19.4 Parking area with river access on right. Route enters Battenkill Special Trout Fishing Area.
- 22.1 Vermont state line: the halfway point of the ride.
- 25.5 Pass Wayside Country Store, a snack stop, on the right.
- 28.8 Enter West Arlington. Battenkill Canoe Rentals on the right.
- 28.8 Turn right onto Rte. 7A toward Bennington.
- 28.9 Left onto E. Arlington Rd., opposite a doctor's office.
- 29.9 Right on unmarked Warm Brook Rd. It comes just before the road turns left. Cross Rte. 313.
- 39.9 Left on Maple Hill Rd., which soon becomes a maintained dirt road. In a quarter mile follow it to the right as a poorly maintained dirt road continues straight.
- 33.9 At the fork bear left onto East Rd., which is also unpaved. Maple Hill Rd. continues straight, then turns to the right toward Rte. 7A. The next mile presents this ride's most demanding hill, a steady grade up a rough surface. The road becomes paved again, at the end of a long climb, beyond the Peter Matteson Tavern Museum on the left.
- 38.9 Right on unmarked Buck Hill Rd., the first paved road to the right. Look for some guardrails on the corner. Following a short climb, Buck Hill Rd. descends almost 500 feet in 2 miles of swooping turns. Buck Hill Rd. becomes East Rd. again toward the bottom.

- 41.0 Continue straight across Rte. 7A (Main St.) and onto Church St. in South Shaftsbury.
- 41.3 Bear left onto Rte. 67 at stop sign, immediately after crossing railroad tracks. *Caution:* This is a blind curve for traffic coming from the right.
- 43.0 Follow Rte. 67 as it turns left, becoming Upper Main St., into North Bennington..
- 43.1 Return to train station on the left.

36

Chester Country Weekend: Saxtons River Cruise

Chester—Grafton—Cambridgeport—Saxtons River—Westminster—Saxtons River—Bartonsville—Chester

The southeastern corner of Vermont offers some of the finest cycling in New England. The Chester Country Weekend explores this countryside of hills, river valleys, and bucolic Vermont villages, with two days of riding that start and end in Chester. The first day's Saxtons River Cruise, 45 or 25 miles long, rolls southeast toward the Connecticut River. The second day's companion West River Challenge loops for 52 or 30 miles southwest to the boundary of the Green Mountain National Forest.

Whether you choose the longer or the shorter options, or plan to spend only one day on the bike, combine your rides with a country inn stay for a weekend of R&R and exercise. Cycle Inn Vermont, an affiliation of inns that transport baggage and cater to guests biking between them, can provide packages for touring cyclists (802–228–8799). The Chester Chamber of Commerce operates an information booth in the center of town and can help with accommodations, especially if you call ahead.

The initial stretch of the Saxtons River Cruise follows an old stagecoach route over hilly terrain, ending with a beautiful descent into the classic New England town of Grafton. This town was home to 10,000 sheep and several woolen mills before the Civil War. In the past several decades, the private Windham Foundation has spurred the town's revival. These efforts have paid off. The Hidden Orchard Farms and the Grafton Village Cheese Company are worth detours for those interested in seeing the sights (and getting fed too).

From Grafton the route follows the Saxtons River to the town of the same name. The shorter option turns north from here, directly back to Chester. The longer option continues south over rolling terrain toward Westminster, a calm village located on the mile-wide plain of one of the Connecticut River Valley's terrace formations. This 45-miler then returns to Saxtons River and follows the same route as the 25-mile ride back to Chester. Both rides cross many short hills. The longer option adds a gradual 2-miler as well.

If you're a covered bridge fan—and what better excuse for a rest is there—look for the recently rebuilt Saxtons River bridge on the right just a mile before you return to Saxtons River. The reconstruction used the same building techniques originally employed back in 1867. There's also a covered bridge at the Grafton Village Cheese Company, and two more covered bridges lie slightly off the ride route, both spanning the Williams River off Route 103 in Bartonsville.

If you arrive back in Chester with an unplanned afternoon still ahead, consider exploring by bike or foot the many handsome historic buildings and short local trails in and around Chester.

The Basics

Start: At the Historic Village Green in Chester, on Rte. 11, just west of the junction with Routes 35 and 103. Located 8 miles southeast of Springfield, Chester is most easily reached from exit 6 off I–91. Follow Rte. 103W for 10 miles into town. Route distances are measured from Chester's main intersection, where Routes 103, 11, and 35 converge.
Length: 45.0 or 25.4 miles.
Terrain: Hilly, with one 2-mile climb on the longer option.
Food: Grafton Village Store, Hidden Orchard Farms, and other places in Grafton at 7 miles and in Saxtons River at 14 miles (and again at 34 miles on the longer option).

Traffic/Safety: The fastest traffic is on Rte. 103 at the end of the ride.

Miles and Directions

- 0.0 From Chester ride south on Rte. 35, a rolling road with some steep climbs, toward Grafton.
- 7.0 Left onto Rte. 121E, following the Saxtons River downstream toward the Connecticut River.

  To visit Grafton turn right onto Rte. 121W. The Village Store is only 0.2 mile distant. The Hidden Orchard Farms is another 1.5 miles down Rte. 121W, which becomes ridable dirt here. For an additional excursion turn left after the Village Store at the sign for Brattleboro and Stratton, passing the Old Tavern on your right as you turn. The Grafton Village Cheese Company and a covered bridge lie 1 mile down the road.

- 10.9 Bear left crossing the bridge, staying on Rte. 121E. Follow the sign toward the town of Saxtons River.
- 11.1 Pass Cambridgeport Post Office and General Store.
- 13.8 Pleasant Valley Rd. joins Rte. 121 from the left. The longer and shorter options diverge here.

  To complete the 25.4-mile ride, turn left onto Pleasant Valley Rd., going uphill. Then bear right, staying on Pleasant Valley Rd. At 21.3 miles turn left onto Rte. 103N, which returns you to downtown Chester at 25.4 miles. For the longer option this intersection is the knot at the center of a figure-eight circuit; you will return on Pleasant Valley Rd. after completing the loop through Westminster.

- 14.1 In Saxtons River turn right across the bridge with the railing, following signs to Putney.
- 14.4 Bear right, staying on the main road.
- 20.0 Bear left at the Y, staying on the paved road. The Maple Grove Schoolhouse is up on the right.

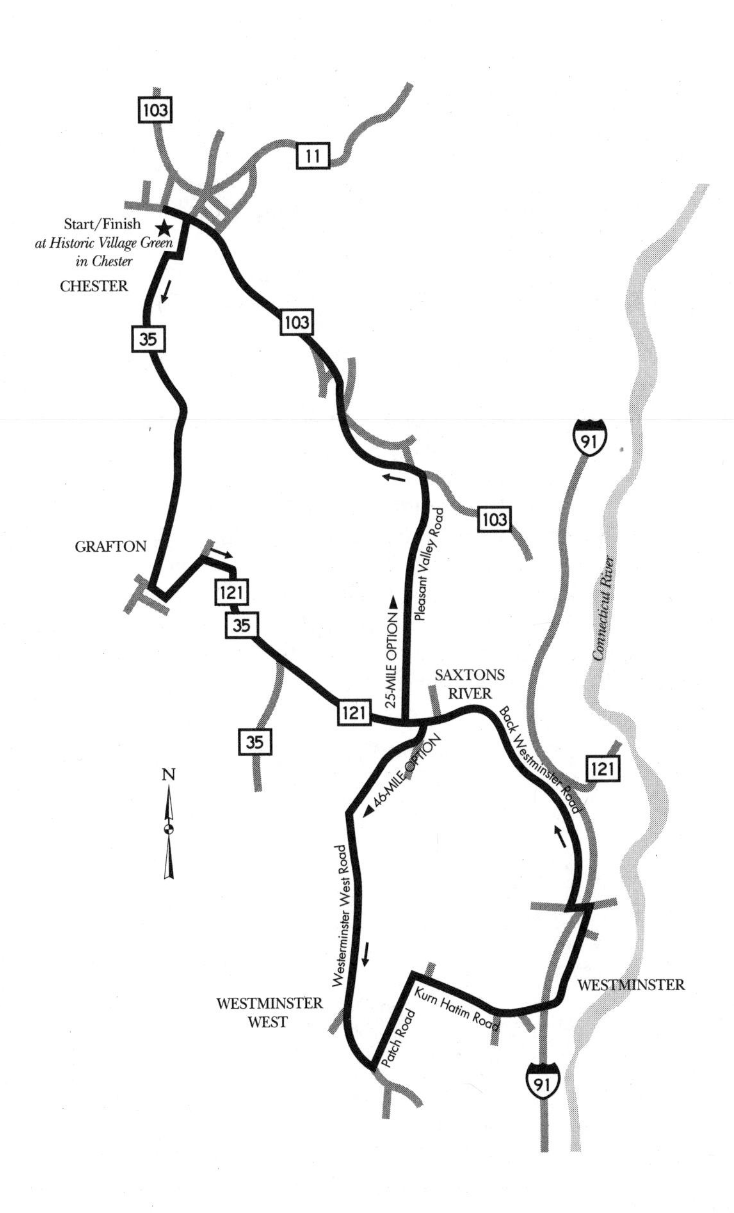
103
11
Start/Finish
at Historic Village Green in Chester
CHESTER
35
103
103
91
Pleasant Valley Road
GRAFTON
121
35
25-MILE OPTION
Connecticut River
SAXTONS RIVER
121
35
Back Westminster Road
46-MILE OPTION
121
N
Westerminster West Road
WESTMINSTER
Kurn Hatim Road
WESTMINSTER WEST
Patch Road
91

- 21.2 Turn left at the Y onto Patch Rd. just before the bridge. (This is also known as Kurn Hatim Rd.) Begin 2-mile gradual climb.
- 25.4 Kurn Hatim Children's School is on the left.
- 25.9 Pass over I–91 and continue straight. I–91 will be on your left for about 2 miles.
- 27.8 Left at the stop sign, passing under I–91.
- 28.3 Right at the T onto Back Westminster Rd., following signs to Saxtons River and Grafton.
- 31.0 Left at the stop sign onto Rte. 121W. Look for a covered bridge on the right.
- 32.3 Continue straight on Rte. 121 across a bridge and through the town of Saxtons River.
- 33.5 Bear right, staying on Rte. 121W.
- 33.8 Bear right onto Pleasant Valley Rd., going uphill.
- 34.0 Bear right, staying on Pleasant Valley Rd.
- 38.5 Left at stop sign onto Rte. 103N, which follows Williams River into Chester for the next 6 miles.
- 42.3 Chester General Store on the left.
- 44.8 Return to intersection with Routes 11 and 35 in Chester and then the Historic Village Green.

37

Chester Country Weekend: West River Challenge

Chester—Weston—Londonderry—Jamaica—West Townshend—Windham—Chester

The West River Challenge explores the eastern foothills of the Green Mountains. A 31-mile and a 54-mile loop each cross from Chester to the West River's valley, where restored villages cluster in the shadows of forested mountains. Both rides feature challenging but rewarding climbs that pass through hilltop settlements off the beaten track.

The ride reaches its first stop in Weston, situated at the north end of the West River Valley. Lay down your bike and rest by the bandstand on the green (which was a pond before the Civil War). Visit the columned Weston Playhouse, the oldest continuously operated summer theater in Vermont, or the Weston Bowl Mill, which sells wood products.

The longer and shorter rides diverge in Londonderry. The shorter option turns back toward Chester from this ski town, going downhill for 2.5 miles to the base of the Magic Mountain Ski Area and then climbing 2 miles. The longer option loops south, then the two rejoin at North Windham.

The 54-mile route adds both distance and a difficult climb. First, a 2-mile roller-coaster ride uphill along combined Routes 30 and 100 passes the access road to Ball Mountain Lake State Park. Controlled releases from the dam across the West River here create an excellent stretch of white water downstream for an annual canoe race. Jamaica State Park, off Route 100 on the other side of Ball Mountain, has a swimming and picnic area.

The loop turns north from West Townshend, located on the plain above a wide oxbow bend in the river, and follows a backroad that climbs steeply up Windham Hill for about 2 miles along Turkey Mountain Brook. At the end of the climb is Windham, at 2,000 feet the second highest village in Vermont.

Finally, the challenge cruises along an upland river valley, crossing and recrossing the rocky Williams River back to Chester.

The Basics

Start: Chester. Located 8 miles southeast of Springfield, Chester is most easily reached from exit 6 off I–91. Follow Rte. 103 west for 10 miles into town. Park along Rte. 11 west of its junction with Routes 103 and 35.
Length: 54 or 31 miles.
Terrain: Hilly.
Food: Several places in Jamaica.
Traffic/Safety: The shoulder along Rte. 100S can be eroded in places.

Miles and Directions

- 0.0 From the intersection of Routes 11, 103, and 35, ride west on Rte. 11 toward Weston and Londonderry.
- 3.9 Right onto paved road, following sign to Weston and Andover.
- 6.4 Bear right at Y, staying on the main road.
- 6.9 Bear left at Y. (Don't climb East Hill to the right.)
- 7.3 Horse Shoe Acres marks the beginning of a 3-mile climb with rests.
- 10.2 Top of hill.
- 11.1 Fresh springwater on the left. (This is easy to miss on a descent. There's a small turnoff on the right.)

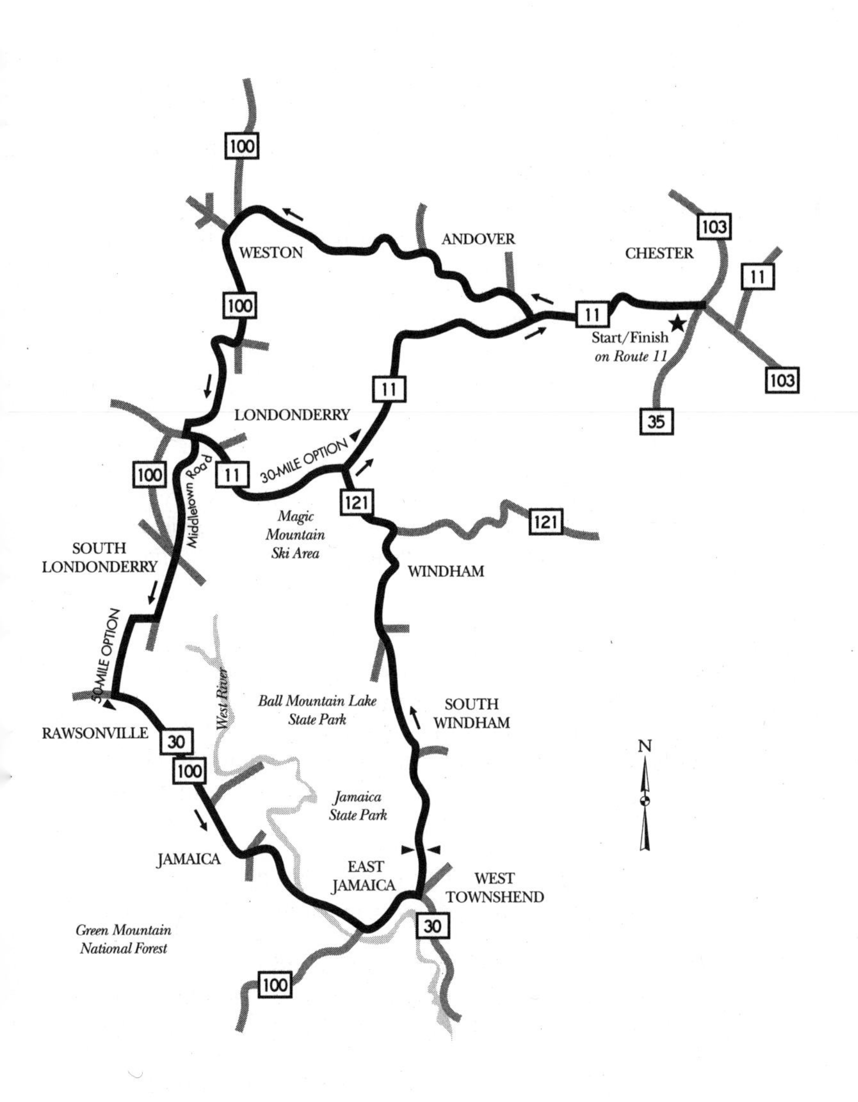

100
WESTON
ANDOVER
CHESTER
103
11
Start/Finish
on Route 11
35
LONDONDERRY
Middletown Road
30-MILE OPTION
121
Magic
Mountain
Ski Area
WINDHAM
SOUTH
LONDONDERRY
30-MILE OPTION
West River
Ball Mountain Lake
State Park
SOUTH
WINDHAM
RAWSONVILLE
30
Jamaica
State Park
N
JAMAICA
EAST
JAMAICA
WEST
TOWNSHEND
Green Mountain
National Forest

- 11.7 Left at the stop sign onto Rte. 100S. (Weston Bowl Mill is on the corner.)
- 11.9 Pass through Weston; its oval common and bandstand make an inviting rest stop. Continue on Rte. 100S toward Londonderry.
- 12.1 The Inn at Weston on the right marks the beginning of a gradual 2-mile climb.
- 17.0 Turn left in Londonderry onto Rte. 11E, riding across the bridge ahead. Then almost immediately . . .
- 17.1 Turn right onto the first paved road, Middletown Rd., and begin a mile-long climb.

The shorter, 31-mile ride diverges here by continuing straight on Rte. 11E to Chester. A 2.5-mile descent to the entrance to the Magic Mountain Ski Area is followed by a 2-mile climb, the only major obstacle remaining. From the junction with Rte. 121, continue on Rte. 11E downstream alongside the middle branch of the Williams River for the final 10 miles to Chester.

- 18.4 As you continue up Middletown Rd. on the longer ride, a cemetery on your right marks the top of the climb. (There's a stop sign at the end of the descent.)
- 19.6 Continue straight at the stop sign onto Rte. 100S.
- 23.6 Left at the stop sign onto combined Routes 30 and 100S, following the signs to Jamaica. Begin 2-mile, up-and-down climb.
- 26.8 A 2-mile descent into Jamaica.
- 28.5 Cross bridge into Jamaica and continue straight through town. *Note:* For a detour to a great swimming hole, turn left just *before* the bridge. You will see the pool down the embankment to your right, about 100 yards from the bridge. You could turn this into a lunch stop by first riding a bit farther into town and picking up food at the Jamaica Country Market or a couple of other eateries.
- 31.9 Continue straight on Rte. 30S as Rte. 100S turns right.
- 33.4 Left onto paved Windham Hill Rd. in West Townshend. The West Townshend Country Store is opposite the turn on the

right. *Note:* This is the last place to pick up food and water on the ride. Now begins a steep 3-mile climb, with some rests.

- 41.7 Left at four-way intersection onto Rte. 121W (although this may not be marked), and begin a short climb.
- 42.1 Top of hill at Timberline Ski Area at Magic Mountain. From here to Chester it's downhill, with only one small hill on Rte. 11.
- 43.7 Right at the stop sign onto Rte. 11E, which follows the middle branch of the Williams River back to Chester.
- 53.9 Back in Chester.

38

Middletown Springs Cruise

Middletown Springs—Poultney—Wells—Pawlet—Danby Four Corners—Tinmouth—Middletown Springs

This ride, recommended by Vermont Country Cyclers, gives you a choice of three loops of 26, 35, or 40 miles. All feature excellent picnicking and swimming along the rocky banks of the Poultney River and the sandy shores of Lake St. Catherine. The roads lead through a landscape of orchards, farms, summer homes, and small villages. In the nineteenth century Middletown Springs was a health spa, where Victorian-era men and women took "the cure" at iron and sulphur springs. Perhaps the atmosphere will rejuvenate you too.

The first town west from Middletown Springs is East Poultney, where Ethan Allen and the Green Mountain Boys frequented the Eagle Tavern in the 1790s—maybe they were still celebrating their capture of Fort Ticonderoga from the British at the outset of the American Revolution.

Route 30 runs close above the shoreline of Lake St. Catherine, which stretches southward among low hills. New York's Taconic range is visible across the water, and the slate ledges of St. Catherine Mountain press in on the left. Just beyond, an access road crosses the lake's southern neck, giving you the opportunity to explore its opposite shore.

At the town of Wells, at Lake St. Catherine's end, the shortest route option comes up: A road turns east, crossing the hill back to Middletown Springs along a partially dirt road.

The longer rides continue to the town of Pawlet, which is crowded into a narrow valley where Flower Brook and the Mettawee River join. Visit the general store (where you can look through the grate in the back to the river below) and other establishments. Beyond Pawlet the middle-distance option turns north for the final 10 miles back to Middletown Springs.

The 41-mile ride climbs for 2 miles to the mountain settlement of Danby Four Corners, situated on a plateau of farmland, then turns north through the smaller upland village of Tinmouth. Tinmouth was an iron and forge town in the early nineteenth century. Dairy farming, however, evolved as the leading industry over the next hundred years. Now many old pastures have grown over, and the town is dotted with remaining farms and summer homes.

The Basics

Start: Middletown Springs, just southeast of Rutland. Follow Rte. 140W for 9 miles from Rte. 7. Ride distances are measured from the Middletown Springs Inn, on the right just before Rte. 133 turns left.
Length: 26.5, 34.2, or 40.2 miles.
Terrain: The longest ride tackles two steep hills leading to Danby Four Corners. Otherwise, all three options feature rolling hills with only moderate climbs.
Food: Each of the five towns along the way has its general store. Pawlet, at 23 miles, offers the most options—a general store, an ice cream shop, and a restaurant. Those on the shortest option can snack on the town green in Wells.
Traffic/Safety: Traffic is light, but the first third of the ride has narrow shoulders on through roads. The stretch along Lake St. Catherine is particularly narrow. Also, expect more traffic in fall foliage season.

Miles and Directions

- 0.0 Turn right from Middletown Springs Inn onto Rte. 140W.
- 0.1 Continue straight at the stop sign, staying on Rte. 140W for the next 8 miles.
- 6.8 Pass through East Poultney; a general store and town green are on the left.
- 8.3 Left at stoplight, following signs for Rte. 30S. (To visit Green Mountain College and the Original Vermont Store, continue straight on Rte. 140W into Poultney.)
- 8.4 Left at blinking red light, following signs for Rte. 30S and Lake St. Catherine.
- 8.7 Bear right, crossing the Poultney River. Stay on Rte. 30S for the next 8 miles.
- 11.5 Lake St. Catherine State Park. Swimming, picnic area, rest rooms, and refreshments on the right. *Caution:* This road has no shoulder.
- 14.2 Access road to West Shore. Check it out if you wish, but return to Rte. 30S.
- 16.7 Enter village of Wells. The two longer rides bear to the right at the town green here, then immediately turn left onto Wells Rd. just past Nancy's General Store.

The shortest, 26.5-mile option turns left onto Tinmouth Rd., past Nancy's General Store on the right and the town green on the left. Tinmouth Rd. will soon begin a 3-mile climb, with a mile-long unpaved section. Turn left at the stop sign at 21.4 miles, onto Rte. 133N. It's mostly downhill from here back to the intersection with Rte. 140 in Middletown Springs.

- 19.2 Left at the stop sign back onto Rte. 30S, cresting the hill to your left.
- 22.6 Left onto Rte. 133 in Pawlet. As noted above, this is a fine spot to stop for lunch.
- 23.9 Continue straight if riding the longest, 40.2-mile ride.

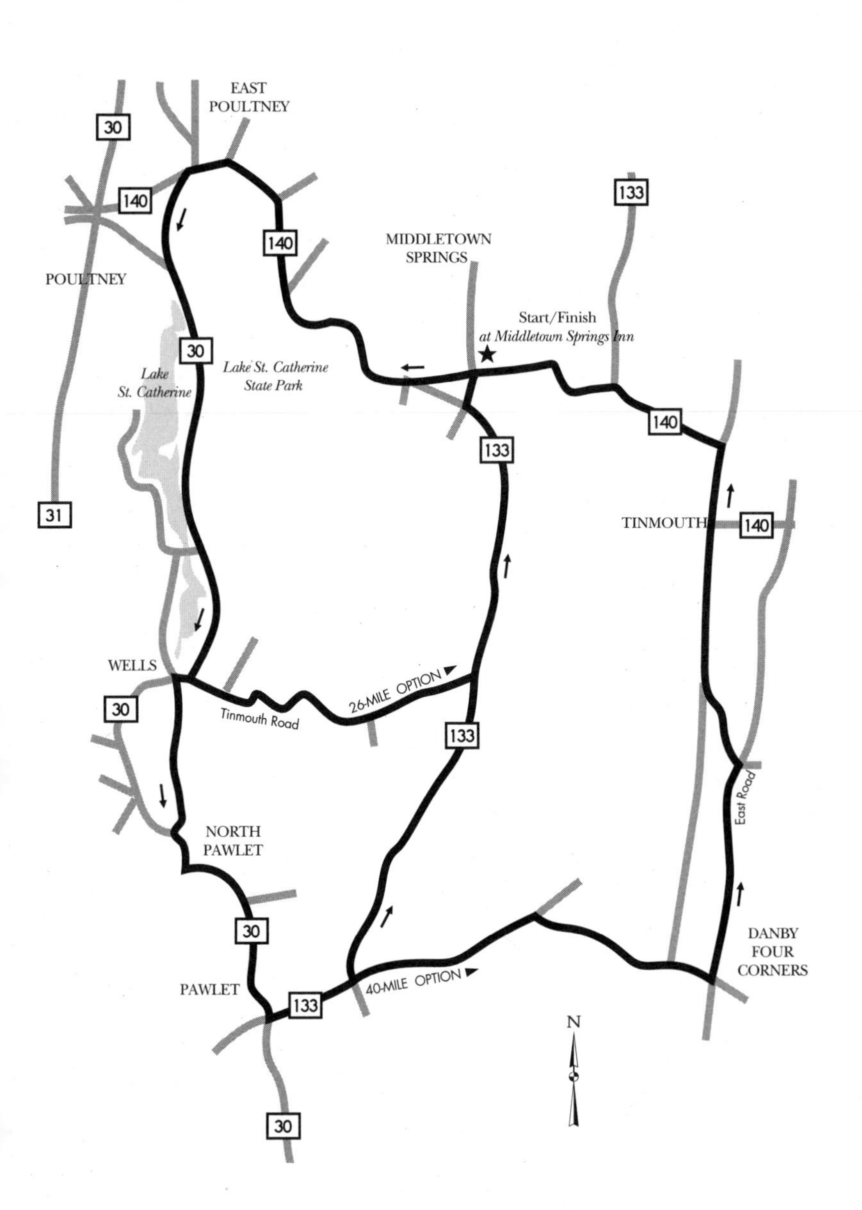

EAST
POULTNEY
30
140
140
133
MIDDLETOWN
SPRINGS
POULTNEY
Start/Finish
at Middletown Springs Inn
30
Lake St. Catherine
State Park
Lake
St. Catherine
140
133
31
TINMOUTH
140
WELLS
26-MILE OPTION
30
Tinmouth Road
133
East Road
NORTH
PAWLET
30
DANBY
FOUR
CORNERS
PAWLET
133
40-MILE OPTION
N
30

The 34.2-mile ride bears left with Rte. 133N, which climbs gradually for 5 miles and then descends for another 5 all the way back to the intersection with Rte. 140 in Middletown Springs. The longest option continues straight, passing a yellow house and large red barn on the left.

- 25.1 Begin steep 2-mile climb.
- 27.0 Barn on the right marks the top.
- 28.5 Left at stop sign in Danby Four Corners. General store on the right. You will be on East Rd. now for 3 miles.
- 31.5 Left onto paved side road marked TH2 (watch closely). A small house will be on your right after you turn. Be careful not to continue straight toward Danby.
- 34.9 In Tinmouth continue straight onto Rte. 140W at the fire station. Stay on Rte. 140 for the next 3 miles. Sharp turns and hills ahead.
- 38.2 Left at stop sign onto combined Routes 140W and 133S, following sign to Middletown Springs.
- 40.2 Arrive back at Middletown Springs Inn, just before intersection where Rte. 133 turns left.

39

Champlain Valley Cruise

Middlebury—Chimney Point—Vergennes—Weybridge—Middlebury

Out-of-staters normally think of Vermont as a land of mountains and hills, with hardly a stretch of level cycling. But biking in Vermont does not necessarily mean pedaling toward the clouds. The Champlain Valley Cruise, nominated as one of New England's finest rides by several local touring leaders, proves this point (although the first 8 miles contain some hills). The tour rolls over a series of moderate north-south ridges from Middlebury, before leveling out near the shores of Lake Champlain; along the way it passes cow pastures, cranberry bogs, and a waterfowl preserve. In October the skies sound with ducks and geese winging south.

The ride next heads north along the shore of Lake Champlain—the sixth largest body of freshwater in the United States. Long and slender, the lake stretches for 110 miles along the border between Vermont and New York. Nearly one hundred mostly uninhabited islands dot its surface. The town square in Vergennes, the self-proclaimed "smallest city in America," offers a resting point two-thirds of the way along the loop. From there the ride follows Otter Creek, the state's longest river, back to Middlebury.

If you love horses, stop to visit the Morgan Horse Farm in Weybridge, located 2.5 miles north of Middlebury (take Seymour Street and Horse Farm Road). The farm is owned by the University of Vermont. Visitors may tour the large barn, where the descendants of the original Justin Morgan horse are bred, trained, and housed.

(Tours run daily from 9:00 A.M. to 4:00 P.M., May through October, and cost $3.00.) If you like birds, stay on Route 17 and pick up the directions at Quaker Village Road through the Dead Creek Waterfowl Area. In Middlebury, you can look into eighteenth-century home life at the Sheldon Museum on Park Street.

Although this tour is more than 40 miles long, beginning-to-intermediate cyclists should have no trouble completing it. Just go slow, enjoy the views, and stop to rest at the high points along the way.

The Basics

Start: Middlebury. Park at the town green. Look for PARKING signs on Main St.
Length: 42.7 miles.
Terrain: Fairly hilly for first 8 miles, then mostly flat to Vergennes. Mildly rolling hills from Vergennes to Middlebury.
Food: The Bridge Family Restaurant at the intersection of Routes 125 and 17, at 15.6 miles, offers lunch, either inside or on picnic tables. There are a general store and a water fountain at the Vergennes town green, at 29.7 miles.
Traffic/Safety: Traffic is generally light except in Middlebury and Vergennes, with an increase during the usual commuting times. There are two brief encounters with busier Rte. 22A. Be prepared to pull over for trucks on it.

Miles and Directions

- 0.0 Head west on Rte. 125 out of Middlebury, passing the Middlebury College campus at the edge of town.
- 8.7 Right at T. Rte. 125 joins Rte. 22AN.
- 9.0 Almost immediate left, at Pratt's Gulf station. Rte. 125 separates from Rte. 22A.
- 15.0 Reach Lake Champlain and see Chimney Point bridge ahead. Views of lake and Crown Point, New York.

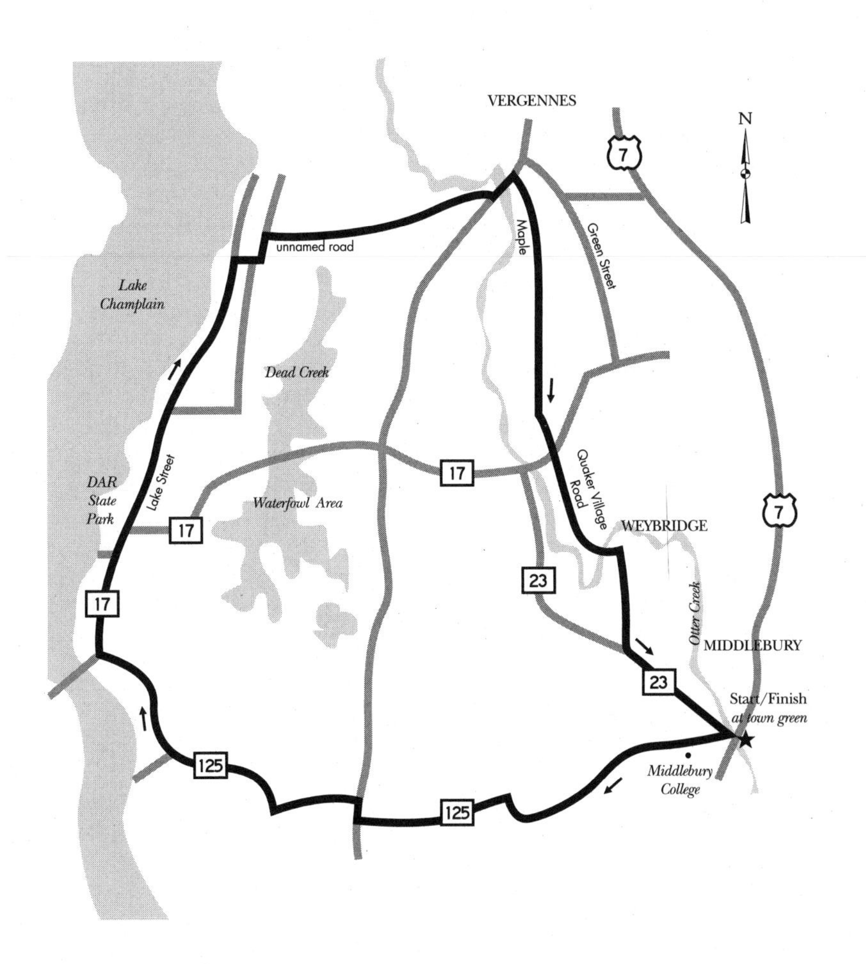
VERGENNES
N
7
unnamed road
Maple
Green Street
Lake
Champlain
Dead Creek
Lake Street
17
Quaker Village
Road
DAR
State
Park
Waterfowl Area
17
WEYBRIDGE
7
23
17
Otter Creek
MIDDLEBURY
23
Start/Finish
at town green
125
Middlebury
College
125

- 15.6 At the Bridge Family Restaurant, turn right on Rte. 17E toward DAR State Park. There is swimming in the park.
- 17.7 Bear left onto Lake St. at Jean's Country Store. An easy turn to miss, this is the first left after you pass the DAR Strong House, a half mile back. (Ahead on Rte. 17 is the Dead Creek Waterfowl Area.)
- 23.6 Lake St. turns right, becoming Pease Rd. Do not continue straight onto gravel road.
- 24.3 Left at T onto unnamed road, just down the hill from a small cemetery on the left.
- 25.5 Turn right on second road just before Burnett's Country Store, toward Vergennes.
- 28.6 WELCOME TO VERGENNES—THE SMALLEST CITY IN THE U.S.A.
- 29.4 Left onto Rte. 22A, Main St.; cross Otter Creek and climb 2 steep blocks.
- 29.7 Right on Maple St., marked as north maple st. on left side of Main St., at City Barber Shop. (For water bottle refills, continue straight to the town square, where there is a water fountain.) At 33.3 miles you'll pass the Sunset View Cemetery, offering outstanding views of Snake Mountain to the southwest, the Otter Valley, and the Adirondack range beyond.
- 35.4 Cross Rte. 17, continuing straight on what is now Quaker Village Rd.
- 37.7 Enter Weybridge, crossing Otter Creek as it pours through a turbine dam on its way to Lake Champlain.
- 39.7 Bear left onto Rte. 23 at Weybridge Hill, with a cemetery on right.
- 42.7 Arrive in Middlebury. Rte. 23 ends at T with Rte. 125.

40

Tour of Scenic Rural Vermont Classic

Jamaica—Rawsonville—Londonderry—Ludlow—Sherburne Center—Stockbridge—Granville—Waitsfield

Today more than half the states in the United States have an annual cross-state bike ride, some of them drawing thousands of avid cyclists. In the case of Vermont, it's a smaller-scale, 200-mile tour sponsored by the American Youth Hostels (AYH). Called the Tour of Scenic Rural Vermont (TOSRV, pronounced like "cause rev"), the ride is celebrating its twenty-fifth anniversary in 1996.

Since 1971, when three friends organized the first TOSRV tour in Vermont, it has become a tradition, drawing fifty or more experienced cyclists to the Green Mountain State each June. Not for the fainthearted, this "vertical" cross-state ride follows the north-south Route 100 northward for just over 100 miles on the first day and returns on the next day. For less experienced riders there's a "mini-TOSRV" too, covering 60 miles each day.

This back-to-back "century" ride attracts cyclists ranging from the eccentric to the merely enthusiastic. One past participant rode to the starting point in southern Vermont from Cape Cod, completed the tour, and pedaled home. Another came fueled by a day's worth of bananas taped to his frame tubes. A couple rode a tandem over the 204 miles—in a single day. But most riders are just active cyclists, either those who return year after year or first-time TOSRV-ites.

Highlights of any long-distance bike tour on Route 100, the state's most famous highway, will include cruising past several ski resort mountains (Killington, Sugarbush, and Mad River); enjoying good views from Granville Notch; riding for 10 miles through the scenic, undeveloped Granville Gulf State Park; and cruising past countless lakes, brooks, farms, and more vistas. There are a few memorable climbs too: Terrible Mountain and then descending into Ludlow, as well as reaching the Killington Ski Area, which is a less rigorous climb.

The two AYH tours, held in June and costing about $70, both offer a sag wagon and official checkpoints. You can get more information about them by contacting the Eastern New England Council of AYH, 1020 Commonwealth Avenue, Boston, MA 02215 (617–731–6692). They often fill up in advance.

If you organize your own Route 100 tour, be sure to reserve accommodations in advance and train adequately. Also, be aware that Route 100 is a well-traveled road—not a backcountry lane. Finally, if you're looking for a longer, more challenging ride, check out the 350-mile, three-day, six-state Tour of New England, sponsored by the Boston-area Charles River Wheelmen (617–325–BIKE).

The Basics

Start: Two good places to start: The AYH ride now begins at the Vagabond hostel in East Jamaica, on Route 100, about 16 miles south of Londonderry. Another starting point is in Rawsonville, 7 miles south of Londonderry on Rte. 100. For convenience the distances below begin at the intersection of Routes 100 and 30 in Rawsonville.

Length: Just over 100 miles one-way (either from Jamaica to Waitsfield or from Rawsonville to Waterbury Center).

Terrain: Hilly, with two major climbs. If you start in Jamaica, there's also a morning "wake-up" climb up Bald Mountain. At about 30 miles you'll climb Terrible Mountain, just before Ludlow, and there's a less challenging climb at about 50 miles, into the Killington Ski Area. If you continue past Waitsfield, toward Water-

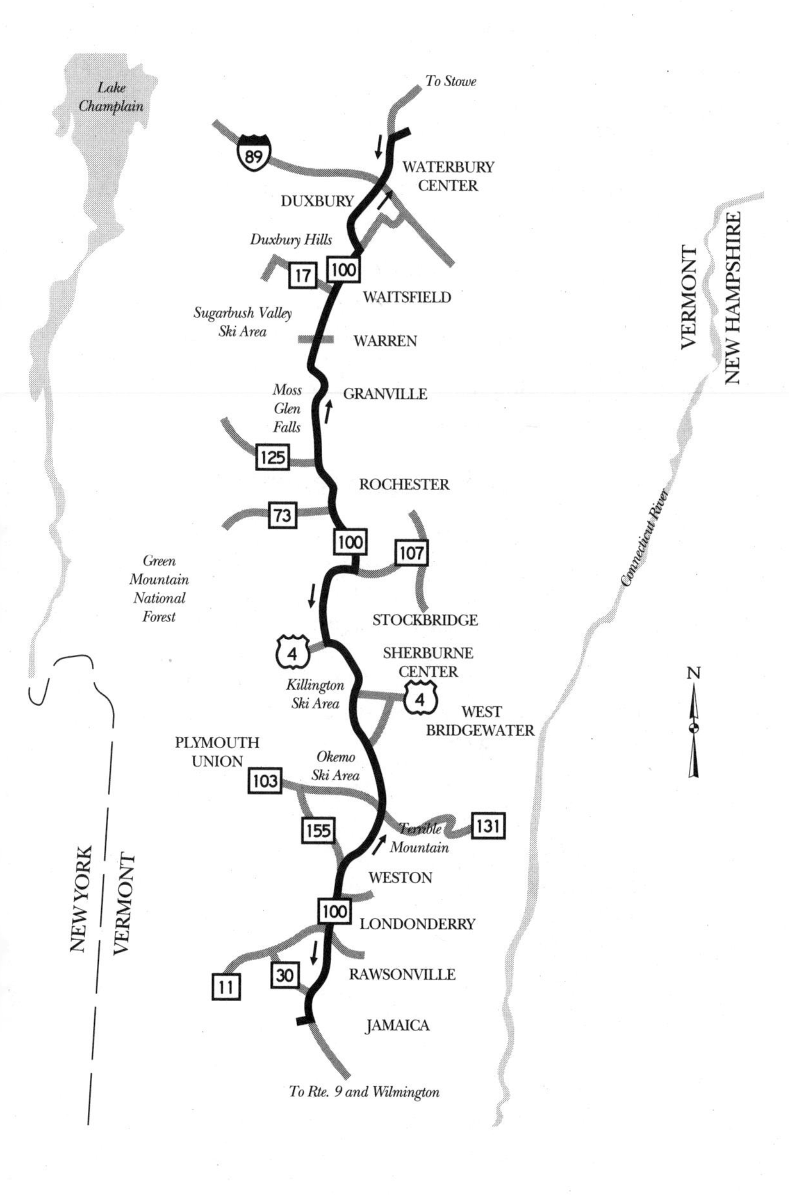

Lake Champlain
To Stowe
89
WATERBURY CENTER
DUXBURY
Duxbury Hills
17
100
WAITSFIELD
Sugarbush Valley Ski Area
WARREN
Moss Glen Falls
GRANVILLE
125
ROCHESTER
73
100
107
Green Mountain National Forest
STOCKBRIDGE
4
SHERBURNE CENTER
Killington Ski Area
4
WEST BRIDGEWATER
PLYMOUTH UNION
Okemo Ski Area
103
155
Terrible Mountain
131
WESTON
100
LONDONDERRY
RAWSONVILLE
30
11
JAMAICA
To Rte. 9 and Wilmington
VERMONT
NEW HAMPSHIRE
Connecticut River
N
NEW YORK
VERMONT

bury, there's a third climb (actually three hills), the Duxbury Hills, in Duxbury.

Food: You'll pass numerous snack and lunch spots along the way. The AYH ride stops for a pancake "breakfast" in Ludlow, at Jim & Zel's in Bridgewater, at the Stockbridge General Store (which has excellent sandwiches) in Stockbridge, and at an ice cream stand in Waitsfield.

Traffic/Safety: To avoid traffic, leaders of the AYH ride recommend riding earlier in the day. Route 100 is a well-traveled north-south route, although cyclists are a common sight on it. Traffic becomes heavier at the northern end, around Waterbury (and Ben & Jerry's), which is one reason that the AYH ride now begins in Jamaica and ends in Waitsfield.

Miles and Directions

- 0.0 From the intersection of Routes 100 and 30 in Rawsonville, head north on Rte. 100, toward Londonderry. Continue on Rte. 100 for the next 100 or so miles. Then relax, hang out for a while, and retrace your route, or have someone pick you up. Below are mileages from Rte. 30, heading northward, into various towns along Rte. 100, including to Duxbury and Waterbury Center, which lie north of Waitsfield.
- 4.0 South Londonderry
- 7.0 Londonderry
- 12.0 Weston
- 23.0 Ludlow
- 32.0 Plymouth Union
- 41.0 Sherburne Center
- 51.0 Pittsfield
- 54.0 Stockbridge
- 62.0 Rochester
- 70.0 Granville
- 81.0 Warren
- 87.0 Waitsfield
- 98.0 Duxbury
- 102.0 Waterbury Center

41

Randolph Challenge

Randolph—Roxbury—
Northfield Center—Williamstown—Brookfield—
Randolph Center—Randolph

This 49-mile tour includes two long climbs. Those who accept the challenge will reap the rewards of a tour through heartland Vermont, past farmlands and forests that still appear much as they did generations ago.

Randolph, the tour's starting point, lies at the head of the White River, three of whose branches fork northward, carving out the ridges and valleys this ride follows. Randolph is an old railroad town known as the home of the first breed of American horses. It was here, in 1795, that Justin Morgan brought the two-year-old colt that founded the Morgan breed. Today Randolph is home to several country inns; Vermont Castings, a premier manufacturer of wood-burning stoves; and a range of local businesses.

Once pedaling north on Route 12A, start enjoying the scenery. The next turn, in Northfield, is more than 20 miles distant. Halfway along Route 12A the river valley narrows as Rice, Adams, and Lost mountains press in on the left. Roxbury State Forest borders the road on the right. A 60-year-old guide to the Green Mountain State notes, "This is one of the last regions in the state where bear can still be found."

The small village of Roxbury is located at the head of the valley. From here the road follows the path of the Dog River toward Northfield Center. A new valley opens in its path.

For cyclists exploring central Vermont, the law of the mountains dictates that while north-south roads roll more or less flat, those crossing from east to west must traverse the ridges separating one long valley from another. The Randolph Challenge proves the law's truth after 22 miles of relatively easy riding. Turning east, Route 64 climbs for 4 miles before finally plunging through hillsides of farmland toward Williamstown.

Four miles south of Williamstown, Route 14 enters Ainsworth State Park and twists through the Williamstown Gulf, where the valley's walls converge to form a deep, narrow pass. This is an ideal resting spot on a hot day. The sun scarcely penetrates this cut, and the fern-covered banks of a roadside stream are a pleasant place to stretch out before you tackle the second big climb.

South of Ainsworth State Park, a 5-mile-long ascent to the town of Brookfield and beyond, occurs in a dozen steps along two roads. Just before Brookfield the route turns south, and a rolling road toward Randolph climbs the crest of an open ridge. This second leg offers views of the Green Mountains that will soon make you forget how long it's been since you rode level ground.

For a rest on the way up this climb, however, detour into the four corners village of Brookfield. To reach Brookfield, simply continue straight on Route 65 past the left turn back toward Randolph. Once in the village you can take a swim and a look at the community's top tourist attraction: the Brookfield Floating Bridge. First built in 1820 of 380 tarred and lashed barrels, the Floating Bridge is the only one of its kind in Vermont and one of only two in the entire country. Thirteen mills once lined Sunset Lake, also known as Mirror Lake or Colts Pond. Also stop by the Newton House, built in 1832 and now maintained as a museum, although it is open only on July and August Sunday afternoons. Organized bike tours frequent the Green Trails Inn, which doubles as a ski-touring center in the winter.

The Basics

Start: Randolph. Take exit 4 off I–89 and follow Rte. 66W for 3 miles. There is public parking behind the Adult Basic Education Center, on the right in the center of town.

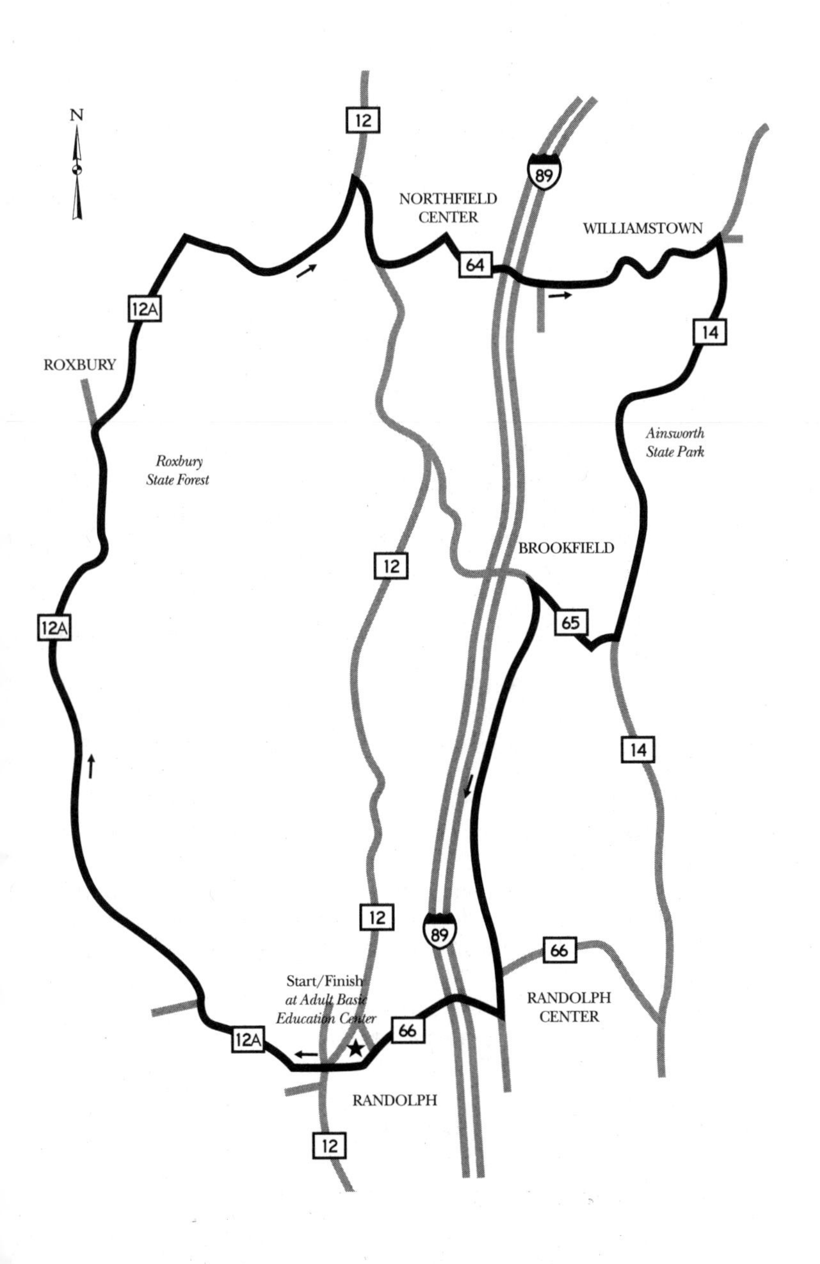
N
12
89
NORTHFIELD
CENTER
WILLIAMSTOWN
64
12A
14
ROXBURY
Ainsworth
State Park
Roxbury
State Forest
BROOKFIELD
12
65
12A
14
12
89
66
Start/Finish
at Adult Basic
Education Center
RANDOLPH
CENTER
66
12A
RANDOLPH
12

Length: 48.8 miles.
Terrain: Two climbs, each exceeding 4 miles long. Otherwise moderate—for Vermont.
Food: General stores in Roxbury, Williamstown, and Randolph Center. Diner and pizza place in Williamstown.
Traffic/Safety: Very light traffic.

Miles and Directions

- 0.0 Leaving the parking lot in Randolph, turn right onto Rte. 66E.
- 0.2 Right onto Rte. 12A at intersection of Routes 66, 12, and 12A. Slab City Bicycles will be on your left as you make this turn. Continue on 12A for 20.8 miles toward Northfield.
- 15.0 Continue straight through village of Roxbury.
- 16.6 Sprint for the Northfield town line.
- 21.0 Right on Rte. 12S.
- 22.1 Left at bottom of short hill onto Rte. 64E toward Williamstown and I–89.
- 26.3 Climb ends 1.3 miles after you pass beneath the I–89 overpass. Rte. 64 begins sweeping downhill run into Williamstown.
- 29.0 Entering Williamstown, right onto Rte. 14S toward Brookfield.
- 33.0 Pass through the thick woods of Ainsworth State Park.
- 36.4 Right onto Rte. 65, which climbs in several large steps toward Brookfield.
- 38.4 Left onto unnamed road immediately after you pass a church on the left. This is the first paved road to the left on Rte. 65. (Or detour straight 0.25 mile to visit the Brookfield Floating Bridge.)
- 45.0 Merge right onto Rte. 66W toward Randolph.
- 45.5 Floyd's General Store on left.
- 45.6 Turn right with Rte. 66 for the final 3-mile downhill into Randolph.
- 48.8 Arrive back in Randolph town center.

42

Orange County Challenge

Thetford—Post Mills—West Fairlee—Vershire—Chelsea—Tunbridge—South Strafford—Thetford

The Orange County Challenge explores an untouristed Vermont of wooded valleys, hilltop farms, and lush pastureland—yet it's conveniently located just off I–91. The tour lies just east of the Randolph Challenge and explores similar river and ridge terrain. Each of the roads along this route, as with most in the hill countries of Vermont and New Hampshire, follows the path of a river or stream. The roads are steepest when they cross a watershed from one trickle to another. The Orange County Challenge features two such ascents, each gaining just over 1,000 feet in elevation. The first begins as a barely perceptible incline along peaceful Route 113 toward Chelsea.

This road follows the Ompompanoosuc River to its source, a string of bubbling springs near the crest of Judgement Ridge. Located halfway along this climb, the small village of Vershire shows little evidence of once having supported a population of more than 2,000. It was the country's leading copper-mining center a century ago. From Judgement Ridge, Route 113 follows the steep downhill course of Jail Brook to the town of Chelsea. Here, 20 miles into the ride, two country stores and a village green provide welcome opportunities to stop, stretch, relax, and refuel.

Bordered on the left by the first branch of the White River, the 8 miles of roadway from Chelsea toward Tunbridge wind through forgotten stretches of Vermont hinterland. The climb from Tunbridge toward Strafford crosses this route's second watershed. A narrow road winds up a hillside whose meadows are dotted with wildflowers throughout the spring, summer, and fall. (This is a steep climb—ride at your own pace, and regroup at a lone roadside maple tree that provides shade from the sun.) After a short rest you can coast for the next 8 downhill miles, braking only for a few sharp turns or the occasional cattle crossing. A monument marks the descent's end at the Strafford village green.

Riding along Route 132 toward South Strafford, do not be surprised if you hear the sudden snorting of horses. Jumping competitions and other equestrian events are often held here, and you may arrive in time for a show. Even empty, though, these pastures are worth a pause.

The broad wooden steps in front of Coburn's General Store in South Strafford provide an opportunity to rest up before the ride's final 9 miles, along the Ompompanoosuc's western branch and across a covered bridge, back to Thetford Hill.

The Basics

Start: Thetford Hill. Take exit 14 off I–91 and follow Rte. 113 west for 1 mile. Park in the lot of the public school on the left.
Length: 46.7 miles.
Terrain: Hilly, with two climbs of almost 4 miles each.
Food: General stores in Post Mills, West Fairlee, Chelsea, Tunbridge, and South Strafford.
Traffic/Safety: Since this is rural Vermont, traffic is generally light, but the roads are narrow, often with little or no shoulder, especially Rte. 110 between Chelsea and Tunbridge.

Miles and Directions

- 0.0 From Thetford Hill proceed west on Rte. 113 toward Thetford Center.

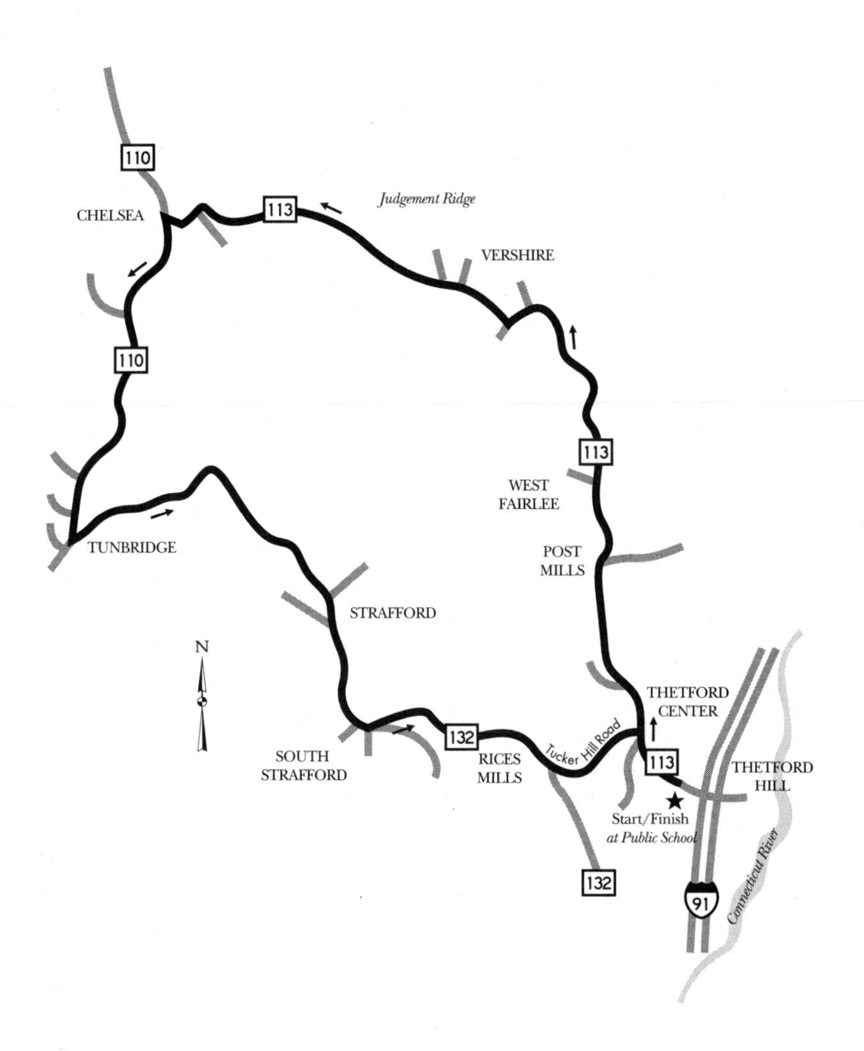

110
CHELSEA
113
Judgement Ridge
VERSHIRE
110
113
WEST
FAIRLEE
POST
MILLS
TUNBRIDGE
STRAFFORD
N
THETFORD
CENTER
132
Tucker Hill Road
SOUTH
STRAFFORD
RICES
MILLS
113
THETFORD
HILL
Start/Finish
at Public School
132
91
Connecticut River

- 5.1 Staying on Rte. 113, pass through Post Mills, following sign toward West Fairlee and Chelsea.
- 7.0 Pass through West Fairlee. Climb begins gradually.
- 12.5 Pass through Vershire. Climb steepens.
- 15.8 Climb ends at Ward's Garage. Begin descent to Chelsea.
- 20.1 At the bottom of the town green in Chelsea, turn left on Rte. 110S toward Tunbridge. Will's General Store and the Chelsea Country Store, established in 1818, are located side by side on the green.
- 27.8 Cross a bridge with concrete railing into Tunbridge and take an immediately sharp left turn. This unnamed road will quickly begin a nearly 4-mile climb. To get to a general store in Tunbridge, detour 0.1 mile off the ride loop by continuing straight after the bridge.
- 31.6 Climb ends. Begin descent to South Strafford.
- 36.1 Bear left at the post office in Strafford.
- 38.3 At the junction with Rte. 132 in South Strafford, continue straight onto Rte. 132E toward Union Village.
- 38.6 Keep on Rte. 132E, which turns left just after Coburn's General Store.
- 43.1 Left on Tucker Hill Rd., just before Rte. 132 crosses a bridge over the west branch of the Ompompanoosuc River.
- 45.1 Cross covered bridge over Ompompanoosuc River.
- 45.4 Right on Rte. 113 at T.
- 46.7 Arrive at school, following a last climb back to Thetford Hill.

43

Smuggler's Notch Challenge

Stowe—Mount Mansfield State Forest—Smuggler's Notch—Jeffersonville—Johnson—Hyde Park—Stowe

The Smuggler's Notch Challenge is a spectacular, exhilarating ride. It is similar to riding on the Kancamagus Highway across the White Mountains in New Hampshire. Just be sure to bring your triple crank, or low gears, and your climbing legs.

You can start with a warm-up stretch along the Stowe Recreation Path. Broad and smooth, it crisscrosses the west branch of the Waterbury River. These opening 2 miles afford clear views of the mountains you will soon be riding through. The Pinnacle, Spruce Peak, Madonna Peak, and White Face mountains march northward. Towering behind them, 4,393-foot Mount Mansfield dominates the skyline.

Once you are on Route 108, the passage through Smuggler's Notch begins to reveal itself. The climb starts in earnest soon after leaving the recreation path. The road enters a dense and cool woodland as it passes the Mount Mansfield Ski Area. Farther along, it becomes clear why the Notch road is often closed in the winter months: Three steep switchbacks snake the road through a landscape of fern-covered glacial rubble.

Several bicycle races have in the past promoted the Notch road as their central challenge. Most cyclists who climb the Notch, however, do not compete to get to the top. They shift into their easiest gear and take their time, enjoying the scenery on the way.

The rewards of this challenging, 4-mile climb more than make up for the efforts. Cyclists can rest at the summit parking area, explore the hillside caves, or just take in the carnival atmosphere that prevails on warm afternoons. The Appalachian Trail crosses here, and the Notch is a popular staging point for hiking and camping expeditions.

Smuggler's Notch acquired its name during the War of 1812. Because it was remote enough not to be watched by revenue officers and had large caves for storage, the Notch became a favorite route for smugglers bringing contraband goods from Canada to Boston.

With its toughest climb behind, the Smuggler's Notch Challenge descends for 8 breathtaking miles to the Lamoille River and its three off-the-beaten-track valley towns. Jeffersonville, at the base of the descent, centers on a broad Main Street that is a pleasure to cycle. From there the challenge follows backroads paralleling the Lamoille River (with fishing and canoeing). Route 15 then rollercoasters its way to Johnson, an old farming and industrial center where a woolen mill and talc plant were once the main industries. Hyde Park, the last town on the way back to Stowe, was one of the earliest settlements in this region. Vermont's pioneers cleared the forest here in 1787.

Stagecoach Road offers a final view toward Mount Mansfield and its neighbors. If you have already expended the energy you'd need to climb these last hills, the directions below will give you the option of following Route 100, more heavily trafficked but flat, back to Stowe.

The Basics

Start: Stowe. Take exit 10 off I–89N. Drive 10 miles north on Rte. 100 through Waterbury Center. Park by the entrance to the Stowe Recreation Path, behind the white Community Church, on the left in the town center.
Length: 44.3 miles.
Terrain: One challenging, long climb through Smuggler's Notch. Otherwise, rolling hills.
Food: There is a grocery/deli halfway down the back side of Smug-

gler's Notch, at 14 miles, and in Jeffersonville, at 18 miles. You may also want to pack a snack to eat on the banks of the Lamoille River, between 20 and 24 miles.

Traffic/Safety: Rte. 108 has a narrow shoulder between Stowe and the top of Smuggler's Notch and can have moderate to heavy traffic during tourist season. Use extreme caution on the final narrow switchbacks. Also, the Stowe bike path is heavily used on weekends.

Miles and Directions

- 0.0 Start warming up along the Stowe Recreation Path, a wide, paved path running parallel to but out of sight of Rte. 108N.
- 2.2 Turning right off recreation path, join Rte. 108N. (The path continues for another 3.5 miles. Stay on it if you wish, joining Rte. 108 farther along.)
- 5.6 Climb to Smuggler's Notch begins in earnest, with a steep half-mile step to the Mt. Mansfield Inn.
- 7.5 Enter Mt. Mansfield State Forest after a short downhill. Begin second step of climb, to the base of the Mt. Mansfield Ski Area.
- 8.4 Begin final stretch of climb. This last half mile features three narrow, exceedingly steep switchbacks.
- 10.2 Reach Smuggler's Notch, at 2,162 feet above sea level. Begin descent to Jeffersonville, almost 8 miles distant. The descent is steep but safe, without the tight switchbacks that marked the climb. On the descent watch for a grocery store on the left.
- 18.1 Enter Jeffersonville; bear right on Rte. 108 as it passes through the center of town.
- 18.3 On the far side of the Main St. stretch, bear left with Rte. 108, following the sign to Rte. 109. Cross Rte. 15 and the Lamoille River.

A scenic option here is to turn right on Rte. 15 and, in a half mile, take the first left, a cutoff to Rte. 109 that has been closed to motor-

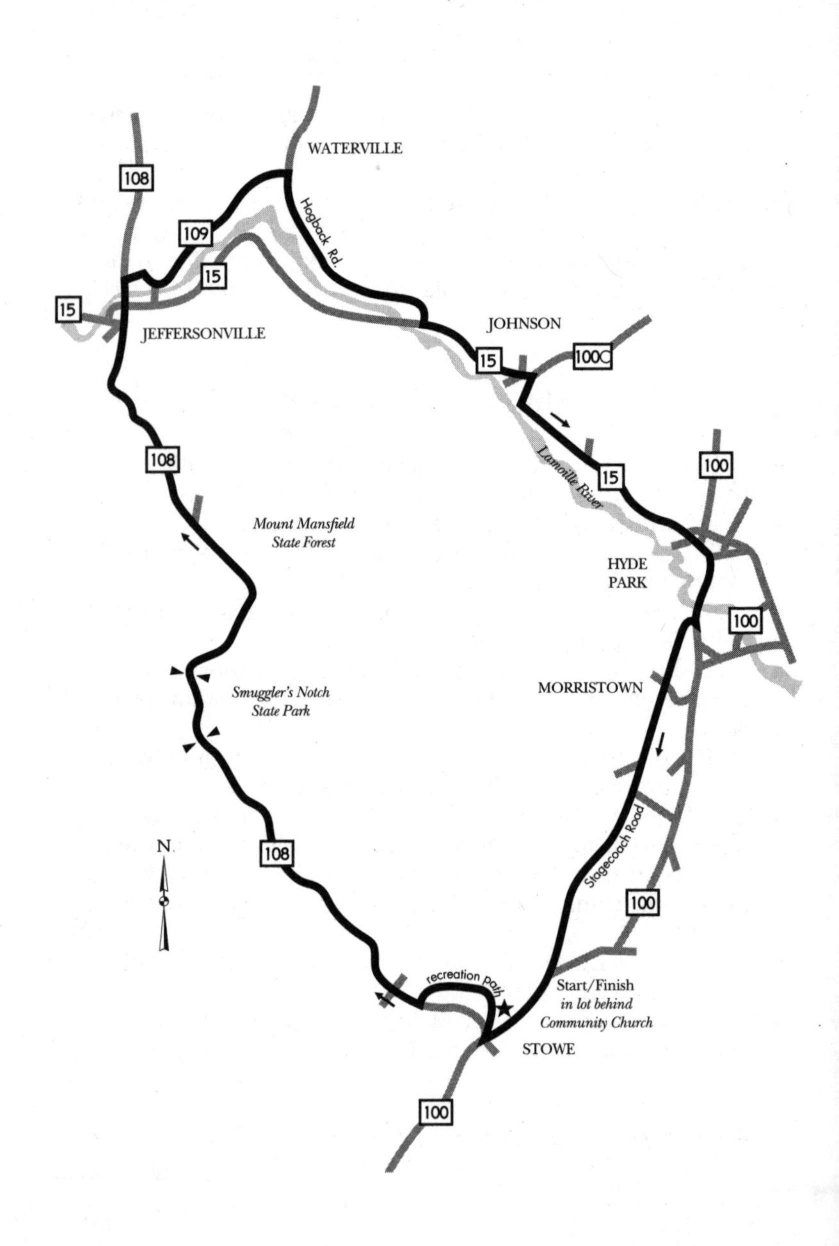
WATERVILLE
108
109
15
Hogback Rd.
15
JEFFERSONVILLE
JOHNSON
15
100C
Lamoille River
15
100
108
Mount Mansfield
State Forest
HYDE
PARK
100
Smuggler's Notch
State Park
MORRISTOWN
Stagecoach Road
N
108
100
recreation path
Start/Finish
in lot behind
Community Church
STOWE
100

ized vehicles but is passable by bike. This route will take you across the Lamoille River via one of Vermont's 108 covered bridges.

- 18.9 Right on Rte. 109N toward Waterville and Belvidere.
- 23.0 Right on an unnamed road 100 yards after crossing a small stream and just as Rte. 109 bears left toward Waterville. This is only the second possible right turn on Rte. 109.
- 27.6 Left on Rte. 15E toward Johnson and Hyde Park.
- 29.3 Pass through Johnson, staying on Rte. 15.
- 30.6 Turn right off Rte. 15 at sign for Hyde Park, at the junction with Rte. 100.
- 34.4 Right, downhill, onto Depot St. at the far end of Main St. There is also a sign for Cady's Falls here. On the descent cross a one-lane bridge. After a short climb and another descent, cross the Lamoille River.
- 35.7 Right, uphill, onto Stagecoach Rd., the backroad to Stowe. (It is unmarked here.) You will pass an old farmhouse on the right.

If you can't face another hill—and Stagecoach Rd. will climb steeply for a short while—continue straight, riding by Lamoille Lake. Then turn right onto Rte. 100, the main road back to Stowe.

- 37.0 Go straight through crossroads, staying on Stagecoach Rd. The hill ahead is the beginning of the last set of steep rollers, with three climbs. You can still bail out, though, by turning left and sweeping downhill to Rte. 100.
- 42.7 Bear right onto Rte. 100, opposite the Foxfire Inn.
- 44.3 Arrive at Community Church in Stowe town center.

44

Northeast Kingdom Challenge

East Burke—West Burke—Westmore—
East Charleston—East Haven—East Burke

From the summit of Burke Mountain, off I–91 north of St. Johnsbury, a glaciated landscape of mountains, forests, lakes, and wide river valleys stretches toward the New Hampshire and Canadian borders. This is Vermont's Northeast Kingdom, the three undeveloped and pristine counties of Orleans, Caledonia, and Essex. Drive up to the peak of Burke Mountain (a seasonal toll road), reached from Route 114 in East Burke, so that you may survey the domain. (It's too steep a road for a warm-up via bike.) Look especially for Lake Willoughby, visible through a mountain gap. It is a highlight of the tour.

The ride itself turns north on Route 5A after a 5-mile-long warm-up along a backroad. Here one of the most famous scenes in Vermont unfolds: Mounts Hor and Pisgah rise abruptly from the otherwise gentle hills as a pair of solitary monadnocks. They are the left and right rims of a U-shaped fold in the earth's crust.

Nestled between them, filling the trough, is 5-mile-long Lake Willoughby, regarded as one of the New England's most beautiful lakes. Its western shores, for the most part surrounded by a state forest, are almost wholly undeveloped. The lake is stocked with fish, and the largest ever caught in Vermont, a 34-pound brown trout, was taken from its 600-foot-deep waters. About 13 miles into the ride, as the road passes directly along the lake's bank beneath the cliffs of Mount Pisgah, a spring bubbles from the rocks on the right. Stop here to fill any empty water bottles. Two general stores and a beach follow.

The ride starts by following the course of the west branch of the Passumpsic River toward Lake Willoughby. It ends with an equally long flat stretch following the Passumpsic River's east branch back to East Burke. The miles in between roll across several long but gradual climbs. This is a popular ride of the Northeast Kingdom's Three Banana Bicycle Club, a touring club that sponsors rides throughout northern Vermont and New Hampshire.

Accommodations in East Burke include the Wildflower Inn, a refurbished farmhouse just south of town; the Old Cutter, located on the road leading to the Burke Mountain Ski Area on the north side of town; and the Garrison Inn, located on the road from East Burke to Burke Hollow. The St. Johnsbury Chamber of Commerce can provide you with additional lodging referrals. As with any ride starting far from home, be sure to reserve accommodations in advance.

The Basics

Start: East Burke. Driving north, take exit 23 off I–91 into Lyndonville. Follow Rte. 5N through Lyndonville, then turn right onto Rte. 114 for the final 5 miles to East Burke. Arriving from the north, take exit 24 onto Rte. 122S into Lyndonville. Then turn north onto Routes 5 and 114 to East Burke. Ride distances are measured from Bailey's General Store in the center of town.
Length: 50.4 or 59.0 miles.
Terrain: Gently rolling backcountry roads, with several long flat stretches.
Food: Fuel up at the Miss Lyndonville Diner in Lyndonville, on the way to East Burke. At the start in East Burke, you can load up on snacks at Bailey's General Store. There are also two general stores and plentiful picnic spots along the shores of Lake Willoughby, starting at 11.0 miles. The East Charleston Store is at 28.8 miles.

There are numerous stores in Island Pond (on the optional route) and several seasonal stores sprinkled all along the ride.
Traffic/Safety: Though this loop is lightly traveled, the shoulders of the roads are mostly narrow, and Rte. 114 is frequented by logging trucks—no problem, but just be aware and ride properly. Tourist traffic may be heavy during peak foliage season (September through October).

Miles and Directions

- 0.0 From Bailey's General Store in the center of East Burke, ride south on Rte. 114.
- 0.1 Right onto the side road toward Burke Hollow and West Burke. This turnoff is directly opposite the Burke Mountain Clubhouse and Community Library. Immediately cross bridge and turn right toward Burke Hollow. The ride starts with a steep 0.6-mile climb and descent.
- 2.9 Descending with caution into Burke Hollow, bear left and then immediately turn right to stay on the main road.
- 3.8 Bear right to stay on main road.
- 5.0 Bear left across a small river as you enter West Burke. Then turn right immediately onto Rte. 5A-N at stop sign. Stay on Rte. 5A for the next 19.2 miles, including 5 miles along the shore of Lake Willoughby. No major climbs until after passing the lake; be aware of summer and fall foliage tourist traffic.
- 11.2 Lake Willoughby. This 5-mile-long lake, wedged between the sheer faces of Mt. Pisgah on the right and Mt. Hor on the left, was dug out by glaciers ages ago. There are swimming beaches at both the south and north ends.
- 12.8 Spring water on the right. Two general stores follow within the next several miles.
- 17.5 Stay on Rte. 5A as Rte. 58 turns left toward Orleans. Continuing north from Lake Willoughby, this circuit passes through some of the Northeast Kingdom's most undeveloped areas. As you crest Rte. 5A out of the Lake Willoughby Gap, you will be treated to gentle downhill and rolling terrain for the next 5.5

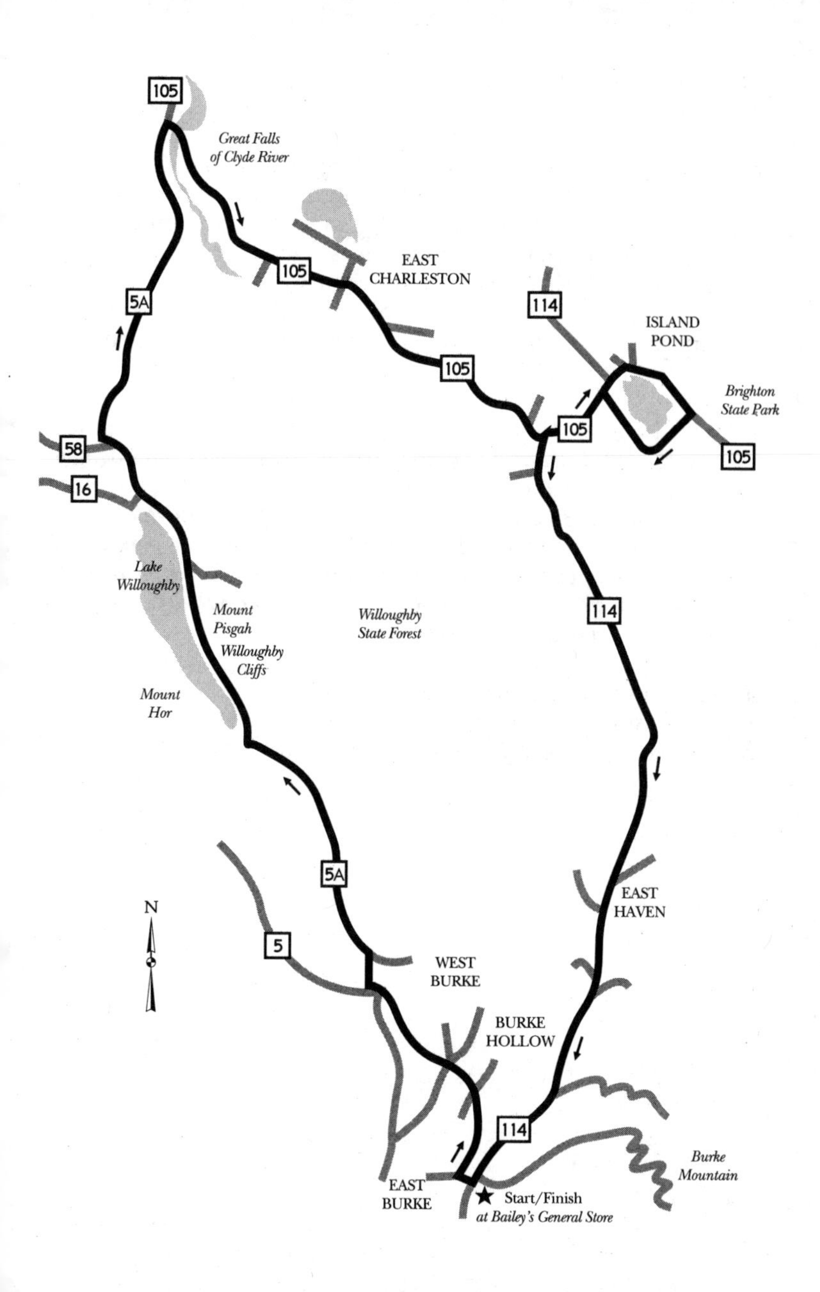
105
Great Falls
of Clyde River
EAST
CHARLESTON
105
114
ISLAND
POND
5A
105
Brighton
State Park
105
105
58
16
Lake
Willoughby
114
Mount
Pisgah
Willoughby
State Forest
Willoughby
Cliffs
Mount
Hor
5A
EAST
HAVEN
N
5
WEST
BURKE
BURKE
HOLLOW
114
Burke
Mountain
EAST
BURKE
Start/Finish
at Bailey's General Store

miles.

- 24.3 Right at junction onto Rte. 105S toward East Charleston and Island Pond. Immediately cross the Clyde River, whose Great Falls cascade through a gorge to the left. Stay on Rte. 105 for the next 10 gradually rolling miles.
- 29.3 East Charleston Store on the right.
- 34.4 Right onto Rte. 114S toward Burke Mtn. *Caution:* This is a popular road for logging trucks en route to and from Canada; be alert for traffic in both directions.

To add roughly 10 miles and a scenic detour to this ride, bear left onto combined Routes 114N and 105E to Island Pond and Brighton State Park. At 36.6 miles turn right onto Rte. 105E in the town of Island Pond. At 38.2 miles turn right off Rte. 105 to Brighton State Park. Continuing around Island Pond after visiting the park itself, turn left onto combined Routes 114S and 105W. Then, at 43.0 miles, turn left to continue on Rte. 114S back to East Burke. Add 8.6 miles to the cumulative mileage below.

- 44.1 Pass through small village of East Haven.
- 50.2 Pass turnoff for Burke Mt. Ski Area to the left.
- 50.4 Return to Bailey's General Store in East Burke.

Appendix

Bicycling and Touring Resources in New England and Beyond

From small "show-and-go" rides leaving from local bike shops on balmy summer evenings, to large weekend rides composed of several dozens cyclists, to touring with commercial outfits that shuttle your luggage from inn to inn, to doing a ride with a friend and this book, there's an ideal way for anyone to explore New England on a bike.

In fact, the region boasts dozens of recreational cycling groups, outing clubs with cycling activities, and commercial touring outfits. Each of the six states also has a tourism bureau that distributes free information of great use to cyclists.

In addition to regular weekly rides, many larger cycling clubs in New England sponsor seasonal or annual long-distance rides that attract cyclists from all over the region. These rides are usually a century (100 miles), a metric century (62 miles), or a half century (50 miles). Two such excursions are documented in this book: the Cape in a Day (or Two) Classic (Ride 22) and the Tour of Scenic Rural Vermont Classic (Ride 40). You can find other such special tours listed in publications like the *Bicycle USA Almanac,* published by the League of American Bicyclists.

Today there's information about local rides, races, and riding club events in many places: national cycling clearinghouses, regional publications like *Ride* magazine in New England, local cycling "hot lines," and, of course, local bike shops, which are usually listed in the yellow pages of telephone directories. Nowadays there's also up-to-the-minute cycling information on the Internet (see below). The following list describes some of the most useful cycling resources in New England and beyond.

National

League of American Bicyclists (LAB; formerly the League of American Wheelmen), Baltimore, Maryland (410–539–3399), the nation's largest recreational cycling organization, with chapters and affiliated clubs throughout New England. LAB members receive a bimonthly magazine, *Bicycle USA,* and two annual publications, *Tour Finder* and *Almanac.* Membership: $30 individual, $35 family.

Adventure Cycling, Missoula, Montana (406–721–1776), a national cycling service organization that publishes maps of touring routes throughout the United States. Members receive a monthly magazine, *Adventure Cyclist,* as well as an annual *Yellow Pages* directory of cycling groups. Membership: $25 individual.

New England

Hostelling International/New England Council of American Youth Hostels (AYH) publishes a monthly magazine, *Footnotes,* that includes many bike rides and events, as well as other local outdoor activities (1020 Commonwealth Avenue, Boston, MA, 02215 (617–731–6692). Membership: $25 adult, $35 family (same household).

Appalachian Mountain Club (AMC) sponsors evening and overnight cycling tours throughout New England and publishes a monthly magazine, *Outdoors,* that lists rides and outdoor activities. 5 Joy Street, Boston, MA 02108 (617–523–0636). Membership: $40 individual, $65 family (same household).

The *Ride,* a monthly cycling magazine for New England and New York, covering rides, events, and other cycling news. Available in most bike shops ($1.00). Karen Hass, editor, 678 Courtland Circle, Cheshire, CT 06410 (203–250–7543), RideZine@AOL.com.

Internet, the electronic information source, carries up-to-the-minute news about local cycling events via free mailing lists sponsored by local cycling clubs. So far, the largest mailing list in New England is maintained by the Charles River Wheelmen (see p. 256).

Subscribing to one of these Internet mailing lists is easy, providing you have the necessary hardware and connection to the Internet via a commercial service like America Online: Simply address an e-mail message to "majordomo@cycling.org" (a national clearinghouse for Internet cycling groups) and, in the body of your message, type these two lines:

subscribe CRW [for Charles River Wheelmen, or another name]
end

It's fully automatic and free, and you can unsubscribe anytime by typing "unsubscribe crw."

Connecticut

Connecticut Tourism Bureau (800–CT–BOUND [282–6863]) offers lots of useful, free information to cyclists, covering attractions, events, lodging, and campgrounds.

Connecticut Bicycle Map shows all the best cycling routes in the state. It's available from the Connecticut Department of Transportation (203–594–2145).

Coalition of Connecticut Bicyclists, P.O. Box 121, Middletown, CT 06457 (203–287–9903), has information about cycling issues throughout the state and has published the *Connecticut Bicycle Book.*

Maine

Maine Tourism Bureau (800–533–9595 or, within the state, 207–623–0363) publishes an annual, free, 200-page book, *Maine Invites You,* that contains all kinds of touring information useful to cyclists.

Maine Freewheelers (P.O. Box 2037, Bangor, ME 04402) is a large and active recreational cycling club in the midstate area, from Bangor to the midcoast around Camden. Its newsletter lists dozens of monthly rides, as well as an annual ride schedule in early spring.

Bicycle Coalition of Maine (P.O. Box 5275, Augusta, ME

04332–5275; 207–865–4842) is a clearinghouse for information about biking advocacy issues (for example, safer roads, safer riders) throughout Maine.

Massachusetts

Department of Environmental Management (617–727–3180) distributes highly useful, free maps of state parks and forests, including camping facilities.

Charles River Wheelmen, the largest cycling club in Massachusetts, sponsors weekend rides and several annual bashes and publishes a newsletter. Its ride hotline: (617) 325–BIKE.

Bicycle Coalition of Massachusetts (617–491–RIDE) has information about many aspects of cycling in Massachusetts.

Regional bicycle maps of Massachusetts and the Boston area are available in many bike shops and bookstores, or contact Rubel Bikemaps, P.O. Box 1035, Cambridge, MA 02140.

New Hampshire

New Hampshire Tourism Office (800–FUN–IN–NH [386–4664]) distributes a 180-page guidebook with all kinds of touring information, as well as a highway map and information on state parks.

Granite State Wheelmen (c/o Dave Topham, 2 Townsend Avenue, Salem, NH 03079; 603–898–9926), is considered the most active recreational cycling club in New England. Its monthly newsletter contains dozens of rides.

Appalachian Mountain Club (AMC); Pinkham Notch, NH 03581; 603–466–2725) is a source of information about camping and other outdoor activities in the White Mountain National Forest.

Rhode Island

Tourism Bureau (800–556–2484 or, within the state, 401–277–2601) distributes many excellent brochures, covering all aspects of touring, camping, accommodations, events, and sightseeing, including a detailed state road map and other maps of Newport and Block Island.

Narragansett Bay Wheelmen (P.O. Box 428, Tiverton, RI 02901), Rhode Island's largest cycling club, maintains a ride hot line (401–246–2753) and publishes the *Spoke 'n Word.*

Vermont

Tourism Bureau (800–VERMONT [837–6668]) offers a packet of information, including the *Vermont Traveler's Guidebook,* a 124-page resource guide with two pages of cycling resources.

Vermont Bicycle Touring (VBT; 800–BIKE–TOUR [245–3868]), offers bike tours for Vermont, Cape Cod, Maine, and western Massachusetts (the Berkshires) between April and November.

Cycle-Inn-Vermont (802–228–8799) in Ludlow, Vermont, is a consortium of five inns that handles luggage and other amenities for touring cyclists.

Bike Vermont (800–257–2226) in Woodstock, Vermont, takes groups of six to twenty cyclists on two- to five-day bike tours from inn to inn.